The Adventure
of Self-Discovery

SUNY Series in Transpersonal and Humanistic Psychology
Richard D. Mann and Jeanne B. Mann, Editors

The Adventure of Self-Discovery

I DIMENSIONS OF CONSCIOUSNESS

II NEW PERSPECTIVES IN PSYCHOTHERAPY

Stanislav Grof, M.D.

STATE UNIVERSITY OF NEW YORK PRESS

Published by
State University of New York Press, Albany

© 1988   State University of New York

All rights reserved

For information, address State University of New York
Press, State University Plaza, Albany, N.Y., 12246

Library of Congress Cataloging in Publication Data

Library of Congress Cataloging-in-Publication Data

Grof, Stanislav, 1931–
    The adventure of self-discovery.

    (SUNY series in transpersonal and humanistic
psychology)
    Includes bibliographies and index.
    1. Psychotherapy. 2. Hallucinogenic drugs.
3. Consciousness — Research. I. Title. II. Series.
[DNLM: 1. Consciousness. 2. Psychotherapy. 3. Self
Concept.   WM 420 G874a]
RC480.5.G76 1987   616.89'14   87-17967
ISBN 0-88706-540-6
ISBN 0-88706-541-4 (pbk.)

20 19 18 17 16 15

To Christina and my mother Marie who have helped me to understand the archetype of the Feminine.

Contents

Contents

III
Appendix A: Psychedelics in Self-Exploration
and Psychotherapy 275

Appendix B: Table of Basic Perinatal Matrices 299

Bibliography 303

Index 311

Introduction

*

If you will know yourselves,
then you will be known and
you will know that you are
the sons of the Living Father.
But if you do not know yourselves,
then you are in poverty
and you are poverty. — Jesus, *The
Gospel According to Thomas, Logion 3.*

*

Knowing others is wisdom;
Knowing the self is enlightenment.
Mastering others requires force;
Mastering self needs strength.
— Lao Tsu, *Tao Te Ching XXXIII*

*

Gnotis te auton (Know thyself).
— Socrates

SEVERAL profound personal experiences with psychedelic substances and clinical observations of their effects in psychiatric patients attracted my attention early in my professional career to the remarkable healing and transformative potential of nonordinary states of consciousness. Systematic exploration of the theoretical significance and practical value of these states has been the central focus on my research for over three decades.

During the first twenty years, this work focused almost exclusively on various psychedelic substances; it was carried out initially in several research facilities in Prague, Czechoslovakia, and later in the Maryland Psychiatric Research Center in Baltimore, Maryland. This work convinced me that psychedelics — if used properly and judiciously under expert guidance — represent extraordinary tools for psychiatry and psychology. Instead of inducing drug-specific states like other pharmaca, they function more like unspecific catalysts or amplifiers of the unconscious processes. By increasing the energetic *niveau* of the human psyche, they reveal its deep contents and intrinsic dynamics.

Clinical work with LSD and other psychedelics thus is not the study of a powerful and exotic psychoactive substance or a group of compounds, but probably the most promising avenue of research of the human psyche and nature. The findings from psychedelic explorations are directly applicable to other situations in which consciousness is altered by various nonpharmacological means. They throw entirely new light on the material from history, comparative religion, and anthropology concerning the ancient mysteries of death and rebirth, rites of passage of various cultures, shamanic procedures of all times, aboriginal healing ceremonies, spiritual practices of various religious and mystical traditions, and other phenomena of great cultural significance.

Nonordinary states of consciousness that occur in these various contexts are in some instances induced by the use of sacred psychedelic plants (see the discussion in the appendix of this book), and in others by powerful nondrug techniques that combine in various ways respiratory maneuvers, chanting, drumming, monotonous dancing, sensory overload, social and sensory isolation, fasting, and sleep deprivation. It is interesting to notice that the spectrum of experiences induced by psychedelic compounds is practically indistinguishable from those resulting from various nondrug techniques.

Similar phenomena can also be observed in the work with modern laboratory methods that can facilitate nonordinary states of consciousness. Here belong, for example, various forms of biofeedback, sessions in a sensory isolation cabin or tank, application of optical or acoustic overload, sleep and dream deprivation, the use of kinesthetic devices, such as the "witches' cradle" or the rotating couch, photic and acoustic stimulation of the brain, and others. Also the phenomena experienced by some subjects in a hypoxic chamber can resemble psychedelic states.

It is of special interest in view of the main focus of this book that the entire spectrum of experiences observed in psychedelic sessions can be induced by various forms of nondrug experiential psychotherapies, such as exploratory hypnosis, primal therapy, neo-Reichian work, Gestalt practice, nude marathon and aqua-energetics, and different varieties of rebirthing. As I will describe later in detail, this experiential spectrum is also characteristic of holotropic therapy, a powerful technique that my wife Christina and I have been using in the last ten years.

I should also mention in this context two situations where nonordinary states of consciousness occur unsolicited under the circumstances of everyday life. Here belong, above all, episodes of unusual experiences, that certain individuals experience spontaneously for unknown reasons. These are currently seen by traditional psychiatry as medical problems — manifestations of diseases of mysterious etiology. The second category of unsolicited nonordinary states of consciousness are near-death experiences (NDE) that are reported by approximately 40 percent of the individuals facing life-threatening situations (Moody 1975, Ring 1980 and 1984, Sabom 1982).

In some of the situations described above, we have to rely on historical reconstructions. Others require field researach in alien cultures and under difficult conditions, or are too elemental and unpredictable for systematic scientific study. The fact that the phenomena involved have their parallels in psychedelic states offers a unique opportunity to study them under controlled conditions of a clinical or laboratory experiment. This is of particular interest, because the observations of nonordinary states of consciousness have important implications for many other fields of research.

The new data are of such far-reaching relevance that they could revolutionize our understanding of the human psyche, of psychopathology, and of the therapeutic process. Some of the observations transcend in their significance the framework of psychology and psychiatry and represent a serious challenge to the current Newtonian-Cartesian paradigm of Western science. They could change drastically our image of human nature, of culture and history, and of reality.

Because of widespread unsupervised use of psychedelic drugs, and ensuing legal, political, and administrative measures, psychedelic research has become increasingly difficult and unpopular. It has been, therefore, particularly exciting for me to discover during the last decade of my professional work that it is possible to induce practically the entire spectrum of the psychedelic phenomena by simple and safe nonpharmacological means. Together with my wife Christina, I have been able to develop a technique that is particularly effective in this regard.

This approach that we call *holonomic integration*, or *holotropic therapy*, is based theoretically on the observations from psychedelic research. It combines in a particular way controlled breathing, music and other types of sound technology, focused body work, and mandala drawing. Our own experience with this technique has been limited to experiential workshops lasting up to four weeks. We have not had the opportunity to subject it to rigorous evaluation in controlled clinical studies, comparable to my research in psychedelic therapy in Baltimore.

However, most participants in our workshops found this technique to be an effective and exciting tool for self-exploration with an unusual potential for mediating transformative and mystical experiences. They repeatedly described it as being far superior to any form of verbal therapy they had tried earlier. Even within the limited framework of short workshops, we have seen many dramatic improvements of various emotional and psychosomatic conditions, often quite severe and of long duration. In many instances, informal feedback by correspondence, by telephone calls, or during a later meeting, confirmed that these changes were lasting. Several colleagues who had trained with us and later started using this approach in their hospitals reached similar conclusions.

During the last ten years, we have used holotropic breathing with many thousands of participants in our workshops in North and South America, different European countries, Australia, and Asia and have found it equally effective in all these areas of the world, in spite of the great cultural differences involved. This book is a response to repeated requests for a manual presenting the basic information on the theory and practice of holotropic therapy in a simple and easily readable form that could be used both by professionals and general public.

In my previous books, the primary focus was on psychedelic work, which certainly narrowed considerably the circles of interested readers. Because many of the new observations could not be reconciled with traditional conceptual frameworks, I had to present the material in the context of technical discussions about psychological theories and to include the dialogue between Newtonian-Cartesian science and the emerging paradigm. The present book differs from my previous writings in many important aspects. Although it contains many references to psychedelic research and descriptions of psychedelic states, its main emphasis is on simple, nonpharmacological techniques of self-exploration that are easily available to the general public and are not restricted by anti-drug laws and other issues that complicate psychedelic experimentation. All interested readers should be able to find an opportunity to test the claims of this book in special experiential workshops under proper guidance.

I have also refrained from including technical discussions relating the new material to the body of accepted knowledge in psychology and other scientific disciplines. I presume that the general intellectual climate has changed to such an extent that many readers either are familiar with the arguments I would bring forth or will be able to accept the data without it. Since I have covered the above topics in my previous writings, I will include references to these books for those readers who would find the theoretical context necessary, useful, or interesting.

The basic findings of my clinical research with psychedelics are discussed in considerable detail in my book *LSD Psychotherapy* (Grof 1980). The relationship between the new concepts and the major schools of depth psychology has been thoroughly explored in my last book, *Beyond the Brain: Birth, Death, and Transcendence in Psychotherapy* (Grof 1985). The section on the "architecture of emotional disorders" is of particular relevance for the present volume and can be considered its important complement. The book *Beyond the Brain* also has an extensive discussion on scientific paradigms and on the limitations of Newtonian-Cartesian thinking in science. In this context, the data from modern consciousness research are compared with the revolutionary developments in other scientific disciplines and with different aspects of the emerging paradigm.

I would like this book to be an easily readable guide for self-exploration and effective psychotherapy and do not want to burden it by lengthy excursions into related problem areas to justify certain statements or to make them more believable. The ultimate "proof" for the readers will have to be personal experience. Without it, much of what is described in this book will probably remain unconvincing, even when supported by the most elaborate intellectual arguments.

The first part of this book focuses on the extended cartography of the psyche that I have developed during my clinical work with psychedelics. It describes the basic types of experiences that become available to an average person whenever he or she gets involved in serious self-exploration with psychedelics or various powerful non-pharmacological experiential techniques. While the model of the human psyche used in traditional academic psychotherapy is concep-tually limited to the *recollective-analytical level*, this new cartography includes two additional levels that are transbiographical. These are the *perinatal level*, characterized by emphasis on the twin phenomena of birth and death, and the *transpersonal level* that can in principle mediate experiential connection with any aspect of the phenomenal world and with various mythological and archetypal domains. I con-sider the knowledge of this cartography to be indispensable for safe and effective inner quest.

The second part of the present volume discusses for the first time in detail the basic principles of *holotropic therapy*, an eclectic technique of nondrug psychotherapy that I have briefly mentioned earlier. This approach can be used as an independent procedure, as a complement to psychedelic therapy, or in combination with other types of expe-riential psychotherapy and various forms of body work. Although the description and discussion of holotropic therapy presented in this book cannot replace actual training that has to involve personal expe-rience and supervised work with others, it contains all the necessary information for experiencers as well as facilitators.

A special section focuses on those effective mechanisms of healing and personality transformation that operate in nonordinary states of consciousness, whether spontaneous, drug-induced, or occurring during sessions of various nonpharmacological forms of psychother-apy. Although most of these mechanisms represent new principles in the Western therapeutic armamentarium, they are actually ancient; since time immemorial, they have played an important role in sha-manic practices, healing rituals, and rites of passage. They are now being rediscovered and reformulated in modern scientific terms.

The book then closes with a discussion of the potential and the goals of experiential self-exploration utilizing the therapeutic and transformative power of nonordinary states of consciousness. It describes how, in this process, emotional and psychosomatic healing is combined with a movement toward a more fulfilling strategy of life and a search for answers to the fundamental ontological and cosmological questions of existence.

The appendix on psychedelic therapy is included to complete the book, both historically and thematically. As I mentioned earlier, the technique of holotropic therapy grew out of the work with psychedelics and is perfectly compatible with it. Although psychedelic therapy is nowadays practically unavailable, some readers might find this section of interest, either because they already have had some psychedelic experiences, or for purely theoretical reasons. It is my hope that sometime in the not-too-distant future these unique tools will be returned to psychiatry and psychology. If and when that happens, psychedelics could then become part of a therapeutic continuum that would include transpersonally oriented interviews, Jungian sandplay, various forms of meditation, Gestalt practice, body work, holotropic therapy, an entire spectrum of psychedelic substances, and possibly other approaches compatible with the above. All these techniques that complement each other and work in the same direction could then be used with flexibility and sensitivity for safe and effective psychotherapy and self-exploration.

I have written this book in the hope that at least some of the readers would find it a useful companion and guide in their adventure of self-discovery and pursuit of self-knowledge that many great philosophers and sages considered to be among the noblest goals of human beings.

Stanislav Grof, M.D.

January 1986
Big Sur, California

I
Dimensions of Consciousness:
NEW CARTOGRAPHY
OF THE
HUMAN PSYCHE

TRADITIONAL psychiatry, psychology, and psychotherapy use a model of the human personality that is limited to biography and to the individual unconscious as described by Sigmund Freud. This approach might appear adequate in the context of psychotherapeutic self-exploration that uses techniques relying on verbal exchange, such as free associations or face-to-face interviews.

However, such a model is inadequate for understanding the dynamics of emotional and psychosomatic healing, personality transformation, and consciousness evolution that occur with powerful techniques, such as psychedelic therapy, healing trance dance, or certain experiential approaches in modern psychotherapy. Such techniques activate and mobilize deep unconscious and superconscious levels of the human psyche and require a vastly expanded conceptual framework. An individual who uses them for self-exploration or as a therapist has to have a model or cartography of the psyche that includes transbiographical domains. We ourselves consider the knowledge of such a cartography to be a necessary prerequisite for any serious inner work and include its discussion in the preparation for both the psychedelic work and holotropic therapy. Although the model described in the following text was first developed for understanding the dynamics of psychedelic sessions, it is equally applicable to in-depth experiential work with nondrug approaches.

The new cartography includes the traditional *biographical-recollective level* and two major transbiographical levels — the *perinatal domain* related to the experiences of birth and death, and the *transpersonal domain*. The experiences of all the above categories — biographical, perinatal, and transpersonal — are quite readily available for most people. They can be observed in sessions with psychedelic drugs, in those forms of experiential psychotherapy using breathing, music, dance, and body work, and, quite regularly, in dreams. Laboratory mind-altering techniques, such as biofeedback, sleep deprivation, sensory isolation or sensory overload, and various kinesthetic devices can also induce many of these phenomena.

There exists a wide spectrum of ancient and Oriental spiritual practices that are specifically designed to facilitate access to the perinatal and transpersonal domains. For this reason, it is not accidental that the new model of the psyche shows great similarity to those developed over centuries or even millenia by various great mystical traditions. The entire experiential spectrum has also been described by historians, anthropologists, and students of comparative religion in the context of various shamanic procedures, aboriginal rites of passage and healing ceremonies, death-rebirth mysteries, and trance dancing in ecstatic religions. Recent consciousness research has thus made it possible for the first time to review seriously ancient and non-Western knowledge about consciousness and to approach a genuine synthesis of age-old wisdom and modern science (Grof 1984).

The fact that many perinatal and transpersonal experiences can also occur during spontaneous episodes of nonordinary states of consciousness has far-reaching consequences for the understanding and treatment of many conditions that traditional psychiatry interprets as psychotic and thus indicative of mental disease. In the light of the new observations, they can be seen as transpersonal crises or "spiritual

..ergencies." When properly understood and treated, such crises can be conducive to emotional and psychosomatic healing, personality transformation, and consciousness evolution (Grof and Grof, 1986).

The Sensory Barrier and the Recollective-Biographical Level

THE techniques that mediate experiential access to the unconscious tend to activate initially the sensory organs. As a result of this, deep self-exploration starts for many people with a variety of unspecific sensory experiences, such as elementary visions of colors and geometrical patterns, hearing of ringing or buzzing sounds, tactile sensations in various parts of the body, tastes, or smells. These are of a more or less abstract nature; they do not seem to have any deeper symbolic meaning, and have little significance for self-exploration and self-understanding. They seem to represent a *sensory barrier* that one has to pass through before the journey into one's psyche can begin.

As the process continues, the next most easily available realm of the psyche is usually the *recollective-biographical level* and the *individual unconscious*. Although the phenomena belonging to this category are of considerable theoretical and practical relevance, it is not necessary to spend much time on their description. The reason for this is that most of the traditional psychotherapeutic approaches have been limited to this level of the psyche. Abundant professional literature discusses the nuances of psychodynamics in the biographical realm. Unfortunately, various schools contradict each other and there is little agreement as to what the significant factors in the psyche are, why psychopathology develops, and how effective psychotherapy should be conducted.

The experiences belonging to the recollective-biographical level are related to significant biographical events and circumstances of the life of the individual from birth to the present. On this level of self-exploration, anything from the life of the person involved that is an unresolved conflict, a repressed memory that has not been integrated, or an incomplete psychological gestalt of some kind, can emerge from the unconscious and become the content of the experience.

One condition necessary for the emergence of the memory is that the issue be of sufficient emotional relevance. Here lies one great advantage of experiential psychotherapy in comparison with verbal approaches. The techniques that can directly activate the unconscious seem to reinforce selectively the most relevant emotional material and facilitate its emergence into consciousness. They thus provide a kind of inner radar that scans the system and detects material with the strongest charge and emotional significance. This not only saves the therapist the effort of sorting the relevant from the irrelevant, but also relieves him or her from having to make such decisions, which would be necessarily biased by professional training, adherence to a particular school, or personal factors.

By and large, biographical material that emerges in experiential work is in agreement with the Freudian theory or one of its derivatives. However, there are several major differences. In deep experiential psychotherapy, biographical material is not remembered or reconstructed; it can actually be fully relived. This involves not only emotions, but also physical sensations, visual perceptions, as well as vivid data from all the other senses. This happens typically in complete age regression to the stage of development when the original events occurred.

We have been able to demonstrate that the age regression observed in unusual states of consciousness is complete and authentic. A brief neurological examination of a person who is regressed to early childhood would give results characteristic for an infant and not an adult. This includes the presence of the sucking reflex and other so called axial reflexes, and even a positive Babinski — a fan-like extension of the toes in response to stimulation of the lateral part of the sole of the foot by a sharp object.

Another important distinction is that relevant memories and other biographical elements do not emerge separately, but form distinct dynamic constellations, for which I have coined the term *COEX systems*, or *systems of condensed experience*. A COEX system is a dynamic constellation of memories (and associated fantasy material) from different periods of the individual's life, whose common denominator is a strong emotional charge of the same quality, intense physical sensation of a particular kind, or shared additional important elements. Several typical examples of COEX systems, clinical illustrations of their dynamics, and a detailed discussion of their role in experiential self-exploration can be found in my book *Realms of the Human Unconscious: Observations from LSD Psychotherapy* (Grof 1975).

I first became aware of the COEX systems as principles governing the dynamics of the individual unconscious and realized that the knowledge of them was essential for understanding the inner process on this level. However, it later became obvious that the systems of condensed experience represent general organizing principles operating on all levels of the psyche.

Most biographical COEX systems are dynamically connected with specific facets of the birth process. Perinatal themes and their elements then have specific associations with related experiential material from the transpersonal domain. It is not uncommon for a dynamic constellation to comprise material from several biographical periods, from biological birth, and from certain areas of the transpersonal realm, such as past incarnation memories, animal identification, and mythological sequences.

In this context, experiential similarity of these themes from different levels of the psyche is more important than the conventional criteria of the Newtonian-Cartesian world-view, such as the fact that years or centuries separate the events involved, that there ordinarily seems to exist an abysmal difference between the human and the animal experience of the world, or that elements of "objective reality" are combined with archetypal and mythological themes.

The last major difference between verbal and experiential psychotherapies is the emphasis that experiential therapies place on the importance of direct physical traumatization for the psychological history of the individual. In traditional psychiatry, psychology, and psychotherapy, the exclusive emphasis is on psychological traumas. Physical traumas are not seen as having a direct influence on the psychological development of the individual and as participating in the psychogenesis of emotional and psychosomatic disorders. This perspective contrasts sharply with the observations from deep experiential work, where memories of physical traumas appear to be of paramount importance. In psychedelic work, holotropic therapy, and other powerful experiential approaches, reliving of life-threatening diseases, injuries, operations, or situations of near-drowning are extremely common, and their significance exceeds by far that of the usual psychotraumas. The residual emotions and physical sensations from situations that threatened survival or the integrity of the organism appear to have a significant role in the development of various forms of psychopathology, as yet unrecognized by academic science.

Let us consider as an illustration a child who has a serious disease that threatens his or her life, such as diphtheria, and almost chokes to death. The parents call the ambulance and an emergency transfer to the hospital and a tracheotomy saves the life of this child in the last minute. In the context of traditional psychotherapy, the experience of vital threat and extreme physical discomfort would not be considered to be a trauma of lasting significance. Rather, the focus would be on the fact that the child was separated from his or her mother at the time of hospitalization, experienced emotional deprivation, and was frightened by the shrill sound of the ambulance siren, the interaction with strangers, and the stay in an alien environment.

Conversely, a psychosomatic symptom such as asthma, psychogenic pain, or hysterical paralysis would be interpreted as "somatization" of primarily psychological conflicts. Experiential work makes it obvious that traumas involving vital threat leave permanent traces in the system and contribute significantly to the development of emotional and psychosomatic problems, such as depressions, suicidal tendencies, anxiety states and phobias, sadomasochistic inclinations, sexual dysfunctions, migraine headaches, or asthma. As a matter of fact, problems that have clearly psychosomatic manifestations can always be traced to unconscious themes (on the biographical, perinatal, or transpersonal level) that involve physical traumatization as a significant element.

The memories of serious physical traumas represent a natural link between the biographical realm of the psyche and the perinatal realm, which has as its main constituents the twin phenomena of birth and death. Physical traumas involve events from the individual's postnatal life and are thus biographical in nature. However, the fact that they brought the person close to death and involved extreme discomfort and pain connects them to the birth trauma. For obvious reasons, memories of diseases and traumas that involved severe interference with breathing, such as pneumonia, diphtheria, whooping cough, or near drowning, are particularly significant in this context.

Encounter With Birth and Death: Dynamics of the Perinatal Matrices

AS the process of experiential self-exploration deepens, the elements of emotional and physical pain can reach extraordinary intensity. They can become so extreme that the individual involved feels that he or she has transcended the boundaries of individual suffering and is experiencing the pain of entire groups of unfortunate people, all of humanity, or even all of life. It is not uncommon that persons whose inner process reaches this domain report experiential identification with wounded or dying soldiers of all ages, prisoners in dungeons and concentration camps, persecuted Jews or early Christians, mothers and children in childbirth, or even animals who are attacked by predators or tortured and slaughtered. This level of the human unconscious thus clearly represents an intersection between biographical experiences and the spectrum of transpersonal experiences that will be described in the next section.

Experiences on this level of the unconscious are typically accompanied by dramatic physiological manifestations, such as various degrees of suffocation, accelerated pulse rate and palpitations, nausea and vomiting, changes in the color of the complexion, oscillation of body temperature, spontaneous occurrence of skin eruptions and bruises, or tremors, twitches, contortions, twisting movements and other striking motor manifestations. In psychedelic sessions and occasionally in nondrug experiential sessions or in spontaneously occurring states of mind, these phenomena can be so authentic and convincing that the person involved can believe that he or she is actually dying. Even an inexperienced sitter or witness of such episodes can perceive such situations as serious vital emergencies.

On the biographical level, only those persons who actually have had during their lifetime a serious brush with death would be dealing with the issue of survival or impermanence. In contrast, when the inner process transcends biography, the problems related to suffering and death can entirely dominate the picture. Those individuals whose postnatal life history did not involve serious threat to survival or body integrity can enter this experiential domain directly. In others, reliving of serious physical traumas, diseases, or operations functions as an experiential bridge to this realm. Thus reliving of childhood pneumonia, diphtheria, whooping cough or near-drowning can deepen into reliving of the suffocation experienced at birth.

Profound confrontation with death characteristic for these experiential sequences tends to be intimately interwoven with a variety of phenomena that are clearly related to the process of biological birth. While facing agony and dying, individuals simultaneously experience themselves as struggling to be born and/or delivering. In addition, many of the physiological and behavioral concomitants of these experiences can be naturally explained as derivatives of the birth process. It is quite common in this context to identify with a fetus and relive various aspects of one's biological birth with quite specific and verifiable details. The element of death can be represented by simultaneous or alternating identification with sick, aging or dying individuals. Although the entire spectrum of these experiences cannot be reduced just to reliving of biological birth, the birth trauma seems to represent an important core of the experiential process on this level. For this reason, I refer to this realm of the unconscious as perinatal.

The term *perinatal* is a Greek-Latin composite word in which the prefix *peri-* means around or near, and the root *-natalis* denotes relation to birth. It is commonly used in medicine to describe processes that immediately precede childbirth, are associated with it, or immediately follow it; medical texts thus refer to perinatal hemorrhage, infection, or brain damage. In contrast to the traditional use of this word in obstetrics, the term *perinatal* is used in this book in relation to experiences. Current neurophysiology denies the possibility of birth memories; the reason usually given is the lack of maturity of the not yet fully myelinized cerebral cortex of the newborn. However, the existence of authentic perinatal experiences cannot be denied; the frequency of their occurrence and paramount clinical significance should serve as an incentive for brain researchers to review and revise their outdated theories.

The connection between biological birth and perinatal experiences described above is quite deep and specific. This makes it possible to use the clinical stages of delivery in constructing a conceptual model that helps us to understand the dynamics of the perinatal level of the unconscious and even to make specific predictions in relation to the death-rebirth process in different individuals.

Perinatal exeriences occur in typical clusters whose basic characteristics are related through deep experiential logic to anatomical, physiological, and biochemical aspects of those clinical stages of birth with which they are associated. Thinking in terms of the birth model provides new and unique insights into the dynamic architecture of various forms of psychopathology and offers revolutionary therapeutic possibilities (Grof 1985).

In spite of its close connection to childbirth, the perinatal process transcends biology and has important psychological, philosophical, and spiritual dimensions. It should not be, therefore, interpreted in a mechanistic and reductionistic fashion. An individual who is dealing with the powerful dynamics of the perinatal process — experientially or as a researcher — can get deeply immersed in it and tend to see birth as an all-explanatory principle. From a broader perspective, this is a limited approach that must be transcended. Currently, thinking in terms of the birth process is a very useful model whose applicability is limited to the phenomena of a specific level of the unconscious. When the process of experiential self-exploration moves to transpersonal realms of the phyche, an entirely new way of thinking becomes mandatory.

Certain important characteristics of the perinatal process clearly suggest that it is a much broader phenomenon than reliving of biological birth. Observations from clinical work with non-ordinary states of consciousness show that many forms of psychopathology have deep roots in the biological aspects of birth. Experimental sequences of death and rebirth have profound therapeutic effect on various emotional and psychosomatic problems related to the traumatic impact of childbirth, both on the child and the mother. However, they have also important transpersonal dimensions and are conducive to profound changes in the philosophical and spiritual belief system, basic hierarchy of values, and general life strategy.

Deep experiential encounter with birth and death is typically associated with an existential crisis of extraordinary proprotions during which the individual seriously questions the meaning of his or her life and existence in general. This crisis can be successfully resolved only by connecting with the intrinsic spiritual dimensions of the psyche and deep resources of the collective unconscious. The resulting personality transformation and consciousness evolution can be compared to the changes described in the context of ancient death-rebirth mysteries, initiation to secret societies, and various aboriginal rites of passage. The perinatal level of the unconscious, therefore, represents an important interface between the individual and the collective unconscious, or between traditional psychology and mysticism.

The experiences of death and rebirth reflecting the perinatal level of the unconsious are rich and complex. Sequences related to various stages and facets of biological birth are typically intertwined or associated with many mythological, mystical, archetypal, historical, sociopolitical, anthropological, or phylogenetic transpersonal experiences. These tend to appear in four characteristic experiential patterns or constellations, and a deep connection seems to exist between these thematic clusters and the clinical stages of childbirth.

Connecting with the experiences of the fetus in the stages of the biological birth process functions as a selective stencil providing experiential access to specific domains of the collective unconscious involving similar states of consciousness. It has proved very useful for the theory and practice of deep experiential work to postulate the existence of four hypothetical dynamic matrices governing the processes related to the perinatal level of the unconsious and refer to them as basic perinatal matrices (BPMs).

In addition to having specific emotional and psychosomatic content, they also function as organizing principles for material from other levels of the unconscious. From the biographical level, elements of important COEX systems that deal with physical abuse and violation, threat, separation, pain, and suffocation or, conversely, with states of biological and emotional satisfaction, are closely related to specific aspects of BPMs.

The perinatal unfolding is also frequently accompanied by transpersonal experiences, such as archetypal visions of the Great

Mother or the Terrible Mother Goddess, hell, purgatory, heaven or paradise, identification with animals, and past incarnation experiences. As it is the case with the various associated COEX systems, the connecting link between these transpersonal phenomena and the BPMs is similarity of the emotions or physical sensations involved.

The basic perinatal matrices have also specific relations to different aspects of the activities in the Freudian erogenous zones and to various forms of psychopathology (see the synoptic paradigm in Appendix B). In the following text, I will describe the BPMs in the order in which the corresponding stages of birth follow each other during childbirth. This order is seldom repeated in the process of deep experiential self-exploration; here the themes of the different matrices can occur in many variations of sequential patterns.

FIRST BASIC PERINATAL MATRIX (BPM I):
THE AMNIOTIC UNIVERSE

The biological basis of this matrix is the original symbiotic unity of the fetus with the maternal organism at the time of the prenatal intrauterine existence. During episodes of undisturbed life in the womb, the conditions of the fetus can be close to ideal. However, a variety of factors of physical, chemical, biological, and psychological nature can seriously interfere with this state. Also, during later stages of pregnancy the situation might become less favorable because of the size of the child, increasing mechanical constraint, and the relative insufficiency of the placenta.

Perinatal experiences can be relived in a concrete biological form or in combination with a variety of symbolic images and other phenomena with which they are connected. The relationship between the individual stages of birth and the associated themes is quite specific and selective and reflects deep experiential logic. Identification with the fetus in various stages of the birth process seems to provide selective access to themes in the transpersonal domain that involve similar emotional states and psychosomatic experiences. Some of these themes have the form of archetypal sequences; others depict situations from the collective memory banks of humanity, or even from the holographic archives of nature related to the animal, vegetable, or mineral kingdoms.

Thus, the elements of the undisturbed intrauterine state can be accompanied by, or alternate with, experiences that share with it the lack of boundaries and obstructions. Here belong deep experiental identification with the ocean or various aquatic life forms (algae, kelp, anemone, jellyfish, fish, dolphin, or whale) or with the cosmos, interstellar space, galaxy, or with an astronaut floating in weightless condition in cosmic space or in an orbiting spaceship. Also images of nature at its best, which is beautiful, safe, and unconditionally nourishing (Mother Nature), represent characteristic and quite logical concomitants of the blissful fetal state.

Archetypal themes from the collective unconscious that can be accessed in this context involve heavens and paradises of different cultures of the world. This seems to make deep sense, since archetypal descriptions of heavens often refer to vast open spaces, sky, radiant celestial bodies such as the sun or stars, and other elements and characteristics of the astronomical cosmos. Similarly, the images of paradise in different cultures reflect nature at its best, with descriptions of beautiful flowers, luscious fruits, exotic birds, the luster of gold, silver and precious stones, and streams or fountains of the water of life.

All the above experiences have a very strong numinous aspect. However, the extreme expression of the sacred and spiritual quality of BPM I is the *experience of cosmic unity* and *unio mystica*. This is characterized by transcendence of time and space, overwhelmingly strong ecstatic feelings (*Apollonian* or *oceanic ecstasy*), a sense of unity of all existence with no boundaries, and deep reverence and love for all creation.

The disturbances of intrauterine life are associated with images and experiences of underwater dangers, polluted streams, lakes, or oceans, and contaminated or otherwise inhospitable nature, such as toxic soil and mud after volcanic eruptions, industrial dumps and junkyards, deserts and wastelands. These are appropriate images, considering the fact that most intrauterine disturbances involve toxic placentary influences or insufficient nourishment. More violent interferences, such as an imminent miscarriage or attempted abortion, are experienced as some form of a universal threat or are associated with bloody apocalpytic visions of the end of the world.

Equally as common as the above imagery is identification with soldiers exposed to chemical warfare, prisoners dying in the gas chambers of the Nazi concentration camps, and persons or animals who have been poisoned. The most common concomitant archetypal images involve various insidious demons, evil metaphysical forces, and malefic astral influences experienced in the mythological framework of various cultures of the world. In the context of such experiences, the mystical dissolution of boundaries characteristic of blissful fetal episodes is replaced by psychotic distortion and disintegration of all familiar and reliable structures, accompanied by terror and paranoia.

Positive aspects of the first perinatal matrix are closely related to memories of the symbiotic union with mother on the breast, to positive COEX systems, and to recollections of situations associated with relaxation, satisfaction, security, peace of mind, and beautiful natural scenery, and exquisite artistic creations. Similar selective connections exist also to various forms of positive transpersonal experiences with related themes. Conversely, negative aspects of BPM I tend to associate with certain negative COEX systems and with corresponding negative transpersonal matrices.

With regard to the Freudian erogenous zones, the positive aspects of BPM I coincide with the biological and psychological condition in which there exist no tensions in any of these areas and in which all the partial drives are satisfied. Negative aspects of BPM I seem to have specific links to nausea, dyspepsia, and intestinal dysfunction.

I will illustrate the dynamics of the individual perinatal matrices with examples from the records of my own psychedelic training sessions. The following is an excerpt from a high-dose LSD experience (300 micrograms) that was influenced primarily by BPM I. We have observed many similar experiences in sessions of holotropic breathing.

> I felt the need to curl up and had a sense of getting progressively smaller. I was floating in a luminescent liquid surrounded by some translucent gossamer veils. It was easy to identify this state as a deep regression, a return into fetal existence. A subtle, but profound feeling of bliss and imperturbable peace — "peace that passeth all

understanding" — was filling my entire being. My state involved a strange paradox: I was becoming smaller and smaller, shrinking into absolute nothingness, and yet it seemed that I had no boundaries and was reaching into infinity.

My fantasy playfully offered the idea that I was a graceful jellyfish, leisurely floating in the ocean, propelled by gentle squirts of water. This initially tentative, almost dreamlike, identification became gradually more and more real. I had very primitive phylogenetic sensations that were extremely convincing and experienced a variety of strange processes that had nothing to do with ordinary human experience. This slowly changed into equally convincing identification with various kinds of fish, sea horses, anemones, and even kelp, all which were authentic and astonishing in biological detail.

But underlying all these experiences was an overarching feeling of being a fetus floating in the amniotic sac and connected with the maternal organism by the umbilical cord and the placentary circulation. I was aware of a complex and rich exchange between us that was partly biochemical and physiological, partly emotional and even telepathic. At one point the theme of blood as a sacred life-giving substance dominated my experience. I was aware of the placentary connection with my mother and clearly sensed the flow of blood through the arterial and venous circuits, the passage of oxygen and nourishment, and the disposal of metabolic products. This was interspersed with various archetypal, mythological themes focused on the significance of blood and its numinous properties. With a subtle shift of emphasis, I could also connect with a more superficial aspect of the same experience — an authentic identification with a nursing infant, where the sacred nourishing substance was milk.

Occasionally, the positive experiences were interrupted by waves of strong physical and emotional discomfort and a sense of some mysterious undefined threat. This condition seemed to have a definite chemical component — I felt sick, nauseated, intoxicated, poisoned. A horrible taste in my mouth made me want to vomit. At the same time I felt possessed or overtaken by some dark metaphysical forces. When these episodes of demonic assault subsided, my experiential field cleared and I returned to deep oceanic bliss. I concluded that this must have been reliving of situations when the intrauterine conditions were disturbed by some adverse events in the maternal organism.

As the experience was subsiding, the oceanic milieu changed into vast interstellar space. I felt like an astronaut floating in the immense cosmic ocean without boundaries, connected by a life-supporting pipeline to the "mother ship," while simultaneously maintaining identification with a fetus. The starfilled universe with its distinct Milky Way and its millions of galaxies gave me a sense of tranquillity and equanimity that I had never imagined were possible. Its immensity and timelessness made events of any kind and scope appear to be insignificant ripples.

As the session was coming to an end, the experience focused on the earth, yet its timeless quality continued in a somewhat different form. Like a gigantic statue of Buddha that cannot be moved by the turmoil and chaos of human life in repeated cycles of death and rebirth, I became a sequoia tree witnessing unperturbed the passage of time throughout millenia. And as if to emphasize that size is of no import in the world of consciousness, the experience transformed me into a tiny bristle-cone pine in the high Sierra mountains whose existence also bridges thousands of years.

Returning to my normal consciousness, I was filled with gratitude for the miracle of life and the gifts of nature. I saw many images of "Mother Earth" nourishing all her children — green luscious pastures, fields of ripening wheat and corn, orchards abounding in fruits, agricultural terraces of the Peruvian Andes, the life-giving valley of the Nile, and the earthly paradise of the Polynesian islands.

SECOND BASIC PERINATAL MATRIX (BPM II):
COSMIC ENGULFMENT AND NO EXIT

This experiential pattern is related to the onset of biological delivery and to its first clinical stage. Here the original harmony and equilibrium of the fetal existence is disturbed, first by alarming chemical signals and later by mechanical contractions of the uterus. With this stage fully developed, the fetus is periodically constricted by uterine spasms. At this point, the system is entirely closed; the cervix is not dilated and the way out is not yet available. Since the arteries supplying the placenta follow a winding course through the complex spiral, circular and longitudinal fabric of the uterine musculature, each contraction restricts the supply of blood and thus oxygen, nourishment, and warmth to the fetus.

Concrete memories of the threat that the onset of the delivery represents for the fetus have their symbolic concomitant in the experience of cosmic engulfment. This involves overwhelming feelings of increasing anxiety and the awareness of an imminent vital danger. The source of this danger cannot be clearly identified and the subject has a tendency to interpret the world in paranoid terms. This can result in a convinced sense of being poisoned, influenced by hypnosis or by a diabolic machine, possessed by a demonic force, or attacked by extraterrestrials.

Characteristic of this situation is the experience of a three-dimensional spiral, funnel, or whirlpool sucking the subject relentlessly toward its center. A closely related equivalent to this annihilating maelstrom is the experience of being swallowed by a terrifying monster, such as a giant dragon, leviathan, python, crocodile, or whale. Equally frequent in this context are experiences of attack by a monstrous octopus or tarantula. A less dramatic version of the same experience is the theme of descent into a dangerous underworld, realm of the dead, system of dark grottoes, or mystifying labyrinth. Corresponding mythological themes are the beginning of the hero's journey, the fall of the angels, and paradise lost.

Some of these images might appear strange to the analytical mind; however, they show deep experiential logic. Thus the whirlpool represents a serious danger to an organism enjoying free floating in a watery environment and imposes on it a dangerous unidirectional motion. Similarly, the situation of being swallowed changes freedom into a life-threatening confinement comparable to the situation of a fetus wedged into the pelvic opening. An octopus entangles, confines, and threatens organisms living in the oceanic milieu. A spider traps and restricts insects who previously flew freely in an unobstructed world and seriously endangers their life.

The symbolic counterpart of a fully developed first clinical stage of delivery is *the experience of no exit or hell*. It involves a sense of being stuck, encaged, or trapped in a claustrophobic, nightmarish world and an experience of incredible psychological and physical tortures. The situation is typically unbearable and appears to be endless and hopeless. The individual loses the sense of linear time and cannot see the possibility of an end to this torment or any form of active escape from it.

This can be associated with experiential identification with prisoners in dungeons or concentration camps, inmates of insane asylums, sinners in hell, or archetypal figures, such as Ahasuerus the wandering Jew, the Flying Dutchman, Sisyphus, Ixion, Tantalus, or Prometheus. Quite frequent also are images and experiences of people and animals dying lonely deaths of starvation or in inhospitable natural settings, such as deserts and the freezing cold of

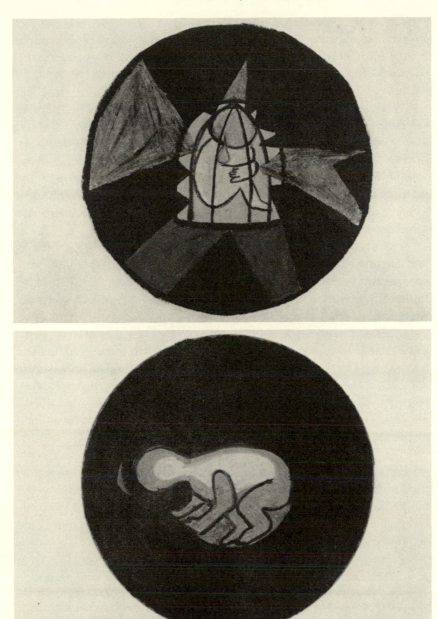

Figure 1ab Two paintings depicting an imprisoned fetus struggling to free herself from the confines of the birth canal. These experiences occurred in a holotropic session dominated by BPM II.

Siberia or of the arctic ice. The logic of these themes reflects the fact that the contractions of the uterus cut off the placentary blood supply for the fetus, which represents not only meaningful connection with the world and human contact, but also the source of nourishment and warmth.

While under the influence of this matrix, the subject is also selectively blinded for anything positive in the world and in his or her life. Agonizing feelings of metaphysical loneliness, helplessness, hopelessness, inferiority, inadequacy, existential despair, and guilt are standard constituents of this state of consciousness. Through the prism of this matrix, human life appears as an absolutely meaningless Theater of the Absurd, as a farce staging cardboard characters and mindless robots, or as a cruel circus sideshow.

As far as the organizing function of BPM II is concerned, it attracts and is connected with COEX systems which involve situations of a passive and helpless victim subjected to an overwhelming destructive force without a chance of escaping. It also has affinity to transpersonal themes with similar qualities.

With regard to the Freudian erogenous zones, this matrix seems to be related to conditions that involve unpleasant tension, pain, and frustration. On the oral level, it is hunger, thirst, nausea and painful stimuli; on the anal level, retention of feces; and on the urethral level, retention of urine. The corresponding sensations on the genital level are sexual frustration and the pains experienced by delivering women in the first clinical stage of labor.

The following account of my psychedelic session with 300 micrograms of LSD is a typical illustration of an experience governed predominantly by BPM II, with a few initial themes bridging the biographical and perinatal levels and with elements of BPM IV in the terminal phase. The experiences characterizing the second matrix are separated in the text by brackets.

> The session started on an optimistic note about forty minutes after the ingestion of the drug. I felt that I was rapidly regressing into the carefree world of a satisfied infant. My physical feelings, emotions, and perceptions were extremely primitive and authentically infantile; this was associated with automatic sucking movements of my lips, profuse salivation, and occasional burping.

This was periodically interrupted by visions depicting various aspects of the hectic and driven life of an average adult, full of tension, conflict, and pain. As I compared these with the paradisiacal state of an infant, I suddenly connected with the deep craving that we all have to return to this primal condition of infantile happiness. I saw the image of the Pope with a bejewelled cross and an ornate ring with a large gem on his hand; masses of people looked up to him full of great expectation. This was followed by visions of countless thousands of Moslems surrounding the Kaaba in Mecca with the same sense of deep longing. And then anonymous crowds with red banners looked up to gigantic images of Communist leaders during a parade in Moscow's Red Square and millions of Chinese worshipped Chairman Mao. I felt strongly that the driving force behind such great religious and social movements was the need to reenact the state of fulfillment and satisfaction experienced in early infancy.

[As the effect of the drug increased, I suddenly felt an onslaught of panic anxiety. Everything became dark, oppressive, and threatening; the entire world seemed to be closing in on me. The images of the everyday misery that had previously appeared as contrasts to the problem-free world of the infant became overwhelming and unrelenting. They portrayed the absolute hopelessness of human existence, fraught with suffering from birth till death. At that point, I understood existential philosophers and authors of the Theater of the Absurd. THEY KNEW! Human life is absurd, monstrous, and utterly futile; it is a meaningless farce and a cruel joke played on humanity.

We are born in suffering, we suffer throughout life, and we die suffering. I felt I was in touch simultaneously with the pain of birth and with the agony of dying. They merged for me into an inextricable amalgam. This led to a truly horrifying realization: Human life ends in an experience that is similar to the one in which it began. The rest is just a matter of time — waiting for Godot! Was this what the Buddha was so clearly aware of?

It seemed essential to me to find some meaning in life to counteract this devastating insight; there had to be something! But the experience was mercilessly and systematically destroying all my efforts. Every image I was able to conjure up to demonstrate there was meaning in human life was immediately followed by its negation and ridicule. The ancient Greek ideal of a brilliant mind in a beautiful body did not last very long. The physical shrines of the most enthusiastic and persistent body builders end in the same senile marasmus to be eventually destroyed by death like all the others. The knowledge accumulated in thousands of hours of voracious study is partially forgotten and partially falls prey to the organic degeneration of the brain that comes with old age. I had seen individuals known for great intellectual

accomplishments who in senility had to struggle with the simplest
and most trivial tasks of everyday life. And the death of the body and
the brain brings the final and complete annihilation of all the
knowledge stored by the efforts of a lifetime. What about having
children — is that not a noble and meaningful goal? But the images of
beautiful smiling children were immediately replaced by scenes
showing them growing, getting older, and ultimately dying, too. One
cannot give meaning to one's life by producing offspring whose lives
are as meaningless as one's own.

The images of absurdity and futility of human life eventually
became unbearable. The world appeared to be full of pain, suffering,
and death. Either I was selectively blinded to any positive aspects of
existence, or there simply were not any. There were only incurable
diseases, of which life was one, insanity, cruelties of all kinds, crime
and violence, wars, revolutions, prisons, and concentration camps.
How was it possible that I did not see all this before? To find anything
positive in life, one must wear distorting rosy glasses and play a game
of perpetual self-deception! It seemed that now my glasses had been
broken, and I would never be able to fool myself again as I did before.

I felt caught in a vicious circle of unbearable emotional and physical
suffering that would last forever. There was no way out of this
nightmarish world. It seemed clear that not even death, spontaneous
or by suicide, could save me from it. THIS WAS HELL! Several times,
the experience actually took the form of archetypal images of infernal
landscapes. However, I was gradually becoming aware that in all this
gloomy philosophical perspective on life, there seemed to be a
dimension that I previously had not noticed. My entire body felt
mechanically squeezed and compressed and the maximum of this
pressure was around my forehead. I realized that all this was
somehow related to reliving of the memory of my biological birth, of
the agonizing experience of the confinement in the birth canal.

If that was the case, maybe there was a way out, maybe the
situation only seemed to be hopeless, as it must have appeared to the
struggling infant. Maybe the task was to complete the reliving of birth
by an experience of emerging into the world. However, for a long time
period that seemed like eternity, I was uncertain that this completion
would actually happen, since it would require finding meaning in life.
That clearly appeared to be an impossible task and if that was a necessary condition for liberation from this hellish situation, there was
not much hope.]

Suddenly, without warning, the pressure was magically lifted in one
single instant, and I was released from the clutches of the infernal birth
canal. I felt flooded with light and indescribable joy and connected in
a new way to the world and to the flow of life. Everything seemed

fresh and sparkling, exploding into brilliant colors, as in the best of van Gogh's paintings. I sensed a healthy appetite; a glass of milk, a simple sandwich, and some fruit tasted like the nectar and ambrosia of the Olympian gods.

Later, I was able to review the experience in my mind and formulate for myself the great lessons about life I had learned. Deep religious and utopian craving in human beings does not reflect only the need for the simple happiness of the infant as I had seen it early in the session, but also the urgency to escape from the nightmarish memories of the trauma of birth into postnatal freedom and the oceanic bliss of the womb. And even that was only the surface. Behind all biologically determined needs there was also clearly a genuine craving for transcendence that could not be reduced to any simple formula of natural sciences.

I understood that the lack of fulfillment in human life results from the fact that we have not come to terms with the trauma of birth and with the fear of death. We have been born only anatomically and have really not completed and integrated this process psychologically. Questions about meaning of life are symptomatic of this situation. Since life is cyclical and includes death, it is impossible to find meaning in it using reason and logic. One must be tuned into the flow of the life energy and enjoy one's existence; then the value of life is self-evident. And I felt after this experience like a surfer riding with great joy the wave of life.

THIRD BASIC PERINATAL MATRIX (BPM III):
THE DEATH-REBIRTH STRUGGLE

Many important aspects of this complex experiential matrix can be understood from its association with the second clinical stage of childbirth. In this stage, the uterine contractions continue, but, unlike in the previous stage, the cervix is now dilated and allows gradual propulsion of the fetus through the birth canal. This involves an enormous struggle for survival, crushing mechanical pressures, and often a high degree of anoxia and suffocation.

I have already mentioned that, because of the anatomical conditions, each uterine contraction restricts the blood supply to the fetus. In this stage of delivery, many complications can further reduce the circulation and cause suffocation. The umbilical cord can be squeezed between the head and the pelvic opening or be twisted around the neck. A cord that is short anatomically or shortened by forming loops around various parts of the body can pull on the placenta and detach it from the uterine wall. This disrupts the connection with the maternal organism and can cause a dangerous degree of suffocation. When the delivery culminates, the fetus can experience intimate contact with various forms of biological material; in addition to fetal liquid, this includes blood, mucus, urine, and even feces.

From the phenomenological point of view, BPM III is an extremely rich and complex experiential pattern. In regressive therapy, it takes the form of a determined *death-rebirth struggle*. Beside actual realistic reliving of different aspects of the struggle in the birth canal, it involves a wide variety of archetypal and other phenomena which occur in typical thematic clusters and sequences. The most important of these are the elements of titanic fight, sadomasochistic experiences, intense sexual arousal, demonic episodes, scatological involvement, and encounter with fire. All these aspects and facets of BPM III again reflect deep experiential logic and can be meaningfully related to certain anatomical, physiological, and emotional characteristics of the corresponding stage of birth.

The *titanic aspect* is quite understandable in view of the enormity of the forces encountered in this stage of the childbirth. At this time, the frail head of the fetus is wedged into the narrow pelvic opening by the power of uterine contractions that oscillates between fifty and one hundred pounds. The subject facing this aspect of BPM III can experience overwhelming streams of energy building up to explosive discharges. One of the characteristic forms that this experience can take is identification with raging elements of nature, such as volcanoes, electric storms, earthquakes, tidal waves, or tornadoes. Another variety of this experiential pattern involves scenes of wars or revolutions and enormous energies generated by high power technology — thermonuclear reactors, atomic bombs, tanks, spaceships, rockets, lasers, and electric power plants.

A mitigated form of the titanic experience includes participation in dangerous adventures, such as hunting of wild animals or physical fight with them, gladiator combats, exciting explorations, and conquest of new frontiers. Related archetypal and mythological themes are images of the Last Judgment, Purgatory, extraordinary feats of superheroes, and battles of cosmic proportions involving the forces of Light and Darkness or Gods and Titans.

Aggressive and sadomasochistic aspects of this matrix reflect the biological fury of the organism whose survival is threatened by suffocation combined with the introjected destructive forces of the birth canal. From this association, it is clear why sadism and masochism form a logical unit, sadomasochism, being two aspects of the same experiential process, two sides of the same coin. Frequent themes occurring in this context are scenes of violent murder and suicide, mutilation and automutilation, torture, execution, ritual sacrifice and self-sacrifice, bloody man-to-man combats, boxing, freestyle wrestling, sadomasochistic practices, and rape.

The experiential logic of the *sexual component* of the death-rebirth process is not as immediately obvious. It can be explained by the fact that the human organism has an inbuilt physiological mechanism that translates inhuman suffering and particularly suffocation into a strange kind of sexual arousal and eventually ecstatic rapture. Examples of this can be found in the history of religious sects and in the lives of individual martyrs, in the material from concentration camps and from the files of the Amnesty International, and in the observations of individuals dying on the gallows.

The experiences that belong to this category are characterized by the enormous intensity of the sexual drive, its mechanical and unselective quality, and its pornographic or deviant nature. The fact that on this level of the psyche sexuality is inextricably connected with death, danger, anxiety, aggression, self-destructive impulses, physical pain, and various forms of biological material (blood, mucus, feces, urine) forms a natural basis for the development of the most important types of sexual dysfunctions, variations, deviations, and perversions. The connection between the sexual orgasm and the orgasm of birth makes it possible to add a deeper and highly relevant perinatal layer to the dynamic interpretations of Freudian analysis which have a superficial biographical and sexual emphasis. The implications of these interrelations for the understanding of various forms of sexual pathology is discussed in detail in my book *Beyond the Brain: Birth, Death, and Transcendence in Psychotherapy* (Grof 1985).

The *demonic element* of this stage can present specific problems for the experiencers, as well as for the therapists and facilitators, since the uncanny quality of the material often leads to reluctance to face it. The most common themes observed in this context are scenes of the Sabbath of the Witches (Walpurgi's Night), satanic orgies and Black

Figure 2a–h   A series of drawings illustrating the progression of the perinatal process in holotropic therapy. The subject identified the emotional and psychosomatic sensations experienced in a magnified form in holotropic sessions as elements underlying her everyday feelings and causing a severe distortion of her self-image.

 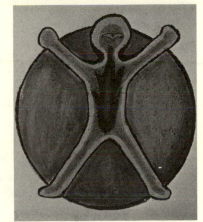

Mass rituals, and temptation by evil forces. The common denominator connecting this stage of childbirth with the themes of the Sabbath or with the Black Mass rituals is the peculiar experiential amalgam of death, deviant sexuality, fear, aggression, scatology, and distorted spiritual impulse that they share.

The *scatological facet* of the death-rebirth process has its natural biological basis in the fact that in the final phase of the delivery, the fetus can come into close contact with feces and other forms of biological material. However, these experiences by far exceed what the newborn might have actually experienced during birth. Experiences of this aspect of BPM III involve scenes of crawling in offal or through sewage systems, wallowing in piles of excrement, drinking blood or urine, or participating in revulsive images of putrefaction. It is an intimate and shattering encounter with the worst aspects of biological existence.

The *element of fire* is experienced either in its ordinary form (with the subjects witnessing scenes of conflagrations and identifying with the immolation victims) or in an archetypal form of purifying fire (*pyrocatharsis*) which seems to destroy whatever is corrupted and to prepare the individual for spiritual rebirth. This thematic motif is the least comprehensible aspect of the birth symbolism. Its biological counterpart might be the overstimulation of the fetus with indiscriminate "firing" of peripheral neurons. It is interesting that it has its experiential parallel in the delivering mother who often feels in this stage that her vagina is on fire.

The religious and mythological symbolism of this matrix focuses particularly on the themes that involve sacrifice and self-sacrifice or combine spiritual pursuit and sexuality. Quite frequent are scenes of Pre-Columbian sacrificial rituals, visions of crucifixion or identification with Christ, experiential connection with deities symbolizing death and rebirth, such as Osiris, Dionysus, Attis, Adonis, Persephone, Orpheus, Wotan, or Balder, and sequences involving worship of the terrible goddesses Kali, Coatlicue, Lilith, or Rangda. Sexual motifs are represented by episodes of phallic worship, temple prostitution, fertility rites, ritual rape, and various aboriginal tribal ceremonies involving rhythmic sensual dancing. A classical symbol of the transition from BPM III to BPM IV is the legendary bird Phoenix who dies in fire and rises resurrected from the ashes.

Several important characteristics of this experiential pattern distinguish it from the previously described no-exit constellation. The situation here does not seem hopeless and the subject is not helpless. He or she is actively involved and has the feeling that the suffering has a definite direction and goal. In religious terms, this situation relates to the concept of purgatory rather than hell.

In addition, the individuals involved do not play only the roles of helpless victims. They are observers and can at the same time identify with both the aggressor and the victim to the point of having difficulty separating the roles. Also, while the no-exit situation involves sheer suffering, the experience of the death-rebirth struggle represents the borderline between agony and ecstasy and the fusion of both. It seems appropriate to refer to this type of experience as *Dionysian* or *volcanic ecstasy* in contrast to the *Apollonian* or *oceanic ecstasy* of the cosmic union which is associated with the first perinatal matrix.

Specific experiential characteristics connect BPM III to COEX systems that include memories of intense sensual and sexual experiences in a dangerous and precarious context, such as parachuting, car racing, exciting but hazardous adventures, wrestling, boxing, fights, battles, conquests, red light districts, rape or sexual orgies, and amusement parks. A special group of memories related to BPM III involves intimate encounter with biological material, such as bedwetting, soiling, toilet training, exposure to blood, or witnessing dismemberment and putrefaction in war or in accidents. Memories of large fires tend to occur during the transition from BPM III to BPM IV.

With regard to the Freudian erogenous zones, the third matrix is related to those physiological activities which bring sudden relief and relaxation after a prolonged period of physiological tension. On the oral level, it is the act of chewing and swallowing of food or conversely vomiting; on the anal and urethral level, the process of defecation and urination; and on the genital level, the build-up to sexual orgasm and the feelings of delivering women in the second stage of labor.

I will use here the record from one of my high-dose LSD sessions (300 micrograms) to illustrate the phenomenology of BPM III that governed the first few hours of this experience. The continuation of the same psychedelic session and its resolution will be described later in the section on the fourth perinatal matrix (p. 35).

The session started with an incredible upsurge of instinctual forces. Waves of orgastic sexual feelings alternated or combined with aggressive outbursts of immense power. I felt trapped by steel-like machinery threatening to choke me to death, yet mesmerized and carried along by this irresistible outpouring of life energies. My visual field was glowing with a spectrum of red colors that had an awesome and numinous quality. I somehow sensed that it symbolized the mystical power of blood uniting humanity in strange ways throughout the ages. I felt connected with the metaphysical dimensions of cruelties of all kinds — torture, rape, and murder — but also to the mystery of the menstrual cycle, birth, delivery, death, ancestral bloodlines, and sacred bloodbonds of brotherhood, true friendship, and loyalty.

The underlying theme behind all this seemed to be a profound identification with an infant's struggle to free himself from the clutches of the birth canal. I felt that I was in touch with the strange force that connects mothers and children in a bond of life and death. I understood instinctively, on a gut level, both the symbiotic and uniting aspects of this relationship and its restricting and suffocating influence that can interfere with independence and autonomy. The strange bond of uterine connection between grandmother, mother, and daughter took on a special significance, as if it were a profound mystery of life from which males were excluded.

Against this background, I was identifying with masses of people connected by some higher cause — revolutionaries and patriots of all ages fighting for freedom against any form of oppression, or pursuing some other collective goal. At one point, I strongly identified with Lenin and felt that I understood intimately the unquenchable thirst for liberation of the masses from oppression that he must have experienced and the fire of revolution that burned in his heart. *Fraternité! Egalité! Liberté!* Images of the French revolution and the opening of the gates of the Bastille flashed through my mind followed by memories of similar scenes from Beethoven's *Fidelio*. I felt moved to tears and sensed profound identification with freedom fighters of all times and all countries.

As I was moving into the second half of the session, the emphasis shifted from death to sex and violence. Colorful images and experiences of rapes, sadomasochistic practices of all kinds, obscene burlesque shows, red light districts, prostitutes, and pimps attacked all my senses with extraordinary power. I seemed to be deeply identified with all the persons involved in the most amazing variety of roles, and yet was also watching it all as an observer. And then picturesque visions, partly figurative, partly woven from the most intricate arabesques, created an irresistibly seductive atmosphere suggestive of oriental harems, *Sheherazade,* and the *Thousand and One Nights.* Gradually a strong spiritual element was added to this highly sensual experience. It seemed that I participated in hundreds of scenes depicting African tribal ceremonies, Babylonian temple prostitution, obscure ancient fertility rites, and some aboriginal ritual orgies involving group sex, which took place possibly in New Guinea or Australia.

And then, without a warning, came a sudden shift. I felt surrounded by some indescribably disgusting stuff, drowning in some kind of archetypal cesspool epitomizing biological garbage of all ages. Foul stench seemed to penetrate my whole being; my mouth was full of excrement that was robbing me of my breath. The experience opened repeatedly into scenes of complex labyrinths of the sewage systems of the world. I felt that I became intimately familiar with the biological fallout of all the metropolises of the world, with every manhole and every leachline there is. This seemed to be a shattering encounter with the worst that can come from biology — excreta, offals, pus, decomposition, and putrefaction.

Amidst this appaling esthetic horror an interesting idea flashed through my mind: What I was experiencing was a typical response of a human adult. A child or a dog might have an entirely different reaction. And there are clearly many forms of life, such as bacteria, worms, or insect larvae, for whom this would be a highly desirable milieu in which they would thrive. I tried to tune into such an attitude and explore it from their perspective. Gradually, I was able to accept and even in a strange way enjoy where I was (see continuation under BPM IV).

FOURTH BASIC PERINATAL MATRIX (BPM IV):
THE DEATH-REBIRTH EXPERIENCE

This perinatal matrix is related to the third clinical stage of the delivery, the actual birth of the child. Here the agonizing process of the birth struggle comes to an end. The propulsion through the birth canal associated with an extreme build-up of anxiety, pain, pressure, and sexual tension is followed by a sudden release and relaxation. The child is born and after a long period of darkness faces for the first time the bright light of the day or the artificial illumination of the delivery room. After the umbilical cord is cut, the physical separation from the maternal organism has been completed. Far-reaching physiological changes have to be accomplished, so that the organism can begin its new existence as an anatomically independent individual providing its own supply of oxygen, digesting its food, and disposing of its waste products.

As in the case of the other matrices, the specific aspects of this stage of birth can be relived as concrete memories of the physiological events and also of the various obstetric interventions involved. Even subjects who do not know anything about the circumstances of their birth can through these experiences correctly identify in great detail the initial position, the mechanism of labor, the type of anesthesia used, the nature of the instrumental or manual intervention, as well as the specifics of postnatal care.

The symbolic counterpart of this final stage of childbirth is the *death-rebirth experience*; it represents the termination and resolution of the death-rebirth struggle. Paradoxically, while only a small step from an experience of phenomenal liberation, the individual has a feeling of impending catastrophe of enormous proportions. This frequently results in a desperate and determined struggle to stop the process. If allowed to happen, the transition from BPM III to BPM IV involves a sense of total annihilation on all imaginable levels — physical destruction, emotional disaster, intellectual and philosophical defeat, ultimate moral failure, and absolute damnation of transcendental proportions. This experience of *ego death* seems to entail an instant merciless destruction of all previous reference points in the life of the individual. The *ego death and rebirth* is not a one-time experience. During deep systematic self-exploration, the unconscious presents it repeatedly with varying emphasis and increasing proportions until the process is completed.

Under the influence of Freudian psychoanalysis, the concept of the ego is associated with one's ability to test reality and to function adequately in everyday life. Individuals who share this limited point of view see the perspective of the *ego death* with horror. However, what actually dies in this process is a basically paranoid attitude toward the world which reflects the negative experience of the subject during childbirth and later in life. It involves a sense of general inadequacy, a need to be prepared for all possible dangers, a compulsion to be in charge and in control, constant efforts to prove things to oneself and others, and similar elements of problematic value.

When experienced in its final and most complete form, the ego death means an irreversible end to one's philosophical identification with what Alan Watts called *skin-encapsulated ego*. When the experience is well integrated, it results not only in increased ability to enjoy existence, but also in better functioning in the world. The experience of total annihilation and of "hitting the cosmic bottom" that characterizes the ego death is immediately followed by visions of blinding white or golden light of supernatural radiance and beauty. It can be associated with astonishing displays of divine archetypal

a. *The Ether Demon*: This painting was done after recognizing that an all-pervasive, non-specific sense of nausea, terror, and electric icy cold was related to the anaesthesia used in birth.

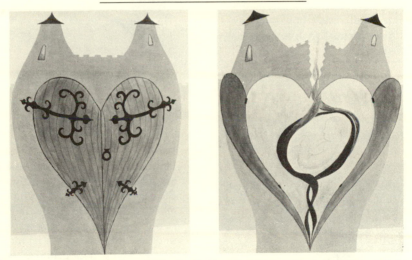

b.,c. *The Pregnant Castle* and *The Castle Opening*: These show first the containment that is present during the anesthesia (the fire in the castle windows) and then the splitting open upward to the light as the incision is made.

d. *The Aztec Priest*: Mixed together with Caesarean birth memory was material related to being an Aztec sacrificial victim. The face of the priest at that death merged with the face of the obstetrician at birth. Both are helpers at a threshold.

---

e. *Revenge on the Priest*: Re-experiencing and releasing the murderous anger engendered by rough handling at birth was mixed with a desire for revenge on the priest. Experiencing this dynamic, active role was the way out of the sense of victimization and helplessness in both cases.

f. *Merging with the Priest*: With both victimization and aggression released, that remained was a strong sense of love for the obstetrician/priest. Once fears related to sexual taboos and transference issues were faced, the love was entered into, leading to a sense of mergence, then cellular consciousness, then galactic, cosmic consciousness.

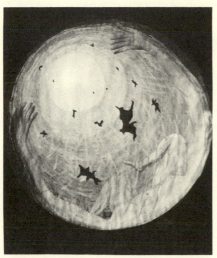

g. *Falling into Form*: While a Caesarean birth is a lifting upward into the light, it, paradoxically, feels like falling into fire, as the full weight of the body is experienced for the first time and the nervous system is intensely stimulated. On a more subtle level, this image relates to a reverse passage through the same tunnel as in near-death experiences. Here consciousness is entering incarnation; there it is leaving.

h. *Fire*: Caesarean birth is an intense ecstatic/terrifying explosion through a red opening into the light. It feels like dying as everything familiar is stripped away.

Figures 3a–h These paintings give a glimpse into the perinatal realms as experienced by a person born non-labor Caesarean. The artist, Jane English, is also author of *Different Doorway: Adventures of a Caesarean Born*, a book which contains more detailed accounts of her experiences, interviews with other Caesareans, and some preliminary conceptual tools for looking at the Caesarean perinatal realm (English 1985). Jane English used a variety of techniques while working on her process; among them was the holotropic breathing that she experienced in our workshops.

entities, rainbow spectra, intricate peacock designs, or pristine natural scenery. The subject experiences a deep sense of spiritual liberation, redemption, and salvation. He or she typically feels freed from anxiety, depression and guilt, purged and unburdened. This is associated with a flood of positive emotions toward oneself, other people, and existence in general. The world appears to be a beautiful and safe place and the zest for life is considerably increased.

It should be emphasized, however, that this description reflects the situation of normal and uncomplicated birth. A prolonged and debilitating course of delivery, the use of forceps, the administration of general anesthesia, and other complications and interventions can introduce specific experiential distortions and abnormalities into the phenomenology of this matrix.

The specific archetypal symbolism of the death-rebirth experience can be drawn from many different realms of the collective unconscious, since every major culture has the appropriate mythical forms for this process. The ego death can be experienced in connection with various destructive deities, such as Shiva, Huitzilopochtli, Moloch, Kali, or Coatlicue, or in full identification with Christ, Osiris, Adonis, Dionysus, or other sacrificed mythical personages. The divine epiphany can involve an entirely abstract image of God as a radiant source of light, or more or less personified representations from different religions. Equally common are experiences of encounter or union with Great Mother Goddesses, as exemplified by the Virgin Mary, Isis, Lakshmi, Parvati, Hera, or Cybelé.

Related biographical constellations involve memories of personal successes, fortuitous terminations of dangerous situations, ends of wars or revolutions, survivals of accidents, or recoveries from serious diseases. In relation to the Freudian erogenous zones, BPM IV is associated on all levels of libidinal development with the states of satisfaction immediately following the activities that released unpleasant tension — satiation of hunger by swallowing of food, relieving vomiting, defecation, urination, sexual orgasm, and delivery of a child.

The following is a continuation of my LSD session described earlier under BPM III. It focuses on the transition between BPM III and BPM IV and then specifically on experiential elements that belong to the fourth matrix.

I was quite pleased with myself, having achieved the demanding and difficult task of accepting an aspect of my biological nature that our culture abhors. However, the worst was yet to come. All of a sudden, I seemed to be losing all my connections to reality, as if some imaginary rug was pulled from under my feet. Everything was collapsing and I felt that my entire world was shattered to pieces. It was like puncturing a monstrous metaphysical abscess of my existence; a gigantic bubble of ludicrous self-deception had burst open and exposed the lie of my life.

Everything that I ever believed in, everything that I did or pursued, everything that seemed to give my life meaning suddenly appeared utterly false. These were all pitiful crutches without any substance with which I tried to patch up the intolerable reality of existence. They were now blasted and blown away like the frail feathered seeds of a dandelion, exposing a frightening abyss of ultimate truth — the meaningless chaos of the existential Void. Filled with indescribable horror, I saw a gigantic figure of a deity towering over me in a threatening pose. I somehow instinctively recognized that this was the Hindu god Shiva in his destructive aspect. I felt the thunderous impact of his enormous foot that crushed me, shattered me to smithereens, and smeared me like an insignificant piece of excrement all over what I felt was the bottom of the cosmos.

In the next moment, I was facing a terrifying giant figure of a dark goddess whom I identified as the Indian Kali. My face was being pushed by an irresistible force toward her gaping vagina that was full of what seemed to be menstrual blood or repulsive afterbirth. I sensed that what was demanded of me was absolute surrender to the forces of existence and to the feminine principle represented by the goddess. I had no choice but to kiss and lick her vulva in utmost submission and humility. At this moment, which was the ultimate and final end of any feeling of male supremacy I had ever harbored, I connected with the memory of the moment of my biological birth. My head was emerging from the birth canal with my mouth in close contact with the bleeding maternal vagina.

I was flooded with the divine light of supernatural radiance and beauty whose rays were exploded into thousands of exquisite peacock designs. From this brilliant golden light emerged a figure of a Great Mother Goddess who seemed to embody love and protection of all ages. She spread her arms and reached toward me, enveloping me into her essence. I merged with this incredible energy field, feeling purged, healed, and nourished. What seemed to be ambrosia, some archetypal essence of milk and honey, was poured through me in absolute abundance.

Then the figure of the goddess gradually disappeared, absorbed by an even more brilliant light. It was abstract, yet endowed with definite personal characteristics and radiating infinite intelligence. It became clear to me that what I was experiencing was the merging with and absorption into the Universal Self, or Brahma, as I have read about it in books of Indian philosophy. This experience subsided after about ten minutes of clocktime; however, it transcended any concept of time and felt like eternity. The flow of the healing and nourishing energy and the visions of golden glow with peacock designs lasted the night. The resulting sense of wellbeing stayed with me for many days. The memory of the experience has remained vivid for years and has profoundly changed my entire life philosophy.

I would like to close this section on perinatal dynamics with an account from a holotropic breathing session of Albert, a clinical psychologist who participated recently in one of our five-day seminars. At the beginning of the workshop, he described himself to the group as a high-strung individual with a strong workaholic life pattern, who thrived on difficult projects and enjoyed challenges and struggles. His breathing session resulted in a profound sense of release and relaxation. This report is a good example of a powerful birth experience that, by its elemental power and meaningful connection to everyday life, convinced an intelligent, skeptical, and scientifically trained individual. It contains a surprising accurate detail.

> At the beginning, I identified with a scaly, wormlike animal and got involved in a number of appropriate movements. I turned repeatedly in a spiral fashion from my back to my belly and back again. Suddenly, I felt on my feet touches that I experienced as bothersome and confining. I began to fight against them, at first lightly and later with increasing strength and determination. This intensified gradually to such an extent that I was sure I was fighting for my life.
>
> I found later that I had to be held down by five persons, because I was moving forcefully into the spaces of other people around me. I developed the idea that I would never give up, even if the entire world were against me. With tricks and strength and loud screaming, I fought against the helplessness and the overpowering foes.
>
> As I was held down, Stan kept repeating that he and the others around me were not my enemies, that they were helping me to get through. After some time I was able to identify this struggle as the reliving of my birth. I have to say that the feeling of helplessness kept triggering in me massive resistance, never resignation. I know a similar pattern also from my everyday life.
>
> My strong movements and loud screams reached a culmination point and then subsided; I moved into a phase of relaxation. At this

point, I decided to sit up. When Stan told me it was too early, a sudden realization flashed through my mind: "I am a premature birth!" I lay down again, got all covered up, and had the feeling that I was able to make up for all the lost time in the uterus. This was very beautiful; I felt happy and was able to let go internally.

Suddenly, I noticed a very intense and full smell of fresh leather; I smelled it again and again and it was very, very pleasant. I was in a state of extreme relaxation, a condition unfamiliar to me from my everyday life. I was able to really enjoy my visions. This strong and intense smell of leather was the most remarkable aspect of my experience. I found it utterly puzzling and did not know what to do with it. During the group sharing, I asked Stan what it could be. He told me that leather (or the smell of it) does not seem to belong to the symbolic and archetypal aspects of birth and that it must somehow reflect the actual circumstances of my delivery.

Later that evening, I found out that my mother worked in a leather shop and on the day of my birth stayed at work till late at night, sewing leather pants (Lederhosen) on her lap. She did not expect the labor to start that day and when her water broke, she misinterpreted it as some kind of bladder problem. Also, my early postnatal life was closely connected to the smell of fresh leather, since my mother continued to work on leather pants at home shortly after my delivery.

I am convinced that I have relived the experience of my birth and that the smell of fresh leather was in some way an authentic memory too.

Beyond the Brain: Transpersonal Dimensions of the Psyche

Like the giraffe and the duck-billed platypus, the creatures inhabiting these remoter regions of the mind are exceedingly improbable. Nevertheless they exist, they are facts of observation; and as such, they cannot be ignored by anyone who is honestly trying to understand the world in which he lives. — Aldous Huxley, *Heaven and Hell*

EXPERIENTIAL sequences of death and rebirth typically open the gate to a transbiographical domain in the human psyche that can best be referred to as *transpersonal*. The perinatal level of the unconscious clearly represents an interface between the biographical and the transpersonal realms, or between the individual and the collective unconscious. In most instances, transpersonal experiences are preceded by a dramatic encounter with birth and death. However, there exists also an important alternative: occasionally, it is possible to access experientially various transpersonal elements and themes directly, without confronting the perinatal level. The common denominator of the rich and ramified group of transpersonal phenomena is the subject's feeling that his or her consciousness has expanded beyond the usual ego boundaries and has transcended the limitations of time and space.

In the ordinary or "normal" states of consciousness, we experience ourselves as existing within the boundaries of the physical body (the body image); our perception of the environment is restricted by the range of our sensory organs. Both our internal perception (interoception) and external perception (exteroception) are confined by the usual spatial and temporal boundaries. Under ordinary circumstances, we can experience vividly and with all our senses only the events in the present moment and in our immediate environment. We can recall the past and anticipate or fantasize about future events; however, the past and the future are not available for direct experience. In transpersonal experiences, as they occur in psychedelic sessions, in self-exploration through nondrug experiential techniques, or spontaneously, one or more of the above limitations appear to be transcended.

On the basis of the above discussion, transpersonal experiences can be defined as experiential expansion or extension of consciousness beyond the usual boundaries of the body-ego and beyond the limitations of time and space. They cover an extremely wide range of phenomena which occur on different levels of reality; in a sense, the entire spectrum of transpersonal experiences is commensurate with existence itself. At this point, before continuing the discussion of the transpersonal experiences, I would like to introduce two new terms, which will be explained and discussed at some length later in the book (p. 239 ff); they refer to two complementary modes of consciousness in which we can experience ourselves and the world.

The *hylotropic*, or matter-oriented, *mode of consciousness* is the term I am using for the normal, everyday experience of consensus reality. The *holotropic mode of consciousness*, or consciousness aiming toward wholeness and totality of existence, characterizes certain nonordinary psychological states, such as meditative, mystical, or psychedelic experiences. It can also be observed in many spontaneously occurring episodes referred to as psychotic by contemporary psychiatry.

In the *hylotropic mode of consciousness*, we experience only a limited and specific segment of the phenomenal world or consensus reality from one moment to another. The nature and scope of this experiential fragment of reality is quite unambiguously defined by our spatial and temporal coordinates in the phenomenal world, the anatomical and physiological limitations of our sensory organs, and the physical characteristics of the environment.

In the *holotropic mode of consciousness*, it is possible to reach, in addition, all the remaining aspects of existence. These include not only access to one's biological, psychological, social, racial, and spiritual history and the past, present, and future of the entire phenomenal world, but access to many other levels and domains of reality described by the great mystical traditions of the world. Comparative study of mystical literature shows that most of these systems seem to agree on a complex, layered, and hierarchical model of reality that includes phenomenal as well as transphenomenal aspects of existence (Wilber 1980).

The *gross experiential realm* reflects the world of ordinary waking consciousness and consensus reality based on the evidence of the sensory organs. The corresponding worldview and way of being in the world is limited to information derived from the physical body and the material world, to linear causality as the only connecting principle, and to Newtonian understanding of space and time. Many systems of perennial philosophy have identified and explored, in addition, several transphenomenal levels or realms of existence, usually referred to as subtle, causal, and ultimate or absolute.

Both the subtle and the causal levels can be further subdivided into lower and higher. The *lower subtle*, or *astral-psychic, level* contains traditionally out-of-body experiences, astral travel, occult and psychic phenomena (precognition, clairvoyance, psychokinesis), auras, and similar experiences. The *higher subtle level* comprises archetypal forms of deities, supreme presences and spiritual guides, experiences of divine inspiration, visions of light, and audible illuminations.

The *lower causal level* is the realm of *sāvikalpa samādhi*, the final

God, creator of all the realms, the audible light of *bija mantra* — the source of all individual deities. The *higher causal realm* is characterized by ultimate transcendence and release into boundless radiance, or *nirvikalpa samādhi*. On this level, there is no subject or object, no self or god, only formless consciousness as such. On the level of the *Absolute*, consciousness awakens to its original condition and suchness, which is also suchness of all of existence — gross, subtle, and causal.

The observations from modern consciousness research with or without psychedelic drugs bring, in general, strong supportive evidence for this understanding of reality. However, in specific details, the cartography of consciousness found in perennial philosophy would have to be extended and modified to fit the findings of experimental psychiatry and the new experiential psychotherapies. In the following text, I will attempt to outline a classification of transpersonal experiences that is based on the scheme of perennial philosophy, but incorporates, at the same time, the findings of modern scientific research.

To create a transpersonal taxonomy that would reflect in an accurate and comprehensive way the introspective data and objective observations from modern consciousness research is not an easy task. The spectrum of transpersonal experiences is not only extremely rich, ramified, and variegated, but includes levels of reality governed by laws and principles that are different from those that rule ordinary reality. Many transpersonal experiences, being ineffable, elude adequate verbal description and occur on levels of reality where those very aspects that could ordinarily serve as *principia divisionis*, such as time, space, duality, and polarity, or linear causality, are transcended. The problem is further complicated by the holographic nature of consciousness and mutual interpenetration of its different levels and domains.

However, I believe that in spite of all these inherent limitations, the following discussion of transpersonal phenomena will reflect the experiential realities to a sufficient degree to provide useful information to future researchers and explorers of these fascinating territories of the human mind. I hope that they will, in turn, complement, refine, and revise in the future, on the basis of their own experiences and observations, the scheme I am proposing here.

Before I start outlining a system of classification of transpersonal phenomena, I would like to clarify the relationship between the holotropic mode of consciousness and transpersonal experiences. Holotropic consciousness has the potential to reach all aspects of existence. This includes the postnatal biography of the individual, events in the future, biological birth, embryonal and fetal development, the moment of conception, as well as the ancestral, racial, karmic, and phylogenetic history. Of these, biographical and perinatal experiences have already been discussed earlier.

In a sense, full reliving of events from childhood and birth (as compared to just remembering) could be seen as true transcendence of time and space. In that case, the individual experiencing a sequence from infancy, childhood, and later life, or the struggle in the birth canal, would not be reconstructing these events from memory engrams in his or her nervous system, but actually connecting directly to the spatial and temporal coordinates of the original events. This would then be comparable to a situation known from science fiction, where astronauts visiting a planet with a strong gravitational field experience time-space loops and can exist simultaneously in two different spatio-temporal frameworks. Under these circumstances, they can actually see and meet themselves at different points of their past.

Full reliving of events from childhood can be occasionally accompanied by experiential identification with the protagonists (e.g., identification with the aggressor), which gives these experiences a distinct transpersonal flavor. Reliving different stages of birth not only involves the possibility of full experiential identification with the delivering mother, but also mediates access to situations in different parts of the world and throughout history that include other individuals experiencing similar emotional states and physical sensations. These connections have been discussed in detail earlier in relation to the phenomenology of basic perinatal matrices.

The most important distinction thus has to be made not between the transpersonal experiences and the biographical or perinatal ones, but between the hylotropic mode — ordinary waking consciousness experienced from one moment to another — and the holotropic mode — nonordinary states of consciousness that mediate access to all other aspects of existence. This includes not only spacetime of the phenomenal world, but also all the transphenomenal levels of reality. It is primarily for didactic reasons that biographical and perinatal experiences are discussed separately from transpersonal experiences. In the following scheme, embryonal, ancestral, racial, karmic, and phylogenetic experiences are included in the transpersonal domain.

In general, transpersonal experiences can be divided according to their content into three large categories. Some of them involve phenomena from the material world of spacetime that our culture sees as objectively real. Others reflect levels of reality denied by Western mechanistic science, but recognized and acknowledged by many ancient and non-Western cultures and by the great mystical traditions of the world, which are described by Aldous Huxley as the perennial philosophy (Huxley 1945).

The first category of transpersonal experiences, which deals with the world of spacetime, can be further subdivided into those experiences that involve transcendence of the ordinary spatial boundaries and those that involve transcendence of linear time. To these we can add a third category of experiences and phenomena that represent strange hybrids between the gross and subtle or causal levels of consciousness. They seem to occur on the interface between the inner world and the external reality, or between matter and consciousness. I have taken the liberty to adopt for this category the term *psychoid phenomena*, used in the past with different connotations by the German biologist and philosopher Hans Driesch (Driesch 1929), one of the main exponents of vitalism; by the Swiss psychiatrist Eugen Bleuler (Bleuler 1925) who coined the term schizophrenia; and, most recently, by Carl Gustav Jung (Jung 1964) in connection with synchronicities and archetypal phenomena. The following classification system is based on the principles discussed above.

Transpersonal Experiences
EXPERIENTIAL EXTENSION WITHIN CONSENSUS REALITY AND SPACE-TIME

1   Transcendence of Spatial Boundaries

  a.   *Experience of Dual Unity*
  b.   *Identification with Other Persons*

c. *Group Identification and Group Consciousness*
d. *Identification with Animals*
e. *Identification with Plants and Botanical Processes*
f. *Oneness with Life and All Creation*
g. *Experience of Inanimate Matter and Inorganic Processes*
h. *Planetary Consciousness*
i. *Extraterrestrial Experiences*
j. *Identification with the Entire Physical Universe*
k. *Psychic Phenomena Involving Transcendence of Space*

2   Transcendence of the Boundaries of Linear Time

a. *Embryonal and Fetal Experiences*
b. *Ancestral Experiences*
c. *Racial and Collective Experiences*
d. *Past Incarnation Experiences*
e. *Phylogenetic Experiences*
f. *Experiences of Planetary Evolution*
g. *Cosmogenetic Experiences*
h. *Psychic Phenomena Involving Transcendence of Time*

3   Physical Introversion and Narrowing of Consciousness

EXPERIENTIAL EXTENSION
BEYOND CONSENSUS REALITY AND SPACE-TIME

a. Spiritistic and Mediumistic Experiences
b. Energetic Phenomena of the Subtle Body
c. Experiences of Animal Spirits
d. Encounters with Spirit Guides and Suprahuman Beings
e. Visits to Other Universes and Meetings with
Their Inhabitants
f. Experiences of Mythological and Fairy-Tale Sequences
g. Experiences of Specific Blissful and Wrathful Deities
h. Experiences of Universal Archetypes
i. Intuitive Understanding of Universal Symbols
j. Creative Inspiration and the Promethean Impulse
k. Experience of the Demiurg and Insights into
Cosmic Creation
l. Experience of Cosmic Consciousness
m. The Supracosmic and Metacosmic Void

TRANSPERSONAL EXPERIENCES OF PSYCHOID NATURE

1   Synchronistic Links between Consciousness and Matter

2   Spontaneous Psychoid Events

    a.   Supernormal Physical Feats
    b.   Spiritistic Phenomena and Physical Mediumship
    c.   Recurrent Spontaneous Psychokinesis (Poltergeist)
    d.   Unidentified Flying Objects (UFO Phenomena)

3   Intentional Psychokinesis

    a.   Ceremonial Magic
    b.   Healing and Hexing
    c.   Siddhis
    d.   Laboratory Psychokinesis

The above classification represents a complete list of the types of transpersonal experiences that I have witnessed in psychedelic research, in sessions of holotropic breathing, and in the work with individuals in spontaneous episodes of nonordinary states of consciousness. In addition, it contains a few transpersonal phenomena of the psychoid type that have been described repeatedly in mystical literature and by some modern researchers, but that I have not observed in my own work.

This cartography is in general agreement with perennial philosophy, although it is more complete and differs in some details. The category of experiences involving extension of consciousness within consensus reality and spacetime roughly corresponds to the astral-psychic domain of the lower subtle realm. Most of the experiences characterized by experiential extension beyond consensus reality and spacetime belong to the higher subtle realms. The experience of the final God or Cosmic Demiurg (*sāvikalpa samādhi*) seems to correspond to the lower causal level and the experience of formless consciousness transcending all dualities (*nirvikalpa samādhi*) or the Void (*śūnyata*) to the higher causal level. The Absolute or the Ultimate then would be the experience of the Suchness of all the levels and consciousness in its original condition.

It is necessary to bear in mind that transpersonal experiences do not always occur in a pure form. It was mentioned before that, for example, perinatal experiences characteristic of the individual matrices are frequently accompanied by specific types of transpersonal phenomena and that biographical experiences can have certain transpersonal features. Various forms of transpersonal experiences also tend to occur in clusters. Thus, embryonal experiences can appear in combination with phylogenetic memories, with the experience of cosmic unity, archetypal images of heavens or paradises, or with visions of various blissful deities or demons. These associations are very constant and they seem to reflect remarkable experiential logic and deep intrinsic interconnections among various phenomena in the world of consciousness.

In the following text, I will briefly describe and discuss the major types of transpersonal experiences and illustrate them with typical examples.

EXPERIENTIAL EXTENSION WITHIN
CONSENSUS REALITY AND SPACE-TIME

1   Transcendence of Spatial Boundaries

Transpersonal experiences which involve transcendence of spatial barriers suggest that the boundaries between the individual and the rest of the universe are not fixed and absolute. Under special circumstances, it is possible to identify experientially with anything in the universe, including the entire cosmos itself. Here belong the experiences of merging with another person into a state of dual unity or assuming another person's identity, of tuning into the consciousness of a specific group of people, or of expansion of one's consciousness to such an extent that it seems to encompass all of humanity. In a similar way, one can transcend the limits of the specifically human experience and identify with the consciousness of animals, plants, or even inorganic objects and processes. In the extremes, it is possible to experience the consciousness of the entire biosphere, of our planet, or of the entire material universe.

a.   Experience of Dual Unity

This type of transpersonal experience is characterized by loosening and melting of the boundaries of the bodyego and a sense of merging with another person into a state of unity and oneness. In spite of feeling fused with another, the subject retains awareness of his or her own identity. In psychedelic states, sessions of experiential psychotherapy, meditation, or spontaneous episodes of nonordinary consciousness, this sense of dual unity can be experienced in relation to the persons in the environment — therapist, sitter, family members, or friends. It can also occur entirely in the inner experiential space in relation to imagined individuals not present in the session.

The experience of dual unity occurs quite regularly in the sessions where the individual is reliving perinatal memories of the symbiotic fusion with the maternal organism ("good womb" and "good breast"). Under these circumstances, it is possible to have alternating experiences of identification with the child, the mother, and both of them simultaneously (dual unity). In states of mystical union with the universe, the state of dual unity can be experienced in relation to any aspect of existence — not only people, but animals, plants, and inanimate objects.

An important example of the experience of dual unity is the sense of fusion with the partner in a sexual situation (with or without the element of genital union). It can occur spontaneously under the circumstances of everyday life or in the context of intentional Tantric practice. In the left-handed path of Tantra (*vāma mārga*), the achievement of the experience of cosmic unity through sexual union with the partner (*maithuna*) is the objective of a complex sacred ritual (*pāncha makāra*). Experiences of dual unity also occur frequently during systematic spiritual practice (particularly in the *bkakti* tradition), where the disciples can experience a sense of union with the guru.

The experiences of dual unity are often accompanied by profound feelings of love and a sense of sacredness (numinosity) of the event. There exist specific exercises in the spiritual traditions and in the human potential movement that can facilitate such experiences by looking into another person's eyes, attending to another person's breath, synchronizing breathing, or listening to each other's heart beat.

The following example from a therapeutic LSD session combines a regressive experience of dual unity with the mother during the intrauterine existence and nursing with an experience of merging with the therapist. The patient was treated by psycholytic therapy for a psychotic condition; the condensed history of her treatment is given in my book *LSD Psychotherapy* (Grof 1980, pp. 246–51).

> At this point, Milada assumed a fetal position and seemed very regressed. I could see a remarkable change in her face. All her wrinkles had disappeared and she looked like a very small infant. She described that she felt a wonderful sense of oneness with her mother. There was no separation between the feelings of her mother and her own. She could shift freely from the experience of being herself as an infant in the womb or on the breast to the complementary experience of being her pregnant or nursing mother. She could also experience both of these roles at the same time, as if it were just one experiential continuum with absolutely no boundaries.
>
> When she opened her eyes, she noticed with great surprise that she was experiencing no boundaries between the two of us. She had the feeling that she could read my thoughts and my emotional processes. I could actually confirm this to be true on the few occasions when she verbalized her perceptions. Conversely, she felt that I had unlimited access to her mind and that I could "read her as an open book." However, this aspect of her experience was clearly a projection and did not reflect correctly my own situation. At a certain point, Milada also showed an element of paranoid fear that all her thoughts were being broadcast not only to me, but to other people and the whole world.

b.   Identification with Other Persons

This transpersonal experience is closely related to the preceding one. While merging experientially with another person, the subject has a sense of complete identification to the point of more or less losing the awareness of his or her own identity. The sense of becoming another person is total and complex. It involves the body image, physical sensations, emotional reactions and attitudes, thought processes, memories, facial expression, typical gestures and mannerisms, postures, movements, and even the inflection of the voice.

There exist many forms, degrees, and levels of this experience. It can happen in relation to persons who are in the presence of the subject, to currently living persons who are absent, or as part of an inner experience involving persons from the subject's childhood, ancestry, or past incarnation. Experiential identifications of this kind can involve famous personages from the present or past human history, or even mythological and archetypal characters.

Reliving of emotionally important memories from childhood, or even later life, that involve other persons is frequently characterized by simultaneous or alternating identification with all protagonists. This mechanism can give a transpersonal flavor to many personal biographical experiences. In this context, the subject can identify with his or her parents, children, other close relatives, important friends, acquaintances, and teachers. This process can also involve prominent politicians, scientists, artists, religious leaders, or typical representatives of other professional, ethnic, or racial groups in the past and present.

Among the famous historical and public figures that subjects have identified with in various nonordinary states of consciousness that I have witnessed were Alexander the Great, Emperor Nero, Cleopatra, Genghis Khan, Leonardo da Vinci, Michelangelo, Saint Francis of Assisi, Saint Theresa, Abraham Lincoln, Vladimir Ilyich Lenin, Joseph Stalin, Martin Luther King, Mohammed Ali, John F. Kennedy, and a variety of famous movie actors. Full identification with Christ and his suffering is a frequent and typical occurrence in the context of BPM III. Unlike the past incarnation experiences, simple identification with another person does not have the experiential quality of a memory and does not involve a sense of actually having been that person.

The experience of dual unity and identification with another person is frequently available to accomplished psychics. Here the experience does not have the unpredictable and elemental form it does in psychedelic states, sessions of experiential psychotherapy, meditation, or in spontaneous episodes of nonordinary consciousness (transpersonal crises), but can be voluntarily invoked and controlled. We have ourselves repeatedly witnessed most accurate and reliable readings by Anne Armstrong that involved, among others, these mechanisms. Also, experienced shamans seem to operate in this way while conducting healing or making psychic diagnosis.

I would like to use here as an example an episode from our own life. It is a powerful experience of identification with another person that occurred to my wife, Christina, at the time when she was lying in bed with a febrile virus disease. It involved a good friend of ours, the late anthropologist and generalist Gregory Bateson. At that time, Gregory was spending the last period of his life at the Esalen Institute, fighting his lung cancer. The surgeons had found during an exploratory operation a tumor the size of a grapefruit located very near to his vena cava. It was inoperable and Gregory was given four weeks to live. He was invited by the Esalen Institute to come and spend the rest of his life in the beautiful setting of the Big Sur Coast. During his stay, he underwent a variety of alternative treatments and, with several ups and downs, he actually lived more than two and half years. We had much interaction with him and his family and became close friends.

One morning, Christina decided to stay in bed because she was not feeling well. Suddenly, she had an overwhelming feeling that she was becoming Gregory. She had his giant body and his enormous hands, his thoughts, and his staunch British humor. She felt connected to the pain of his cancer and somehow knew with every cell of her body that he/she was dying. This surprised her, because it did not reflect her conscious assessment of his situation. His condition was worse in those days, but that had happened many times before, and she had no reason to suspect that this was anything more than a transient setback.

Later that day, Christina saw our friend Carl Simonton, who was visiting Esalen at that time. He was working with Gregory using the method of visualization that he had developed as an adjunct treatment of cancer. Christina found out that Carl and Gregory had worked together that morning. In the middle of the session, Gregory suddenly refused to continue and said: "I do not want to do this any more. I want to die." They called Gregory's wife Lois and started talking about dying instead of healing and fighting cancer. The timing of this episode exactly coincided with Christina's morning experience of identification with Gregory.

Christina felt very ambivalent about this episode. On the one hand, it was an unsolicited intrusion into her consciousness that was very frightening. On the other hand, during the few minutes of this fascinating experience, she learned more about Gregory than she had in years of our ordinary, everyday interaction. It seemed clear that experiences of this kind would be invaluable for diagnostic and therapeutic purposes, if they could be brought under full voluntary control.

c.   *Group Identification and Group Consciousness*

The experience of group identification is characterized by further extension of consciousness and melting of boundaries. Instead of identifying with individual persons, the subject has a sense of becoming an entire group of people who share some racial, cultural, national, ideological, political, or professional characteristics. In some other instances, the common denominator is the quality of physical and emotional experience or the predicament and destiny that brought these people together.

In transpersonal experiences of this kind, the subject can have an overwhelming sense of tuning into the group consciousness of all the Jews who have been persecuted through centuries, of the Christian martyrs tortured and sacrificed by the Romans, of the victims of the Inquisition who were interrogated, tortured and subjected to autos-da-fe, or of the prisoners of all ages suffering in dungeons or concentration camps. In these experiences, one can feel the quality of religious zeal of all the Moslems during their pilgrimage to Mecca, the devotion of the Hindus at the time of worship by the river Ganges, or the fanaticism of the members of extremist religious sects, such as the flagellants, the Russian Skopzy, or the snake-handling Holy Ghost people.

The depth, scope, and intensity of these experiences can reach extraordinary proportions. It is possible to experience the totality of suffering of all the soldiers who have ever died on the battlefields of the world since the beginning of history, the burning desire of the revolutionaries of all ages to overthrow the tyrant, or the love, tenderness, and dedication of all the mothers of the world taking care of their babies.

Progressive melting of boundaries can result in experiences of identification with a social or political group, population of an entire country or continent, all people belonging to a particular race, or all the believers in one of the world's great religions. In the extremes, it is possible to identify with the experience of all humanity and of the human condition — with its joy, anger, passion, sadness, glory, and tragedy.

Numerous descriptions of transpersonal experiences of this kind can be found in the spiritual literature as they occurred in the lives of prophets, saints, and great religious teachers of all ages. The surprising discovery of modern consciousness research has been that transpersonal experiences of this kind are under certain special circumstances available to everyone. A particularly moving modern example is the mystical experience of the American astronaut Rusty Schweickart, who had a powerful sense of identification with all of humanity on a spacewalk while orbiting the earth during the Apollo 9 mission (Schweickart 1985).

I will illustrate this type of transpersonal experience by two examples. The first of these is an excerpt from a high-dose LSD session of a psychiatrist. It took place shortly after his five-week visit to India.

> At this point, I was flooded by memories of my recent trip to India, experiencing again how deeply I was moved by the incredibly broad range of existence that one can encounter in that country — from the profound misery of unimaginable poverty, dirt, disease, and death to the timeless beauty of sublime temple architecture and sculpture and the highest achievements of human spirit. Before I could realize what was happening, the emphasis of my experience shifted. Instead of being a visitor and observer, I actually became identified with what I was perceiving. And then the spectrum of my experience moved beyond the range of my actual memories of India altogether.

Figure 4 A painting symbolizing extreme agony experienced in a session of holotropic breathing. Its source was the trauma of birth, but in its culmination it reached the proportions of experiential identification with the suffering humanity and all pain in the world.

I realized that I became the PEOPLE OF INDIA! As difficult as it might be to imagine in the everyday state of consciousness, I felt I was an immense organism whose ramifications and constituents were the countless millions of people inhabiting the subcontinent of India. The best parallel I can find is that of the human body. Each cell is in a way a separate entity, but also an infinitesimal part of the whole organism. And the consciousness and self-awareness reflects the whole, not the individual parts. In a similar way, I was one single immense conscious entity — the population of India.

However, at the same time, I was also identifying with individual lepers and crippled beggars in the streets of Bombay and Calcutta, peddlers selling *bidi* cigarettes or betel nuts, little children starving or dying by the side of the roads of mouth cancer, pious crowds performing their purification ceremonies on the Ganges or burning their relatives on the cremation *ghats* in Benares, the naked *sadhus* lying in *samadhi* in the ice and snow of the Himalayas, confused adolescent brides joining strangers in marriage ceremonies arranged by their families, and the fabulously rich and powerful maharajas.

All the glory and misery of India appeared in my experience as different elements of one cosmic organism, a deity of immense proportions whose millions of arms were reaching out and becoming all possible aspects of my existence. Unimaginable depth and range of sensations filled my entire being; I felt an indescribable connection with India and her people.

The following example comes from the account of a peyote experience of Crashing Thunder, a Winnebago Indian, who participated in the ceremony to find relief from profound guilt and alienation. He had lied to his people, pretending that he had a vision, and had subsequently ruined his life with drunkenness, womanizing, and even implication in a murder. His life was described in *The Autobiography of A Winnebago Indian* by Paul Radin (Radin 1920).

All of us sitting there, we had all together one spirit or soul. At least that is what I learned. I instantly became the spirit, and I was their spirit or soul. Whatever they thought, I immediately knew it. I did not have to speak to them and get an answer to know what their thought had been.

d.   Identification with Animals

This transpersonal experience involves a complete and realistic identification with members of various animal species. The most frequent objects of identification are other mammals, birds, reptiles, amphibians, and various species of fish. However, it can include organisms that are lower on the evolutionary pedigree, such as insects, gastropods (snails and slugs), brachiopods (shellfish), cephalopods (octopus and squid), and coelenterates (sea anemone and jellyfish).

The experiential identification with various animals can be extremely authentic and convincing. It includes the body image, specific physiological sensations, instinctual drives, unique perception of the environment and emotional reactions to it. These phenomena have certain unusual characteristics that distinguish them clearly from the ordinary human experience. Their nature and specific features often transcend the scope of human fantasy and imagination.

In the holotropic mode of consciousness, it is possible to gain experiential insight into what it feels like when a cat is curious, an eagle frightened, a cobra hungry, a turtle sexually aroused, or when a shark is breathing through the gills. After having had experiences of animal identification, subjects have reported that they obtained full organismic understanding of the drive that propels the eel or sockey salmon on their heroic journeys against the stream and up the rapids, of the impulses and sensations of the spider spinning its web, or of the mysterious process of metamorphosis from the egg through the stages of the caterpillar and chrysalis to the butterfly.

Experiences of this kind can be accompanied by acquisition of extraordinary knowledge about the animals and their processes. Numerous clinical observations of this kind find independent confirmation in a chapter of Bruce Lamb's *Wizard of the Upper Amazon* (Lamb 1971). This most interesting book bears some similarity to Carlos Castaneda's series describing his apprenticeship with the Mexican Yaqui sorcerer, Don Juan. In this story staged in the Amazonian jungle at the beginning of the century, the shaman of the preliterate Amahuaca Indians of Peru sees in his clairvoyant visions induced by *ayahuasca* (*yajé*), a psychedelic potion from the jungle vine *Banisteriopsis caapi*, the arrival of white people looking for rubber. He sends his warriors to capture a specific young man and he trains him for his future role as a cultural broker.

According to this book, the Amahuaca training for hunters included group ingestion of *ayahuasca*. Under the influence of the psychedelic brew, participants invoked visions of animals hunted by

a

b

Figure 5a–c Three paintings depicting experiences from a holotropic breathing session thematically focusing on the perinatal level. They represent successive identification with an archetypal Herculean figure, with a Viking warrior involved in a battle, and with a raging lion.

c

the tribe. They were able to tune into them and identify with them so fully that they got to know intimately their instincts and habits. Following this experience, their success in hunting increased considerably, since they were always able to switch from the consciousness of the hunter to the consciousness of the hunted animal and outwit their prey.

The first example I would like to use here to illustrate this type of experience comes from an unsupervised LSD session of a person involved in serious systematic self-exploration. After having read my books, he decided to share with me his session notes and to receive feedback.

> Then I had a very real experience of being an eagle. I was soaring by skillfully using the air currents and subtle changes of the position of my wings. I was scanning with my eyes the area far below me looking for prey. Everything on the ground seemed magnified as if seen through a binocular I could recognize the most miniscule details of the terrain. It seemed that I was responding to changes in the visual field. When I spotted movement, it was as if my eyes froze and zoomed in. It was something like tunnel vision, looking through a long and narrow tube. The feeling that this experience accurately represented the mechanism of vision in raptor birds (something I had never thought about or had been interested in) was so convincing and compelling that I decided to go to the library to study the anatomy and physiology of their optical system.

The following illustration is a sequence of experiences that occurred during systematic self-exploration of a young woman. They began during holotropic breathing and continued in a psychedelic session. The animal identification is combined here in an interesting way with the motif of a ritual dance representing the animal.

> Several years ago, in a session of breathwork with the Grofs, I experienced becoming a large cat — a tiger or jaguar — striking out, attacking with claws extended. The impression from that experience was very strong and I made a drawing of it.
>
> A year or so later, during a therapeutic psychedelic session, I connected again with the feline energy. I experienced myself as being a young African woman, dancing a ritual dance — dancing an animal, a female lion. In letting my body move with the rhythm of this dance, the movement through my shoulders, upper back, neck, and head became very specific. I had a strong sense that I was not just representing a lioness, but actually became one.
>
> I felt that the lioness does not determine her need for food by feelings in her stomach, but rather that this rubbing of the head back into the area between raised shoulders is her means of finding out whether she needs more food to add to her storage of fat for fuel, which is located between her shoulder blades. I had no doubt as to the function of the large pad on the neck and shoulders of large cats, but did nothing to research and confirm the fact empirically.
>
> Two weeks ago, I was listening to an educational tape on body weight. The speaker, William Bennett, briefly contrasted human adipose fat storage and animal fat storage. He described a type of fat not found in humans, but common in animals, called "brown fat." Brown fat is stored as a pad between the scapulae of some animals and must be maintained at a certain level to ensure sufficient energy and health for the survival of the animal.

The last example is Peter Stafford's report about his animal identifications during a session with *yajé* that he experienced with his friends in the Valley of Fire near Las Vegas (Aaronson and Osmond 1970).

> The surface of the water shimmered and beckoned. Soon we went back down to the water's edge, eager to stretch and swim, to dive, and swirl around. The only drag was keeping on a swimsuit. It seemed so unnecessary and unnatural! Especially since I had become a snake writhing about in the water. I maneuvered in and out of a

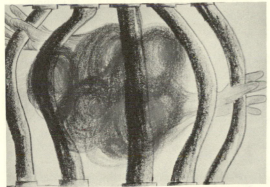

a

b

c

Figure 6a–c Three paintings expressing intense feelings of aggression experienced in a holotropic breathing session focusing on the perinatal level of the unconscious. Powerful destructive energy breaking out of imprisonment takes successively the form of identification with an angry tiger and with a demonic creature.

swamp. Minutes later, I found myself a frog and started propelling myself with long kicks. In both cases, water seemed my natural habitat, and land was distant, alien, somewhat terrifying.

After a while, my mind decided that I would like to climb a small mountain that looked down on this idyllic setting, but by now I was a sea lion, so it was difficult to get myself up and onto dry land. As I waded out, I felt awkward, silly, completely out of my element.

When I say I felt as though I was first one water creature and then another, what I mean goes far beyond merely 'feeling slithery and reptilian.' The experience had a different feel to it, different from anything I had previously felt, both physically and mentally. Under the drug, I was conscious of having different types of memories, and I lost my normal self-awareness. Rather than empathy with what I might imagine a snake or frog might feel, I was sufficiently absorbed in snakeness and frogness as to wonder how the humans around me might feel.

What does it mean that while under the yajé I did not merely 'feel like a snake,' but in some sense, I was a snake, that somehow I had reached a level of experience where I could contact a potential "snakeness" residing within? What does it mean that I felt my perceptions were being sorted in terms of new and different categories?

e.   *Identification with Plants and Botanical Processes*

Transpersonal experiences involving plant life are common in nonordinary states of consciousness, although less frequent than animal identification. An individual tuned into this experiential realm has a convinced sense of identification with various plants, parts of plants, or even physiological and biochemical processes in them. He or she can have a complex experience of becoming a tree, a wild or garden flower, carnivorous plant, kelp, Volvox globator, plankton in the ocean, and even a bacterial culture, or individual bacterium.

In the holotropic mode, it is possible to identify experientially with a root system of a tree involved in the exchange of water and minerals, with the circulation of sap in the cambium, with a leaf in the course of photosynthetic activity, with the germinating seed and the thrust of the seedling, with the process of pollination, or with the cellular divisions during vegetable growth. On occasion, subjects have reported that they witnessed botanical processes on the subcellular and molecular level. They became experientially aware of the activities of the mitochondria or of the biochemical processes underlying the production of auxins, vegetable pigments, oils and sugars, aromatic substances, and various alkaloids.

The experiences of plant consciousness represent an interesting category of transpersonal phenomena. No matter how fantastic and absurd their existence might seem to a traditional scientist and to our common sense, it is not possible to discard them as mere fantasies. They occur independently in many individuals at a certain stage of their consciousness evolution and have a quality of authenticity that cannot be easily communicated in words. They often lead to profound new understanding of the processes involved and are associated with fascinating philosophical and spiritual insights.

The most common of these insights is the awareness of the special quality and purity of the existence of plants that make them important examples for human spiritual life. Unlike animals and man, most plants do not kill or lead a predatory type of existence. They are in direct contact with the sun, the life-giving principle of this planet and the most immediate expression of cosmic creative energy. Plants transform this cosmic energy directly into forms in which it can be useful to other organisms. It seems to be of special significance in this context that they provide oxygen for other life forms. In this way, they are absolutely indispensable for life on this planet. Another important aspect of vegetable life is that it is in direct and immediate contact with all the remaining elements of earth, water, and air.

While not killing, hurting, or exploiting other living organisms, many plants themselves serve as sources of food, minerals, and vitamins for other life forms. In addition, they have many other uses in human life, providing numerous materials and substances and bringing beauty and joy. The life of plants is not confounded by inauthentic ambitions to become something other than what they are, by painful ruminations of the past, by conflicts about the pursuit of alternative goals, or by concerns about the future. They seem to represent pure being in the here and now in full contact with the immediate environment, which is the ideal of many mystical schools. In some subjects, this fascination with the purity of the vegetable kingdom together with the aversion toward slaughter generated by perinatal experiences can result in appreciation of and interest in a vegetarian diet.

Trees known for their longevity, such as the gigantic sequoias and redwoods or the tiny bristlecone pines, are often experienced as representing a state of unperturbed, centered, and timeless consciousness independent of the turmoils and upheavals of the world. Experiences of plant identification also often mediate deep understanding as to why certain plants have been considered sacred by some cultures, such as the banyon tree by the Indians, the lotus by the Indians and Egyptians, the mistletoe by the Druids, or the corn by the North and South American Indians.

More direct and obvious insights into the spiritual aspects of plants are related to those specimens that have been considered sacred and have been used ritually by different cultures and groups because of their psychedelic or entheogenic effects. Among the psychedelic plants that have played a critical role in the spiritual life of humanity are the legendary Vedic sacrament *soma* whose botanical identity is unknown, the African *eboga* (*Tabernanthe iboga*), various parts of hemp (*Cannabis indica* and *sativa*), the fly *agaric* (*Amanita muscaria*), the Mexican sacred mushrooms *teonanacatl* (*Psilocybe mexicana*), the visionary cactus peyote (*Lophophora williamsii*), morning glory seeds or *ololiuqui* (*Turbina corymbosa*), and the Amazonian *liana Banisteriopsis caapi*, the main ingredient of *yajé* or *ayahuasca*. The insights into the numinous role of these plants will naturally be most likely when they are ingested and their specific psychedelic effect is directly experienced.

A typical example of the of experience of plant identification is given later in this book in the context of the discussion of therapeutic mechanisms (p. 245).

f. Oneness with Life and All Creation

In some rare instances, an individual in the holotropic mode can have the experience of consciousness expanding to such an extent that it encompasses the totality of life on this planet, including all of humanity and the entire fauna and flora, from viruses and unicellular organisms to highly differentiated species. Instead of the ordinary identification with one living organism, this experience represents identification with life as a cosmic phenomenon.

In some instances, the experience can focus on a particular aspect of life, such as the power of hunger, of the sexual drive, or of the maternal instinct. It can explore the mandatory nature of the law that life always lives on life, or display the astonishing intelligence governing the life processes on various levels of evolution. Sequences of this kind leave no doubt in the experiencer that the phenomena of life cannot be explained by mechanistic science, and that they prove the existence of creative cosmic intelligence.

Sometimes, the experience of identification with all of life is only horizontal, involving all the complex interactions and interdependences of various life forms in all the permutations of their synergisms and antagonisms that constitute the planetary ecology. Other times, it includes as well the longitudinal, evolutionary dimension of life that will be discussed later (p. 93). Experiences of this kind can result in deep understanding of the cosmic and natural laws, enhanced ecological awareness, and great sensitivity to problems created by rapid technological development and industrialization.

The following is a segment of an LSD session (300 micrograms) of a psychiatrist, in which the identification with the totality of life on this planet was very prominent.

> I seemed to have connected in a very profound way with life on this planet. At first, I went through a whole series of identifications with various species, but later the experience was more and more encompassing. My identity spread not only horizontally in space to include all living forms, but also vertically in time. I became the Darwinian evolutionary tree in all its ramifications. I was the totality of life!
>
> I sensed the cosmic quality of the energies and experiences involved in the world of living forms, the endless curiosity and experimentation characterizing life, and the drive for self-expression operating on many different levels. The crucial question I seemed to be dealing with was whether life on this planet would survive. Is it a viable and constructive phenomenon, or a malignant growth on the face of the Earth that contains some fatal flaw in its blueprint condemning it to self-destruction? Is it possible that some basic error occurred when the design for the evolution of organic forms was originally laid down? Can creators of universes make mistakes as humans do? It seemed at the moment a plausible, but very frightening idea, something I had never considered before.
>
> Identifying with life, I experienced and explored an entire spectrum of destructive forces operating in nature and in human beings and saw their dangerous extensions and projections in modern technology threatening to destroy this planet. In this context, I became all the countless victims of the military machinery of modern warfare, prisoners in concentration camps dying in gas chambers, fish poisoned in polluted streams, plants killed by herbicides, and insects sprayed by chemicals.

This alternated with moving experiences of smiling infants, charming children playing in the sand, newly born animals and newly hatched birds in carefully built nests, wise dolphins and whales cruising the crystal-clear waters of the ocean, and images of beautiful pastures and forests. I felt profound empathy with life, strong ecological awareness, and a real determination to join the pro-life forces on this planet.

g. *Experience of Inanimate Matter and Inorganic Processes*

Experiential extension of consciousness in the holotropic mode is not limited to the world of biology; it can include macroscopic and microscopic phenomena of inorganic nature. Subjects have repeatedly reported that they had experientially identified with the water in rivers and oceans, with various forms of fire, with the earth and mountains, or with the forces unleashed in natural catastrophies, such as electric storms, earthquakes, tornadoes, and volcanic eruptions.

Equally common is identification with specific materials — diamond and other precious stones, quartz crystal, amber, granite, iron, steel, quicksilver, silver, or gold. These experiences can extend into the microworld and involve the dynamic structure of molecules and atoms, the Brownian movement, interatomic bonds, and even electromagnetic forces and the subatomic particles.

On occasion, experiences of this kind involve highly sophisticated products of modern technology, such as jets, rockets and spaceships, lasers, or computers. Under these circumstances, the body image can assume all the qualities of the materials and processes involved, so that they become complex, conscious experiences. It seems that every process in the universe that one can observe objectively in the ordinary state of consciousness also has a subjective experiential counterpart in the holotropic mode.

Experiences of this kind suggest that consciousness and creative intelligence are not products of inanimate matter, but that they play a critical role in the entire fabric of existence. This is a notion that is being increasingly confirmed by modern developments in subatomic physics, astrophysics, biology, thermodynamics, information and systems theory, and other branches of science.

It is of particular interest that experiential identification with the inorganic world is not limited to the secular aspects, but has often distinct numinous or spiritual qualities. The identification with water can thus be experienced simultaneously as a state of consciousness characterized by timelessness, fluidity, melting of boundaries, quiet unassuming strength, purification and cleansing, and the paradoxical combination of immutability and dynamic change.

Similarly, fire can be experienced as a spiritual force of awesome power with its capacity to create and destroy, transform solid forms into energy, comfort and nourish or threaten and hurt, and potentially purify. The element of fire, particularly in the form of the sun, is often experienced as a direct manifestation of the cosmic creative force in the universe, the most immediate manifestation of the divine in the phenomenal world.

In congruence with many mystical systems through the ages, the experiences related to various precious stones and metals, particularly diamond and gold, are associated with very high spiritual states characterized by ultimate purity, immutability, and special radiance. Their images often occur in connection with archetypal visions of paradises, heavens, or celestial cities. Aldous Huxley's famous talk "The Visionary Experience" in which he addresses the question "Why Are Precious Stones Precious?" (Huxley 1983), is particularly relevant from this point of view. His answer is that the enormous value that we attribute to precious stones and metals is based upon the fact that they are surrogates for us of a mystical experience. In our everyday consciousness, they represent the closest approximation to certain experiential characteristics of the visionary states.

Experiential identification with inorganic matter is often accompanied by fascinating insights of a philosophical, mythological, religious, and mystical nature. The intimate relationship between the experiences of the inorganic world and spiritual states can convey an entirely new understanding of animism and pantheism, medieval alchemy, homeopathy, the systems of four and five elements found in Greek philosophy, Chinese medicine, or in Tantric scriptures, and many other ancient and Oriental teachings.

For subjects who have had the experience of identification with water, it is easy to understand why it has such paramount significance in Taoism and is so often used as a spiritual metaphor. On the basis of a deep personal experience, it is also easy to comprehend why the sun has been worshipped by so many cultures as God, or why volcanoes have been perceived as deities of creation and destruction. Similarly, experiential identification with granite can convey a deep insight into why the Hindus see the Himalayas as reclining Shiva, or why various cultures created gigantic granite sculptures.

On a deeper level, these are not images of deities or idols, but the deities themselves. It is the state of consciousness associated with these materials — undifferentiated, imperturbable, unchangeable and transcending linear time — that is the true deity. It is worshipped because it differs so dramatically from the mercurial, turbulent, and erratic states of consciousness characterizing ordinary human existence and the world of biology. The importance of the fact that time is different for different realms of the phenomenal world has been recently emphasized by Ilya Prigogine (Prigogine and Stengers 1984) and Eric Jantsch (Jantsch 1980).

I will illustrate this remarkable type of experience by an account of a session with 150 milligrams of Ketalar (ketamine), a dissociative anesthetic used in surgery and veterinarian medicine. It seems that after the administration of this substance, experiential identification with inorganic matter is particularly frequent.

> The atmosphere was dark, heavy, and ominous. It seemed to be toxic and poisonous in a chemical sense, but also dangerous and evil in the metaphysical sense. I realized I was becoming PETROLEUM, filling enormously large cavities in the interior of the earth. I was flooded with fascinating insights combining chemistry, geology, biology, psychology, mythology, economy, and politics.
>
> I understood that petroleum — immense deposits of mineralized fat of biological origin — had escaped the mandatory cycle of death and birth that the world of living matter is subjected to. However, the element of death was not completely avoided, it was only delayed. The destructive plutonic potential of death continues to exist in petroleum in a latent form and waits for its opportunity as a monstrous time-bomb.
>
> While experiencing what I felt was consciousness of petroleum, I saw the death associated with it manifesting as killing based on greed and lust of those who seek the astronomical profits that it offers. I witnessed scenes of political intrigues and economic shenanigans motivated by oil money. It was not difficult to follow the chains of events to a future world war for the dwindling resources of a substance that has become vital for the survival and prosperity of all the industrialized countries.

It became clear to me that it is essential for the future of the planet to reorient the economic life to solar energy and other renewable resources. The linear policy of fossil fuels that plunders the limited existing reserves and turns them into toxic waste and pollution is obviously fundamentally wrong, being totally incompatible with the cosmic order that is cyclical. While the exploitation of fossil fuels was understandable in the historical context of the Industrial Revolution, its continuation once its fatal trajectory was recognized seemed suicidal and criminal.

In a long series of hideous and most unpleasant experiences, I was taken through states of consciousness related to the chemical industry based on petroleum. Using the name of the famous German chemical combinate, I referred to these experiences as the IG Farben consciousness. It was an infinite sequence of states of mind that had the quality of anilin dyes, organic solvents, herbicides, pesticides, and toxic gases.

Beside the experiences related to these various industrial poisons per se, I also identified with the states of consciousness associated with the exposure of different life forms to the petroleum products. I became every Jew who died in the Nazi gas chambers, every sprayed ant and cockroach, every fly caught in the sticky goo of the fly-traps, and every plant dying under the influence of herbicides. And beyond all that lurked the highly possible future of all of life on the planet — death by industrial pollution.

It was an incredible lesson. I emerged from the session with a deep ecological awareness and a clear sense as to which direction the economic and political development has to take should life on the planet survive.

h. Planetary Consciousness

In this type of transpersonal experience, the consciousness of the subject expands to such an extent that it seems to encompass all aspects of this planet; this includes its geological substance with the entire mineral kingdom, as well as the biosphere with all the life forms including humans. From this point of view, the entire earth seems to be one complex organism, a cosmic entity whose different aspects — geological, biological, psychological, cultural, and technological phenomena — can be seen as manifestations of a sustained effort to reach a higher level of evolution, integration, and self-actualization.

This experience typically involves also the mythological dimension and has a distinctly numinous quality. In this context, the earth can be perceived as Mother Earth or a divine being, in the sense of the Greek goddess Gaia. It is easy to see that the processes on earth are guided by superior intelligence that by far supercedes ours, and that it should be respected and trusted and not be tempered and interfered with from a limited human perspective. This insight that has repeatedly emerged in nonordinary states of consciousness in many individuals has recently received independent support from modern science.

Gregory Bateson, who achieved in his work a brilliant synthesis of the perspectives of cybernetics, information and systems theory, theory of evolution, anthropology, and psychology (Bateson 1979), came to the conclusion that it is not only legitimate, but logically inevitable to assume the existence of mental processes on all the levels of natural phenomena of sufficient complexity — cells, organs, tissues, organisms, animal and human groups, eco-systems, and even the earth and the universe as a whole. In this way of thinking, science has confirmed the old concept of *deus sive natura*, or the existence of immanent God as articulated by Spinoza.

Quite independently, James Lovelock amassed in his remarkable book *Gaia: A New Look at Life on Earth* (Lovelock 1979) fascinating evidence about intricate homeostatic mechanisms maintaining the steadiness of the earth's temperataure and concentration of the key components in the atmosphere, ocean water, and soil, such as salt, oxygen, ammonia, and ozone. His findings are compatible with the assumption that the earth is an intelligent organism. Theodore Roszak in his book *Person/Planet* (Roszak 1978) and Peter Russell in his *Global Brain* (Russell 1983) reached similar conclusions.

The following example of planetary consciousness comes from a holotropic breathing session of a young German woman who attended several years ago one of our five-day workshops.

> The experience of being the Great Mother Goddess, Mother Earth, then changed into actually becoming the planet Earth. There was no question that I — the Earth — was a living organism, an intelligent being trying to understand myself, struggling to evolve to a higher level of awareness, and attempting to communicate with other cosmic beings.
>
> The metals and minerals constituting the planet were my bones, my skeleton. The biosphere — the plant life, animals, and humans —

were my flesh. I experienced within myself the circulation of water from the oceans to the clouds and from there into little creeks and large rivers and back into the sea. The water system was my blood and the meteorological changes — the evaporation, air currents, the rainfall, and the snow — insured its circulation, transport of nourishment, and cleansing. The communication between plants, animals, and humans, including modern technology — the press, telephone, radio, television, and the computer network — was my nervous system, my brain.

I felt in my body the injury of the industrial insults of strip mining, urbanization, toxic and radioactive waste, and pollution of air and water. The strangest part of the session was that I was aware of rituals among various aboriginal peoples and experienced them as very healing and absolutely vital for myself. It seems somewhat weird and bizarre to me now, when I have returned to my everyday rational thinking, but during my experience it was extremely convincing that doing rituals is important for the Earth.

i. Extraterrestrial Experiences

In these experiences consciousness extends to celestial bodies, parts of the universe, and astronomical processes that are outside of the terrestrial sphere. The individual can have a sense of travel to the moon, sun, other planets, stars, and galaxies and can experience explosions of supernovas, contraction of stars, quasars and pulsars, and passage through black holes. This can occur in the form of simply witnessing such events, or actually becoming them and experiencing in one's own experiential field all the processes involved.

Like the identification with inorganic matter described above, these experiences often have spiritual concomitants and counterparts. Thus, for example, experimental identification with the thermonuclear processes inside the sun can be associated with a sense of contact with the creative power of cosmic consciousness. The experience of passage through the black hole typically involves experiential collapse of time, space, and of the philosophical belief in the material reality of the phenomenal world. The experience of the interstellar space connects similarly with the spiritual experience of the Void described later in this chapter (p. 147).

Extraterrestrial experiences seem to be unusually frequent in the nonordinary states of consciousness of John Lilly, the famous neuroscientist known for his research of nonhuman intelligence and interspecies communication, as well as for his unparalleled marathons in psychedelic self-experimentation. In his sessions, he experienced numerous visits to alien worlds and encounters or communication with strange beings and presences. Here is his description of one of such events facilitated by the injection of 75 milligrams of the dissociative anesthetic Ketalar (ketamine) and his stay in a sensory isolation tank (Lilly 1978).

> I have left my body floating in a tank on the planet Earth. This is a very strange and alien environment. It must be extraterrestrial, I have not been here before. I must be on some other planet in some civilization other than the one in which I was evolved. I am in a peculiar state of high indifference. I am not involved in either fear or love. I am a highly neutral being, watching and waiting.
>
> This is very strange. This planet is similar to Earth but the colors are different. There is vegetation but it is a peculiar purple color. There is a sun but it has a violet hue to it, not the familiar orange of Earth's sun. I am in a beautiful meadow with distant, extremely high mountains. Across the meadow I see creatures approaching. They stand on their hind legs, as if human. They are a brilliant white and seem to be emitting light. Two of them come near. I cannot make out their features. They are too brilliant for my present vision. They seem to be transmitting thoughts and ideas directly to me. There is no sound. Automatically, what they think is translated into words that I can understand.

j. Identification with the Entire Physical Universe

This rare experience represents a further logical extension beyond the planetary and extraterrestrial experiences. Here the subject has the feeling that his or her consciousness has expanded to such an extent that it has encompassed the entire physical universe. All the cosmic processes are then experienced as intraorganismic and intrapsychic phenomena within this immense being. This is typically associated with the insight that while various entities of the phenomenal world are experiencing only certain specific aspects of the material reality, the cosmic or divine consciousness has a complete and total simultaneous experience of everything there is, both from the point of view of the individual separate units of consciousness and from that of the undivided whole as experienced from the center.

k. *Psychic Phenomena Involving Transcendence of Space*
(Out-of-Body Experiences, Traveling Clairvoyance
and Clairaudience, "Space-Travels", and Telepathy)

This subgroup of ESP phenomena traditionally studied by parapsychology can be seen as transpersonal experiences involving transcendence of spatial barriers and distances. They can occur in a pure form or in combination with simultaneous transcendence of linear time. The experience of consciousness detaching from one's body, or out-of-body experience (OOBE), has various forms and degrees. It can take the form of isolated episodes, or can occur repeatedly as part of psychic opening and other types of transpersonal crises.

Among the circumstances that are particularly conducive to OOBEs are vital emergencies, near-death situations, experiences of clinical death, sessions of deep experiential psychotherapy, and ingestion of psychedelic substances, especially the dissociative anesthetic Ketamine (Ketalar). Classical descriptions of OOBEs can be found in spiritual literature and philosophical texts of all ages, particularly in the *Tibetan Book of the Dead* (*Bardo Thötröl* or *Thödöl*) and other similar literature. These descriptions were not taken seriously by traditional science until recently, when modern research in experimental psychiatry and thanatology confirmed their authenticity.

During less extreme forms of OOBE, one has a sense of leaving the body, detaching from it, and seeing oneself from various distances as an object (héautoscopy). In more advanced forms of OOBE, the individual experiences himself or herself in other rooms of the building, in remote locations (astral projection), flying above the earth, or moving away from it. A particularly dramatic and moving description of an OOBE in a near-death state can be found in the autobiography of Carl Gustav Jung (Jung 1961). In these states, the subject can accurately witness events in the areas to which detached consciousness projects. Although this should be, in principle, impossible according to Cartesian-Newtonian science, the authenticity of this phenomenon has been repeatedly confirmed and is beyond any doubt.

The research of Raymond Moody (Moody 1975), Kenneth Ring (Ring 1980 and 1984), Michael Sabom (Sabom 1982), Elisabeth Kübler-

Ross (Kűbler-Ross 1985), my own study (Grof and Halifax 1977), and work of many others have repeatedly confirmed that clinically dead people can have OOBEs, during which they accurately witness the resuscitation procedures from a position near the ceiling, or perceive events in remote locations. According to Elisabeth Kübler-Ross (Kübler-Ross 1984), even blind persons have under these circumstances the ability to perceive the environment visually in colors. Modern thanatological research thus confirms the descriptions from the *Tibetan Book of the Dead*, according to which an individual after death assumes the "bardo body" that transcends the limitations of time and space and can freely travel around the earth.

Observations from psychedelic research, holotropic breathing, and other types of experiential psychotherapy similarly confirm the possibility of authentic OOBEs during visionary states, as they have been reported in various mystical sources and in anthropological literature. Clairvoyance and clairaudience of remote events can occur without a sense of actually being there, in the form of astral travel to the location involved, or as instant astral projection. In rare instances, the subject can actually actively control and direct the astral space travel. The famous OOBE veteran and researcher Robert Monroe (Monroe 1971), who had struggled for many years with spontaneous and elemental OOBEs, not only learned how to control them, but also developed specific exercises and electronic technology to facilitate their occurrence.

The authenticity of OOBEs has been demonstrated in controlled clinical experiments by the famous psychologist and parapsychologist Charles Tart at the University of California at Davis (Tart 1974). A highly successful series of scientifically designed "remote viewing" experiments has been conducted at the Stanford Research Institute in California by the physicists Russell Targ and Harold Puthoff (Targ and Puthoff 1977). Among the most remarkable performances in "remote viewing" were the sessions with the psychic Ingo Swann, who repeatedly demonstrated his ability to describe accurately any place on the globe when given the numerical coordinates for its longitude and latitude. However, even more interesting were the findings of these scientists indicating that practically everybody can be trained to perform successfully in these experiments.

Telepathy is direct access to the thought processes of another individual without the mediation of words, nonverbal clues, or other conventional means of communication. Telepathic flashes occur occasionally in ordinary states of consciousness. However, the incidence of telepathic exchange increases considerably when the individual moves into the holotropic mode induced by meditation, experiential techniques of psychotherapy, ingestion of psychedelics, or vital emergency. Although it might not always be easy to distinguish telepathy from other types of parapsychological and transpersonal experiences, careful research leaves little doubt that it is a genuine phenomenon.

The following example is a remarkable out-of-body experience with accurate perception of a remote location reported by Kimberly Clark, who works as a social worker in Seattle. The circumstances of this case were so extraordinary and convincing that the event instigated in her a lasting interest in OOBEs (Greyson and Flynn 1984).

My first encounter with a near-death experience involved a patient named Maria, a migrant worker who was visiting friends in Seattle and had a severe heart attack. She was brought into the hospital by the rescue squad one night and admitted to the coronary care unit. I got involved in her care as a result of her social and financial problems. A few days after her admission, she had a cardiac arrest. Because she was so closely monitored and was otherwise in good health, she was brought back quickly, intubated for a couple of hours to make sure that her oxygenation was adequate, and then extubated.

Later in the day I went to see her, thinking that she might have some anxiety about the fact that her heart had stopped. In fact, she was anxious, but not for that reason. She was in a state of relative agitation, in contrast to her usual calmness. She wanted to talk to me about something. She said: "The strangest thing happened when the doctors and nurses were working on me: I found myself looking down from the ceiling at them working on my body."

I was not impressed at first. I thought that she might know what had been going on in the room, what people were wearing, and who would be there, since she had seen them all day prior to her cardiac arrest. Certainly she was familiar with the equipment by that time. Since hearing is the last sense to go, I reasoned that she could hear everything that was going on, and while I did not think she was consciously making this up, I thought it might have been a confabulation.

She then told me that she had been distracted by something over the emergency room driveway and found herself outside, as if she had "thought herself" over the emergency room driveway and, in just that instant, she was out there. At this point, I was a little more impressed, since she had arrived at night inside an ambulance and would not have known what the emergency room area looked like. However, I reasoned that perhaps at some point in time her bed had been by the window, she had looked outside, and this had been incorporated into the confabulation.

But then Maria proceeded to describe being further distracted by an object on the third floor ledge on the north end of the building. She "thought her way" up there and found herself "eyeball to shoelace" with a tennis shoe, which she asked me to try to find for her. She needed someone else to know that the tennis shoe was really there to validate her out-of-body experience.

With mixed emotions, I went outside and looked up at the ledges but could not see much at all. I went up to the third floor and began going in and out of patients' rooms and looking out their windows, which were so narrow that I had to press my face to the screen just to see the ledge at all. Finally, I found a room where I pressed my face to the glass and looked down and saw the tennis shoe!

My vantage point was very different from what Maria's had to have been for her to notice that the little toe had worn a place in the shoe and that the lace was stuck under the heel and other details about the side of the shoe not visible to me. The only way she would have had such a perspective was if she had been floating right outside and at very close range to the tennis shoe. I retrieved the shoe and brought it back to Maria; it was very concrete evidence for me.

The experience of extraordinary perception can be associated with deep metaphysical fear, since it challenges and undermines the world view that the Western culture subscribes to and associates with sanity. The following episode from my psychedelic training session with 250 micrograms of LSD at the Maryland Psychiatric Research Center can be used here as an example. A similar situation involving an out-of-body experience with directed space travel was described in my book *Realms of the Human Unconscious* (Grof 1975, pp 187–90).

When I was feeling strongly the effects of the drug, my guide for the session (Walter Pahnke) introduced his ESP experiment as we had agreed upon before we started. It was a modification of the famous Zener deck of cards. I was given a keyboard with five different symbols — a circle, square, cross, star, and two wavy lines resembling the astrological sign for Aquarius; the keys were also color-coded. This keyboard was connected to an identical one in the adjacent room, on which the keys could be lit either manually by the experimenter or electronically following a pattern based on the table of random numbers. The experiment was structured so that the subject operated with or without feedback as to the success of the guesses.

At first, my approach was very casual and playful. I was either pressing one of the keys automatically, or was using as a clue the nature and color of my visions. After a while, I started feeling that this experiment was a serious matter. Testing of ESP cannot be isolated from some very fundamental questions about human consciousness, role of the psyche in the world, and the nature of reality. What we were testing was not the existence or non-existence of extrasensory perception, but the validity of the current scientific worldview. Unquestionably positive results would destroy the present belief system and shatter the sense of certainty and security that an average Westerner draws from it.

At the same time, it seemed clear that this alternative worldview was obvious and self-evident; extrasensory perception seemed an easy task, a child's play. I felt total identification with John (Lennox) who was in the other room supervising the keyboard. I could taste the menthol flavor of the gum he was chewing on and was sure that I could see the panel through his eyes. It also seemed that, in a similar way, I could use Helen (Bonny), who was much more emotional and sensitive, to connect with the colors.

Just at this time, Walter announced through the microphone that he would give me feedback about correct and incorrect guesses. I got the first symbol correct and started having a strange sense of excitement and adventure. When I got the next one correct immediately following the first, this feeling increased enormously. The third correct answer in a row sent me into a state of metaphysical panic. The possibility of transcending the limitations of space and time was becoming a reality, confirmed by objective scientific testing.

I saw clearly the image of the fourth symbol, but became strangely afraid to report it to the experimenters. I decided to name a different one, choosing on purpose a one to four probability that I was right, instead of risking the certainty of another correct guess. (As I checked after the session, the image I saw, but decided not to report was the correct one; this was a result that could occur by chance in one of 625 trials.) At this point, I refused to continue any further, to Wallie's great disappointment. The reason for discontinuing the experiment was a strange mixture of conviction that it was absurd to test the obvious and of fear to have this confirmed by the methods of Western science.

2   Transcendence of the Boundaries of Linear Time

In nonordinary states of consciousness, many subjects experience concrete and realistic episodes which they describe as fetal and embryonal memories. It is not unusual under these circumstances to identify with the embryo in very early stages of its intrauterine development, or even with the sperm and the ovum at the time of conception. Sometimes the historical regression goes even further and the individual has a convinced feeling of reliving memories from the lives of his or her ancestors, or even drawing on the memory banks of the racial or collective unconscious. When such sequences are associated with a sense of personal memory from one's spiritual rather than biological history, we can refer to them as *karmic* or past incarnation experiences. On occasion, subjects report experiences in which they identify with specific animal ancestors in the evolutionary pedigree, or with the entire phylogenetic tree. It is even possible to experience the history of the Universe before the origin of life on earth and witness dramatic sequences of the Big Bang, formation of the galaxies, birth of the solar system, and the early geophysical processes on this planet.

a.   Embryonal and Fetal Experiences

I have already briefly mentioned some experiences of this kind in the context of the first perinatal matrix (BPM I). Since the concept of perinatal experiences and matrices refers to processes immediately associated with biological birth, only intrauterine experiences in advanced stages of pregnancy belong to BPM I. However, in the process of systematic self-exploration with psychedelics, powerful nondrug techniques of psychotherapy, or meditation, the subject can connect experientially with any stage of embryonal and fetal development.

These experiences portray in a concrete, realistic, and detailed way various prenatal situations, usually those that are dramatic and associated with a strong emotional charge. The sequences of undisturbed intraterine existence are experienced as episodes of oceanic ecstasy with a mystical connection to life and to the cosmic creative force, while the various crises of prenatal development are experienced as states of anguish, paranoia, physical distress, and attacks of demonic forces. Both types of prenatal sequences typically associate with other types of transpersonal phenomena, most frequently with phylogenetic, karmic, and archetypal experiences and with organ, tissue, and cellular consciousness. These phenomena will be discussed later in this book.

Many prenatal experiences are related to intrauterine psychotraumatization resulting from various noxious and disturbing stimuli of a mechanical, physiological, or biochemical nature. Observations from psychedelic and holotropic sessions suggest that the fetus can experience not only gross disturbances of the intrauterine existence, such as imminent miscarriage and attempted abortion, intense mechanical concussions and vibrations, loud sounds, toxic influences, and somatic disease of the mother, but also share the mother's emotions. Many subjects have repeatedly reported that during experiences of intrauterine existence they could clearly participate in their mothers' emotional shocks, anxiety attacks, outbursts of hate or aggression, depressive mood, and sexual arousal, or, conversely, in their feelings of relaxation, satisfaction, happiness, and love.

This complex exchange and experiential sharing is not limited to intense and dramatic physical and emotional events. It can often include nuances and subtleties of feeling qualities and even telepathic transfer of thoughts and images. During the reliving of episodes from intrauterine existence, subjects have repeatedly reported that they were keenly aware of being unwanted and resented, or, conversely, desired and loved. It was as if they were receiving a clear organismic message expressing their mothers' feelings about the pregnancy, as well as specific loving or hostile communications directed toward them.

For many individuals, memories of fetal traumatization seem to be among important factors underlying general emotional instability and various specific forms of psychopathology. Similarly, the question of having been wanted or unwanted by one's mother appears again and again as an issue of critical importance that requires much time and effort in deep experiential therapy of any kind. For those individuals who were born as twins, the problems of sharing the womb with a partner and competitor represent a special challenge and can have profound effects on future psychological development.

The authenticity of embryonal memories in experiential psychotherapy with or without psychedelics is an important question that has far-reaching practical and theoretical implications. It is comparable to the problems related to reliving memories from early infancy, only more difficult and fundamental. Perinatal and prenatal material has been repeatedly reported in psychoanalytic literature, but with a few exceptions, such as Otto Rank (Rank 1929), Sandor Ferenczi (Ferenczi 1938), Nandor Fodor (Fodor 1949), and Lietaert Peerbolte (Peerbolte 1975), it has not been taken seriously. While postnatal events remembered or reconstructed by patients during psychoanalysis, unless too fantastic and incredible, have always been given serious consideration as possibly reflecting real events, references to birth and to the intrauterine state have been routinely referred to as fantasies.

Having witnessed over the years countless episodes of embryonal and fetal experiences in other people and having experienced several prenatal episodes myself, both in psychedelic sessions and in nondrug contexts, I find it impossible to discard them simply as figments of imagination. Many professionals from various fields have repeatedly reported their astonishment about the authenticity of these phenomena and the richness of information concerning anatomy, physiology, embryology, obstetrics, and even histology that they entailed. Even lay persons often volunteer descriptions of such details as certain characteristics of the heartbeat of the mother and child, murmurs in the blood vessels and in the intestinal tract, specific details about the position and behavior of the fetus, relevant facts about fetal circulation, and even about exchange of blood in the placentary villi. Sophisticated and well-educated individuals have often emphasized that experiences of this kind had occurred in their sessions in spite of the fact that they did not believe in the possibility of prenatal memories and that the existence of this phenomenon was contrary to their scientific worldview.

The authenticity of prenatal experiences as well as the richness of information that they mediate have given me sufficient confidence in the importance of this phenomenon. Whenever possible, I would make every effort to get independent information from the mother, prenatal records, the obstetrician, the relatives, or some other sources, and compare it with the subjective account of the client. This has often brought astonishing confirmation of the insights reached during the reliving of prenatal memories concerning various crises of pregnancy, attempted abortions, and emotional upheavals or physical diseases of the mother. These observations provide more than sufficient reason for a future serious and systematic research of this fascinating phenomenon.

On occasion, the experiences of prenatal existence depict very early stages of the individual's biological history, including identification with the sperm and the ovum on the cellular level of consciousness, ovulation, passage of the ovum or spermatozoids through the Fallopian tube, the moment of conception, implantation of the fertilized egg in the mucous membrane of the uterus, and the early embryonal growth. Sequences of this kind can be associated with insights into hereditary influences, cosmobiological and astrological energy fields, or spiritual, karmic, and archetypal forces governing the development of the embryo.

The example I would like to use here to illustrate the phenomenon of fetal experience comes from the psychedelic therapy of Richard, a gay male suffering from chronic suicidal depressions. The condensed history of his treatment was described in my earlier book *Realms of the Human Unconscious* (Grof 1975, p. 57–60). The same book also contains a detailed description of a cellular memory of the germinal cells and of conception (p. 192–3).

> In one of the LSD sessions of his psycholytic series, Richard described what appeared to be an authentic intrauterine experience. He felt immersed in fetal liquid and fixed to the placenta by the umbilical cord. He was aware of nourishment streaming into his body through the navel area and experienced wonderful feelings of symbiotic unity with his mother. They were connected with each other through the placentary circulation of blood that seemed to be a magical life-giving fluid. Richard heard two sets of heart sounds with different frequencies that were merging into one undulating acoustic pattern.
>
> This was accompanied by peculiar hollow and roaring noises that Richard identified after some hesitation as those produced by the blood gushing through the pelvic arteries and by movements of gas and liquid during the peristaltic movements of the intestines adjacent to the uterus. He was fully aware of his body image and recognized that it was very different from his adult one. He was small and his

head was disproportionately large as compared with the body and the extremities. On the basis of various experiential clues and with the use of adult judgment, he was able to identify himself as being a mature fetus just before delivery.

In this state, he suddenly heard strange noises coming from the outside world. They had a very unusual echoing quality, as if they were resounding in a large hall or coming through a layer of water. The resulting effect reminded him of the sound quality that music technicians achieve on purpose through electronic means in modern recordings. He finally concluded that the abdominal and uterine walls and the fetal liquid were responsible for this effect and that this was the form in which external sounds reach the fetus.

He then tried to identify what produced these sounds and where they were coming from. After some time, he could recognize human voices that were yelling and laughing and what seemed to be sounds of carnival trumpets. Suddenly, the idea came to him that these had to be the sounds of the fair, held annually in his native village two days prior to his birthday. After having put together the above pieces of information, he concluded that his mother must have attended this fair in an advanced stage of pregnancy.

Richard's mother, when asked independently about the circumstances of his birth, without being told about his LSD experience, volunteered among other things the following story. In the relatively dull life of the village, the annual fair was an event providing rare excitement. Although she was in a late stage of pregnancy, she would not have missed this opportunity for anything in the world. In spite of strong objections and warnings from her own mother, she left home to participate in the festivities. According to her relatives, the noisy environment and turmoil of the mart precipitated Richard's delivery. Richard denied ever having heard this story and his mother did not remember ever having told him about this event.

b.   Ancestral Experiences

This group of transpersonal experiences is characterized by a strong sense of historical regression along biological lines to periods preceding the subject's conception and by an authentic identification with one's ancestors. Sometimes these experiences are related to comparatively recent family history and to more immediate ancestors on the maternal and paternal side, such as parents and grandparents. However, in their extreme form, they can reach back several generations and even centuries.

In general, the content of these experiences is always compatible with the individual's racial history and cultural background. Thus, a Jewish subject may experience ancestral episodes from the *holocaust* during World War II, from medieval pogroms, or from tribal life in Israel during Biblical times and may develop a deep bond with his or her racial, cultural, and religious heritage. A person of Scandinavian origin may witness various scenes from the adventurous explorations and conquests of the Vikings; these scenes may be accompanied by vividness of detail with regard to garments, weapons, jewelry, or techniques of navigation and naval warfare. Similarly, an Afro-American can relive sequences from the lives of African natives that involve daily village activities, rites of passage, healing ceremonies, and various festivities, or traumatic events from the history of slavery. Such experiences are usually associated with interesting psychological insights; the subject can relate these archaic elements to his or her present personality and current psychological problems.

Ancestral experiences are multiform and complex. Sometimes they take the form of the actual reliving of short episodes or entire sequences from the life of one's ancestors that are concrete, specific, and rich in detail. They can involve full experiential identification with the ancestors, including the body image, facial expression, gestures, emotional reactions, and thought processes. Other times, they are of a much more generalized and diffuse nature; here the subject senses the emotional atmosphere and quality of interpersonal relations in the family, clan, or tribe, and can reach intuitive insights into cultural attitudes, belief systems, customs and habits, traditions, idiosyncrasies, prejudices, and superstitions.

Some subjects have reported in this context that as a result of such experiences they have developed a new understanding of their personality structure and some of their problems and conflicts that did not make sense before. They could trace them back to various incongruences, incompatibilities, and friction points between their maternal and paternal lineages. What they had tried to understand without success as personal problems suddenly appeared to be introjected and internalized conflicts between generations of their dead ancestors.

There are two important characteristics of ancestral experiences that differentiate them from the following group of racial and collective phenomena. The first of these is an experiential quality that is hard to describe. The subject who has an ancestral experience has a firm subjective feeling that the protagonist belongs to his or her own bloodline, that the experience involves "reading" of the genetic code of the DNA. In addition, objective investigation, if it can be carried out, typically brings results that are congruent with the subject's experience. In several instances where there was a seeming discrepancy — for example, in the case of an ancestral memory of an Anglo-Saxon that involved a gypsy or a black person — exploration of the family pedigree confirmed the accuracy of the experience.

I will illustrate this phenomenon by an interesting observation from a session of holotropic breathing that we conducted in our last workshop in Stockholm, Sweden. Two additional examples of ancestral experiences can be found in my book *Realms of the Human Unconscious* (Grof 1975); the first one reaches back one generation (p. 164–5), the other over three centuries (p. 165–167).

A young woman who had come to the seminar from Finland experienced during this session a very powerful sequence of scenes involving aggression and killing in various types of war. It was happening in the context of the death-rebirth process and reliving of biological birth. All of these sequences had typical features of BPM III.

One of these scenes was unusual and different from the others. She experienced herself as a young soldier participating in a battle during World War II that had taken place fourteen years before she was conceived. She suddenly realized that she actually became her father and experienced this battle from his point of view. She was fully identified with him and felt his body, his emotions, and his thoughts. She could also perceive very clearly what was happening in the environment around her. At one moment, as she/he was hiding behind a tree, a bullet came and scraped her/his cheek and ear.

The experience was extremely vivid, authentic, and compelling. She did not know where it came from and what to make of it. Intellectually she knew that her father had participated in the Russo-Finnish war, but was sure that he had never talked about the above episode. Finally, she concluded that she must have connected with her father's memory of an actual historical event and decided to check it out by telephone.

She came back to the group very excited and in awe. When she called her father and told him about her experience, her father was absolutely astounded. What she experienced was an episode that had actually happened to him in the war; her description of the scene and of the environment was absolutely accurate. He also reassured her that he had never discussed this particular event with her or other members of the family, because it was not sufficiently serious.

c. Racial and Collective Experiences

These experiences represent a further movement away from one's individual life and history. In racial experiences, the protagonists involved are not the ancestors connected with the individual by bloodlines, but are any of the members of the same race. In collective experiences, this process transcends even racial barriers and extends to humanity as a whole. These phenomena are clearly related to Carl Gustav Jung's concept of the racial and collective unconscious and thus represent important supportive evidence for one of the most controversial aspects of his conceptual framework (Jung 1959).

Individuals in nonordinary states of consciousness who tune into these experiential realms participate in dramatic, usually brief, but occasionally complex and elaborate, sequences that take place in more or less remote historical periods and in various countries and cultures. These scenes can be experienced from the position of an observer, but more frequently from experiential identification with the protagonists. This is typically associated with many general, or specific and detailed insights concerning social structure, religious practices, rituals, moral codes, art, and technology of the cultures and the historical periods involved.

Collective memories can be related to any country, historical period, racial group, or culture, although there seems to be a certain preference for ancient civilizations with highly developed spiritual, philosophical, and artistic traditions. Sequences from ancient Egypt, India, Tibet, China, Japan, pre-Columbian Mexico and Peru, Greece and Rome tend to occur with surprising frequency. The choice of the cultures and geographical areas can be quite independent from the subject's own racial and ethnic background, country of origin, cultural tradition, and/or even previous education and interests.

Thus an individual of Slavic origin can experientially participate in the conquests of Genghis Khan's Mongolian hordes, identify with African Kalahari Bushmen during their trance dance, experience a ritual initiation of the Australian Aborigines, or identify with a sacrificial victim of the Aztecs. An Anglo-Saxon can experience dramatic sequences from the history of Afro-American slavery or participate in the role of an American Indian in the massacres during the conquest of the Wild West and develop as a result of it a new awareness of and sensitivity to American racial problems. A person of Jewish heritage can tune into the cultures of the Far East and acquire as a result of profound experiences in this context surprising understanding of the Japanese, Chinese, or Tibetan psyche, certain aspects of Taoist or Buddhist teachings, martial arts, or oriental music and drama.

Sometimes the above experiences can be accompanied by complex gestures, postures, and movement sequences that correctly and accurately reflect certain specific aspects of the culture or tradition involved. We have repeatedly observed in psychedelic and holotropic sessions that naive subjects have assumed at appropriate times and in the right context symbolic gestures (*mudras*) and postures (*asanas*) from the yogic tradition and have spontaneously discovered their meaning. In several instances, subjects experientially tuned into a specific cultural context felt a strong need to dance. Without any previous specific training or even intellectual knowledge of the culture involved, they were able to perform spontaneously various dance and movement forms, such as the *!Kung Bushmen* trance dance, whirling of the dervishes in the Sufi tradition, Indonesian dances performed in Java or Bali, and symbolic dancing of the Indian Kathakali or Manipuri schools.

During collective memories, the individual has the feeling that he or she is witnessing episodes from human history, displays of cultural diversity and the richness of mankind, or illustrations of the cosmic drama and divine play (*lila*). These experiences are not associated with the sense of "reading the DNA code" characteristic for ancestral memories, with racial belonging usually accompanying racial memories, or with a sense of personal recall and spiritual or karmic continuity which is a regular concomitant of past incarnation phenomena.

The following example of racial experiences comes from an unsupervised LSD session of a Jewish subject who subsequently shared with me some highlights of his inner quest.

> I suddenly realized that shame was a split common to all of humanity. Being ashamed of my father, just like my father was! I had a strong feeling that shame is communicated at birth and has something important to do with sexual organs. I felt tired and old, like my father, and his father, and his father's father before him. It was the fatigue before death and a desire to die. I sensed a deep connection with my Jewish heritage through the whole line of male ancestors and the thousand years of Rabbis.
>
> And then I felt a burning and itching pain around my penis and I realized that I was going through circumcision. The wine of the ceremony and my father's presence seemed to be related to the tired feeling. This was the deep source of shame! All the men participating in the ceremony were subconsciously ashamed and embarassed at the incident and communicated their feelings to the infant, passing the feelings of pain, shame, and tiredness to the infant along with the religious tradition.
>
> I felt deeply ashamed of myself. "Aren't you ashamed of yourself? You should be ashamed of yourself!" My mother and my father telling me hundreds of times to be ashamed of myself. I am so ashamed that I am being ashamed to be ashamed! Ashamed of my needs, ashamed of my feelings. The common bond of the Jewish people is shame. The wedding song in *Fiddler on the Roof* contains a wish: "May God keep you from shame!" Adam ate the apple and knew shame. The legacy handed down from father to son from the time of Abraham is shame. The covenant of Abraham, passed on to the male infant for 4,000 years!
>
> I found myself holding my penis and my testicles. All of a sudden came a vision that totally clarified everything for me. Circumcision was a substitute for child sacrifice! Abraham brought Isaac as a sacrifice to God, but then was ordered to circumcise him instead! Circumcision is symbolic castration. The offering of the most precious part of a male child to God, sacrificing his manhood instead of life. The castrating Jewish mother syndrome! My father offered me up for sacrifice to win my mother's approval. The sacrifice of the first-born! Jesus was the son of God and he was sacrificed. It is as though God originally allowed Abraham's son to live, but all his offspring belonged to God and will be claimed in the latter days. That is why the Jews are the "Chosen People" — chosen for sacrifice!
>
> Later, I decided to do some historical research related to the insights from this experience. A local Jewish authority asssured me that

nothing like sacrifice of the first-born had ever taken place in the Jewish tradition. He referred me to the Jewish Encyclopedia and the Fast of the First-Born. However, I was able to find numerous references to sacrifices of the first-born that had been practiced for 2,000 years, up until the time of the Judges. My experience of deep identification with this ancestral heritage convinced me that it has left an indelible mark on the racial unconscious of the Jews and other Mediterranean people.

d.   Past Incarnation Experiences

This is probably the most fascinating and controversial group of transpersonal phenomena. As I suggested earlier, past incarnation memories resemble in many ways ancestral, racial, and collective experiences. However, they are usually dramatic and are associated with an intense emotional charge of a negative or positive quality. Their essential experiential characteristic is a convinced sense of remembering something that happened once before to the same entity, to the same unit of consciousness. The subjects participating in these dramatic sequences maintain a sense of individuality and personal identity, but experience themselves in another form, at another place and time, and in another context.

This sense of reliving something that one has seen before (*déjà vu*) and experienced before (*déjà vécu*) in a previous incarnation is basic and cannot be analyzed any further. It is comparable to the ability to distinguish in everyday life our memories of events that actually happened from our dreams, fantasies, and daydreams. It would be difficult to convince a person who is relating to us a memory of something that happened last week that the event involved did not really occur and that it is just a figment of his or her imagination. Past incarnation memories have a similar subjective quality of authenticity and reality.

Past incarnation experiences usually involve one or several other persons. In rare instances, various animals can appear as protagonists in dramatic scenes of this kind. The individual then feels that he or she became "karmically imprinted" on a scene in which they were killed by a tiger, trampled to death by a wild elephant, gored by a frenzied bull, or bitten by a venomous snake. Sequences of this kind seem to be similar to karmic scenes in their lasting impact on the individual, but they lack the reciprocity of repetition in subsequent incarnations. They thus resemble situations where the psychological effect transcending individual incarnations involves impersonal causes. Typical examples of such situations would be bitterness, hatred, and envy associated with a painful and disabling disease or a crippling injury, and the anxiety and agony experienced in connection with an accidental death under a rockslide, in swamps or quicksand, or during a volcanic eruption or fire.

Karmic experiences fall into two distinct categories characterized by the quality of the emotions involved. Some of them reflect highly positive connections with other persons — deep friendship, passionate love, spiritual partnership, a teacher-disciple relationship, blood bonds, life-and-death commitment, extraordinary mutual understanding, or nourishing and supportive exchange. More frequently, they involve dramatic negative emotions. The experiences belonging to this category cast subjects into various internecine past life situations characterized by agonizing physical pain, murderous aggression, inhuman terror, prolonged anguish, bitterness and hatred, insane jealousy, insatiable vengefulness, uncontrollable lust, or morbid greed and avarice.

Many individuals who have experienced negative karmic experiences were able to analyze the nature of the destructive bond between the protagonists of such sequences. They realized that all these seemingly different emotional qualities — such as murderous passion, insatiable desire, consuming jealousy, or mortal anguish — when intensified beyond a certain point, actually begin to resemble each other. There seems to exist a state of high biological and emotional arousal in which all the extreme affective qualities converge and attain metaphysical dimensions. When two or more individuals reach this universal "melting pot" of passions and instincts, they get imprinted on the situation that caused them, irrespective of the role which they played.

In situations of extreme experiential intensity, the sadistic arousal of the torturer and the inhuman pain of the victim increasingly resemble each other, and the rage of the murderer merges at a certain point with the anguish and suffering of the dying victim. It seems that it is this emotional fusion that is instrumental in karmic imprinting, rather than a specific role in the experiential sequence. Whenever two individuals get involved in a situation where their emotions reach the state described above, they will have to repeat in subsequent lives in alternating roles the same pattern until they reach the level of awareness which is necessary for the resolution of a karmic bond.

Sophisticated subjects familiar with spiritual literature equated this state of undifferentiated emotional arousal that generates karmic bondage with the Buddhist concept of *tṛṣṇā* or *tanha*, the "thirst of flesh and blood," the force that drives the cycle of death and rebirth and is responsible for all human suffering. Others reported their insights into the deep similarity between this state and the strange experiential mixture characterizing the final stages of biological birth (BPM III), where murderous aggression, vital anguish, extreme sexual arousal, demonic tendencies, scatological indulgence, and religious fervor merge into a strange, inextricable amalgam. Biological birth thus seems to represent something like a transformation station, where the intangible "morphogenetic fields" of the karmic record (referred to as the *"akashic* record" in the spiritual literature) enter the biopsychological life of the individual.

The opening of the realm of past incarnation experiences is sometimes preceded by or associated with complex insights and instructions communicated by nonverbal means. In this way, the individual is introduced to the understanding that the law of karma is an important part of the cosmic order mandatory for all sentient beings. On the basis of this new comprehension, he or she accepts responsibility for the deeds in previous lifetimes that at the time are still covered by amnesia. In addition to this general information, such insights can include details of the mechanisms involved in the cycles of rebirth and the necessary strategies for attaining liberation from karmic bonds.

To reach a complete resolution of a karmic pattern or bond, the individual has to experience fully all the painful emotions and physical sensations involved in a destructive past incarnation scene. In addition, it is necessary to transcend the event emotionally, ethically, philosophically, and spiritually, to rise above it entirely, and to forgive and be forgiven. Such a full liberation from a karmic pattern and the bondage involved is typically associated with a sense of paramount accomplishment and triumph that is beyond any rational comprehension. When it occurs, it is associated with an overwhelming feeling that one has waited for this moment and worked for the achievement of this goal for centuries. At this point, nothing in the world seems more important than to free oneself from karmic bondage.

This is typically associated with an ecstatic rapture and feelings of overwhelming bliss. In some instances, the individual can see a rapid replay of his or her karmic history and have clear insights as to how this pattern repeated itself in different variations through ages and has contaminated lifetime after lifetime. Several subjects reported in this context the experience of something like a cleansing "karmic hurricane" or "cyclone" blowing through their past and tearing their karmic bonds in all the situations that involve the pattern that they just resolved.

Past incarnation phenomena are extremely common in deep experiential psychotherapy and have great therapeutic potential. They also have far-reaching theoretical significance, since several of their aspects represent a serious challenge to the mechanistic and materialistic world view. A therapist who does not allow experiences of this kind to develop in his clients or discourages them when they are spontaneously happening is giving up a powerful mechanism of healing and personality transformation. Since the major hindrance in this sense is a philosophical disbelief in reincarnation and karma based on insufficient knowledge of the facts, I would like to explore this issue at some length.

It seems clear that the past incarnation phenomena observed in deep experiential psychotherapy, in meditation, and in spontaneous episodes of nonordinary states of consciousness are identical with those that are responsible for the fact that the belief in reincarnation is so widespread and universal. The concept of karma and reincarnation represents a cornerstone of Hinduism, Buddhism, Jainism, Sikhism, Zoroastrianism, the Tibetan Vajrayana Buddhism, and Taoism. Similar ideas can be found in such geographically, historically, and culturally diverse groups as various African tribes, American Indians, pre-Columbian cultures, the Polynesian kahunas, practitioners of the Brazilian *umbanda*, the Gauls, and the Druids. In ancient Greece, several important schools of thought subscribed to it; among these were the Pythagoreans, the Orphics, and the Platonists. This doctrine was also adopted by the Essenes, the Pharisees, the Karaites, and other Jewish and semi-Jewish groups, and it formed an important part of the kabbalistic theology of medieval Jewry. It was also held by the Neoplatonists and Gnostics and in modern times by the Theosophists, Anthroposophists, and certain Spiritualists.

It is not very well known that concepts similar to reincarnation and karma existed also among the early Christians. According to St. Jerome (340–420), reincarnation was given an esoteric interpretation that was communicated to a selected elite. The most famous Christian thinker speculating about the pre-existence of souls and world cycles was Origen (186–253), one of the greatest Church Fathers of all times. In his writings, particularly in the book *On First Principles* (*De Principiis*) (Origenes Adamantius, 1973), he expressed his opinion that certain scriptural passages could only be explained in the light of reincarnation. His teachings were condemned by the Second Council of Constantinople, convened by the Emperor Justinian in 553, and became a heretical doctrine. The Constantinople Council decreed: "If anyone assert the fabulous pre-existence of souls and shall submit to the monstrous doctrine that follows from it, let him be anathema." However, some scholars believe that they can detect traces of the teachings in the writings of St. Augustine, St. Gregory, and even St. Francis of Assissi.

In addition to the universality of the concept of reincarnation, it is important to emphasize that past life experiences occur in experiential sessions without any programming and often despite the disbelief of the therapist and client. I have observed experiences of this kind long before I, myself, became open to their existence and started taking them seriously. On many occasions, they emerged in sessions of scientists who had previously considered the belief in reincarnation to be an absurd superstition and a cultural delusion of primitive nations, or even a manifestation of individual psychopathology.

In several instances, subjects who had not been familiar with the concept of karma and reincarnation not only experienced dramatic past life memories, but also gained complex and detailed insights into various specific aspects of this doctrine, identical with those found in various spiritual systems and occult literature. I can mention as an example an uneducated patient who participated in our program of psychedelic therapy for cancer patients in Baltimore, Maryland. He was almost illiterate and worked as an unskilled laborer; despite this, he experienced in his psychedelic session complex insights into reincarnation and the cycles of rebirth and emerged from this session a firm believer in the continuity of lives. The experience helped him greatly to face the grim reality of his terminal cancer with its multiple metastases and ultimately to die with equanimity. The condensed history of this patient and the account of his psychedelic session can be found in my book *The Human Encounter with Death* (Grof and Halifax 1977, pp. 80–83).

After this general introduction, I would like to describe certain specific aspects of past life experiences that are extremely interesting and deserve serious attention of researchers of consciousness and of the human psyche. The persons who experience karmic phenomena often gain amazing insights into the time and culture involved and occasionally even into specific historical events. In some instances, it is beyond any doubt that they could not possibly have acquired this information in the conventional way, through the ordinary sensory channels. In this sense, past life memories are true transpersonal experiences that share with the other transpersonal phenomena the capacity to provide instant and direct extrasensory access to information about the world.

Another interesting aspect of karmic experiences is that they are clearly connected with various emotional, psychosomatic, and inter-personal problems of the individual. Most frequently, they represent the deepest roots of problems, in addition to specific biographical and perinatal determinants. In some instances, they immediately and directly underlie psychopathological symptoms. In the latter case, deep experiential therapy will activate these symptoms and lead the individual instantly to the karmic theme that explains them and provides the context for their resolution. These experiences thus not only contribute to the understanding of psychopathology, but also represent one of the most effective therapeutic mechanisms.

Among the characteristic features of past life phenomena that cannot be explained by mechanistic science is their association with astonishing synchronicities in the Jungian sense (Jung 1960). I have observed in many instances that individuals experiencing karmic sequences identified the protagonists in these scenes as specific people in their lives — parents, children, spouses, boyfriends and girlfriends, superiors, and other important figures. When they completed the reliving of the karmic pattern and reached a sense of resolution and forgiveness, they often felt that the respective partner was in some sense involved in the process and must have felt something similar.

When I became sufficiently open-minded to make attempts at verification of the relevance of these statements, I discovered to my great surprise that they were often accurate. I found out that in many instances the persons the subject denoted as protagonists in the karmic sequence experienced at exactly the same time a dramatic shift of attitude in the direction that was predicated by the resolution of the past incarnation pattern. This transformation happened in a way that could not be interpreted by linear causality. The individuals involved were often hundreds or thousands of miles away, they did not know anything about the subject's experience, and the changes in them were produced by an entirely independent sequence of events. They had a deep transformative experience of their own, received some information that entirely changed their perception of the subject, or were influenced by some other independent development in their environment. The timing of these synchronistic happenings was often remarkable; in some instances they were minutes apart. This aspect of past life experiences suggesting nonlocal connections in the universe seems to bear some similarity to the phenomena described by Bell's theorem in modern physics (Bell 1966, Capra 1982).

To clarify my position on past life experiences, I would like to emphasize that I do not consider their characteristics described up to this point to be necessarily a proof that we have lived before. However, I feel very strongly that this phenomenon cannot be adequately explained by mechanistic science and represents a serious conceptual challenge to the existing paradigms in psychiatry and Western science in general. It is certainly conceivable that some of the essential features of the karmic memories — universality, sense of authenticity, experiential quality of a memory, accurate intuitive insights into the time and culture involved, therapeutic potential, and synchronistic events surrounding them — could be explained by a modern paradigm that would not require the assumption of a separate entity surviving biological death and carrying responsibility for its past deeds. The semantic model based on probability theory developed by the Soviet mathematician V. V. Nalimov can be mentioned here as an example of such an effort (Nalimov, 1982).

It is interesting to notice that in the mystical tradition literal belief in reincarnation of separate individuals is seen as an inferior and less sophisticated interpretation of karmic experiences. In its complete form, the reincarnation theory suggests that all divisions and boundaries in the universe are illusory and arbitrary. In the last analysis it is only the creative principle, or cosmic consciousness, that actually exists. An individual who penetrates to this ultimate knowledge will see the realm of karnic appearances as just another level of illusion. The Hindu concept of the universe as divine play (lila) of one supreme being (Brahma) can be used here as example.

In rare instances, the evidence supporting the reincarnation theory can be much more specific. A small fraction of past life experiences involve unambiguous information about the personality and life of the individual that the subject feels karmically connected with. This can be names of persons and places, dates, descriptions of objects of unusual shapes, and many others. On occasion, the nature of this material and the circumstances can be such that they allow for independent testing. In these cases, historical research brings often extraordinary surprises in terms of verification of these experiences, down to miniscule details.

There exists another most interesting independent source of data on reincarnation. It is the study of children who claim that they remember various things from their previous lives. This can include the name of the place where they were born, detailed knowledge of its topography, names and life histories of their alleged former relatives, acquaintances and friends, and other details. Ian Stevenson, who has studied many such cases in different parts of the world, has described his findings in his famous book *Twenty Cases Suggestive of Reincarnation* (Stevenson 1974) and in a sequel to this work (Stevenson 1984).

It is interesting to mention in this context the Tibetan tradition of testing the identity of the reincarnated *lama* by presenting the child, discovered by a special delegation of priests on the basis of various clues and omens, an extraordinary test. To confirm the authenticity of his incarnation, the boy has to identify from several series of similar objects those that belonged to the deceased.

I hope that the above analysis of the available data will leave the reader with the impression that the area of past life experiences and the phenomena surrounding them deserve systematic and careful research. While the observations cannot be interpreted as unambiguous evidence for the continuity of separate individual existence through lifetimes and for the law of karma, it is hardly possible for an unbiased and informed scientist to discard this possibility on the basis of metaphysical adherence to a mechanistic worldview. In the following text, I will illustrate some important aspects of past life experiences by an interesting case history. The protagonist in this story started his self-exploration in a primal group that had separated itself from Janov because of his narrow conceptual framework. Later, he participated in one of our Esalen month-long seminars, where we used the technique of holotropic breathing.

During the time when Karl was reliving in primal therapy various aspects of his birth trauma, he started experiencing fragments of dramatic scenes that seemed to be happening in another century and in a foreign country. They involved powerful emotions and physical feelings and seemed to have some deep and intimate connection to his life; yet none of them made any sense in terms of his present biography.

He had visions of tunnels, underground storage spaces, military barracks, thick walls, and ramparts that all seemed to be parts of a fortress situated on a rock overlooking an ocean shore. This was interspersed with images of soldiers in a variety of situations. He felt puzzled, since the soldiers seemed to be Spanish, but the scenery looked more like Scotland or Ireland.

As the process continued, the scenes were becoming more dramatic and involved, many of them representing fierce combat and bloody slaughter. Although surrounded by soldiers, Karl experienced himself as a priest and at one point had a very moving vision that involved a bible and a cross. At this point, he saw a seal ring on his hand and could clearly recognize the initials that it bore.

Being a talented artist, he decided to document this strange process, although he did not understand it at the time. He produced a series of drawings and very powerful and impulsive finger paintings. Some of these depicted different parts of the fortress, others scenes of slaughter, and a few his own experiences, including being gored by a sword, thrown over the ramparts of the fortress, and dying on the shore. Among these pictures was a drawing of the seal ring with the initials.

As he was recovering bits and pieces of this story, Karl was finding more and more meaningful connections with his present life. He was discovering that many emotional and psychosomatic feelings, as well as problems in interpersonal relationships that he had at that time in his everyday life, were clearly related to his inner process, involving the mysterious event in the past.

A turning point came when Karl suddenly decided on an impulse to spend his holiday in Ireland. After his return, he was showing for the first time the slides that he had shot on the Western coast of Ireland. He realized that he had taken eleven consecutive pictures of the same scenery that did not seem particularly interesting. He took the map and reconstructed where he stood at the time and in which direction he was shooting. He realized that the place which attracted his attention was the ruin of an old fortress called Dunanoir, or *Forte de Oro* (Golden Fortress).

Suspecting a connection with his experiences from primal therapy, Karl decided to study the history of Dunanoir. He discovered, to his enormous surprise, that at the time of Walter Raleigh, the fortress was taken by the Spaniards and then besieged by the British. Walter Raleigh negotiated with the Spaniards and promised them free egress from the fortress, if they would open the gate and surrender to the British. The Spaniards agreed on these conditions, but the British did not hold their promise. Once inside the fortress, they slaughtered mercilessly all the Spaniards and threw them over the ramparts to die on the ocean beach.

In spite of this absolutely astonishing confirmation of the story that he laboriously reconstructed in his inner exploration, Karl was not satisfied. He continued his library research until he discovered a special document about the battle of Dunanoir. There he found that a priest accompanied the Spanish soldiers and was killed together with them. The initials of the name of the priest were identical with those that Karl has seen in his vision of the seal ring and had depicted in one of his drawings.

e. *Phylogenetic Experiences*

This type of transpersonal experience is closely related to animal identification, described earlier. It shares with it the sense of total anatomical, physiological, psychological, and even biochemical identity with various members of other species of living organisms. These experiences also resemble animal identification in that they offer amazing new insights into the life forms involved. The main difference is a convinced sense of regression in historical time. Instead of transcending only spatial barriers and identifying with currently existing animals, the subject identifies with the members of various species in the evolutionary history of life.

a

b

Figure 7a–j   A series of drawings and paintings illustrating various aspects of Karl's past life experience involving the battle of Dunanoir. **a.** A view of the fortress situated on the cliffs and overlooking the ocean. **b.** A semisymbolic picture showing the blood flowing over the ramparts, down the cliffs, and coloring the beach and the ocean.

c

d

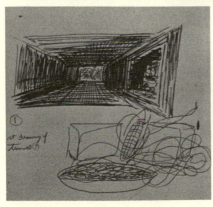

e

c. Sketches showing the external architectural design and layout of the fortress.
d. and **e.** Drawings depicting various aspects of the interior of the fortress —
living quarters, dormitories, corridors, and storage rooms for ammunition and
food supplies seen during various experiential sequences.

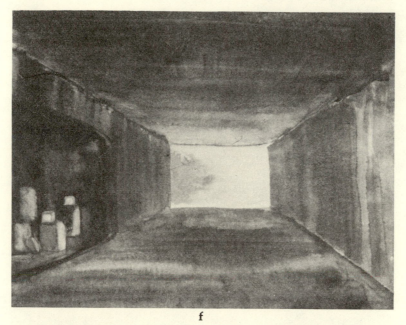

f

f. Watercolor painting of one of the corridors of the fortress.

g

g. Picture of an underground tunnel leading to the beach.

h

i

j

h. Drawing of the design on the seal-ring with the initials of the priest's name.
i. An impulsive finger-painting depicting the experience of being gored by the
sword of a British soldier. **j.** A drawing representing the death on the beach.

Some of these experiences involve a feeling of exploring personal biological history and identifying with one's animal ancestors. They thus represent a logical extension of previously described embryonal, ancestral, and racial experiences. Others involve experiential identification with various aspects of the evolution of life on earth or with the phylogenetic tree of life in its totality. The insights accompanying these experiences often provide intuitive understanding not only of the life forms the subject identifies with, but also of the forces that rule evolution — creative intentions of cosmic intelligence, archetypal dynamics, phylogenetic logic, and instinctual drives. In this context, the individual can identify with the totality of life and ask such questions as: Is life a viable cosmic phenomenon? Does it have a built-in self-destructive propensity? Are the constructive aspects of life that foster survival and evolution stronger than the destructive and self-destructive ones? (see p. 61).

This report, from a high-dose LSD session (250 micrograms) conducted in the context of the training program for mental health professionals at the Maryland Psychiatric Research Center in Baltimore, can be used here as a good example of a typical phylogenetic experience.

> Most of these experiences were related to the age of the large reptiles — the Triassic, Jurassic, and Cretaceous period — and seemed to focus on various forms of survival struggle. One of them is particularly vivid in my memory. I experienced a vicious fight with a monstrous carnivorous reptile of a Tyrannosaurus variety from the position of some kind of a large dinosaur. I would like to emphasize that the experience was unbelievably real. All its elements were absolutely authentic, far beyond anything I could possibly conjure up from my ordinary human experience.
>
> I was in a huge, clumsy body, experiencing a mixture of elemental fear and primitive blind rage. I felt the pain and sensed my flesh being torn; the quality of these experiences certainly was not human. But the most astonishing aspect of the situation was a peculiar taste in my mouth that was a combination of the taste of blood and of the stale, putrid water of the primeval swamp. I experienced vividly my loss in this fight. My head was driven into the mud by the blows of the aggressor and I died. This was by far the clearest and most vivid episode, although there were sequences involving other specimens.

f. Experiences of Planetary Evolution

In this type of experience, the subject can witness panoramic images of the evolution of the entire planet, including its origin as part of the solar system, the early geophysical processes, the situation in the primeval ocean, and the origin and evolution of life. All this can be experienced in the role of the observer; the subject can also identify experientially with the totality of the planetary evolution or with any of its aspects. This is clearly related to the experience of identification with Gaia mentioned earlier, but with a dynamic evolutionary perspective. Like the other types of transpersonal experiences, sequences of this kind can provide deep understanding of the processes involved that clearly transcend the subject's intellectual knowledge of the specific areas and often also his or her general educational background.

g. Cosmogenetic Experiences

Experiences of this group represent a logical extension of the previous one. Here the sense of evolutionary exploration involves the entire universe. The subject can witness or identify with the birth and development of the cosmos involving dimensions and energies of unimaginable scope. This can be various episodes from the cosmogenetic history — the Big Bang, the creation of matter, space, and time, the birth of galaxies and their expansion, explosions of novas and supernovas, and the contraction of large suns ending in black holes. Occasionally, the entire history of the cosmos is played out with extraordinary changes of the subjective sense of time.

Sophisticated subjects — some of them mathematicians and physicists — reported in this context remarkable experiential insights into various problems related to astronomy and astrophysics that can be expressed in mathematical equations, but cannot be fully intuited in the ordinary state of consciousness. These insights included Einstein's concept of an infinite but self-enclosed universe, non-Euclidean geometries of Lobatchevsky and Riemann, Minkowski's spacetime, the "event horizon", the collapse of time, space, and natural laws in a black hole, and other difficult concepts of modern physics.

These insights from nonordinary states indicating that consciousness and creative intelligence are intimately involved in cosmogenesis throw a new light on the so-called anthropic principle, a concept formulated recently by theoreticians of astrophysics (Davies 1983). It refers to the fact that the conditions during cosmogenesis required too many fortuitous accidents to result in a universe that could support life. This seems to suggest that the intention to create a universe in which life would exist was present in the process of creation from the very beginning.

The following account from a psychedelic session of the famous British-American writer and philosopher Alan Watts is a vivid and articulate description of a psychedelic experience that retraced evolution through his personal history and the history of organic life to the origins of the galaxy and of the universe (Watts 1962).

> I trace myself through the labyrinth of my brain, through the innumerable turns by which I have ringed myself off and, by perpetual circling, obliterated the original trail whereby I entered this forest. Back through the tunnels — through the devious status-and-survival strategy of adult life, through the interminable passages which we remember in dreams — all the streets we have traveled, the corridors of schools, the winding pathways between the legs of chairs where one crawled as a child, the tight and bloody exit from the womb, the fountaineous surge through the channels of the penis, the timeless wonderings through the ducts and spongy caverns. Down and back through ever-narrowing tubes to the point where the passage itself is the traveler — a thin string of molecules going through the trial and error of getting itself into the right order to be a unit of organic life. Relentlessly back through endless and whirling dances in the astronomically proportioned spaces which surround the original nuclei of the world, the centers of centers, as remotely distant on the inside as the nebulae beyond our galaxy on the outside.
>
> Down and at last out — out of the cosmic maze — to recognize in and as myself, the bewildered traveler, the forgotten yet familiar sensation of the original impulse of all things, supreme identity, inmost light, ultimate center, self more than myself.

h. Psychic Phenomena Involving Transcendence of Time (Precognition, Clairvoyance and Clairaudience of Past and Future Events, Psychometry, Time Travels)

The existence of psychic phenomena (and other types of transpersonal experiences) transcending spatial barriers described earlier clearly suggests that events in the universe are connected in a way that disregards linear distances. This group of PSI indicates that, in addition to these nonlocal or translocal links, all events have also intricate nontemporal or transtemporal connections that transcend linear time as we know and experience it in everyday life. The PSI events in this category cannot be explained through conventional transfer of energy and information in the material world.

In nonordinary states of consciousness and occasionally in everyday life, it is possible to experience clear anticipation and precognitive flashes of future events that show far-reaching correspondence with the actual events to come. In some instances, subjects can experience complex and detailed scenes from the future involving all the senses. Particularly frequent are vivid pictorial representations of future sequences and their acoustic concomitants. These range from sounds, words, and sentences from ordinary life to dramatic noises accompanying accidents or injuries (fire engines, car brakes, crashing sounds, ambulance sirens, or blowing horns). Verification of these phenomena has to be done with particular care; unless these instances are reported and recorded at the time when they happen, there is a great danger of contamination of data. Loose interpretation of events, memory distortions, and déjà vu are the major pitfalls involved. Despite this fact, there is no doubt that genuine precognition and clairvoyance of the future can occur.

Clairvoyance and clairaudience related to various events in the past can be observed as an isolated phenomenon or in connection with transpersonal experiences transcending time (ancestral, racial, collective, karmic, or evolutionary). A special example in this category is psychometry, where the experiences are triggered by holding an object and are specifically related to this object's history. This can involve emotions, thoughts, and a variety of sensory qualities, such as visions, sounds, smells, and physical sensations.

I have observed repeatedly, in psychedelic sessions and in holotropic therapy, verified instances of precognition, clairvoyance of past and future events, and psychometry. I have also had the privilege to witness repeatedly reliable performance in these areas by such accomplished psychics as Anne Armstrong and Jack Schwartz. Of particular interest in this context are controlled experiments of future remote viewing conducted at the Stanford Research Institute by Russell Targ, Harold Puthoff, and Keith Harary not only with famous psychics, but also with many ordinary people not known for having special psychic ability (Targ and Puthoff 1978, Targ and Harary 1984). In their two recent successful remote viewing experiments, Russell Targ and Keith Harary used a Soviet subject who was able to describe not only a randomly chosen target location in the United States visited by the "beacon" person (the person who visits the target area at the time the psychic is trying to describe it) but also the one that would be visited in the future.

In some instances, the subject can transcend the ordinary temporal limitations at will and choose the points of time that he or she wants to visit. This situation, somewhat reminiscent of H. G. Wells' time machine or similar contraptions of other science fiction writers, can be referred to as time travel. This is usually combined with a similar voluntary choice of the location where the events take place. The sense of free choice distinguishes these experiences from the spontaneous and involuntary reliving of historical events in childhood, birth, ancestral, racial, or collective experiences. Directed time travel can also be conducted under the influence of hypnosis; here the subject can be either guided to a specific time indicated by the hypnotist, or can look for a specific past event. A beautiful artistic representation of spontaneous and elemental time travels is Vonnegut's *Slaughterhouse Five* (Vonnegut 1974).

Experiences involving transcendence of linear time represent a serious challenge to the Newtonian-Cartesian worldview. The possibility of direct access to the information about various aspects of the past without the mediation of the central nervous system violates the basic metaphysical dogma of mechanistic science about the primacy of matter over consciousness. It suggests the astonishing possibility of memory without a material substrate. The possibility of obtaining information about the future then undermines the deeply ingrained belief of Western civilization in the linearity of time. However, these observations from modern consciousness research are compatible with some interesting alternative models of time and the future, such as the chronotopology of Charles Musès (Musès 1985), or the probabilistic concepts of V. V. Nalimov (Nalimov 1982).

The following example of a precognitive experience is an excerpt from the session with 30 milligrams of psilocybine that the famous American parapsychologist Stanley Krippner experienced in the context of the Harvard University Psilocybine Research Project. It involved anticipation of the assassination of J. F. Kennedy, preceding by more than a year-and-a-half the actual event (Aaronson and Osmond 1970).

> From Baltimore, I traveled to the nation's capitol. I found myself gazing at a statue of Lincoln. The statue was entirely black, and the head was bowed. There was a gun at the base of the statue and someone murmured: "He was shot. The President was shot." A wisp of smoke rose into the air.
>
> Lincoln's features slowly faded away, and those of Kennedy took their place. The setting was still Washington, D.C. The gun was still at the base of the black statue. A wisp of smoke seeped from the barrel and curled into the air. The voice repeated: "He was shot. The President was shot." My eyes opened; they were filled with tears.
>
> In 1962, when I had my first psilocybine experience, I gave this visualization of Kennedy little thought, as so many other impressions came my way. However, it was the only one of my visualizations that brought tears in my eyes, so I described it fully in the report I sent to Harvard. Nineteen months later, on November 23, 1963, the visualization came back to me as I mourned Kennedy's assassination.

3   Physical Introversion and Narrowing of
      Consciousness: Organ, Tissue, and
      Cellular Consciousness

In transpersonal experiences characterized by spatial extension of consciousness, the subject's awareness appears to transcend what is traditionally considered to be the individual, that is, the body-ego. In this group, conscious awareness remains within the body, but extends to anatomical areas and to processes that are not available for conscious exploration under ordinary circumstances. Instead of experiencing the psychological inner space, the individual accesses the physical inner space. Phenomena of this kind thus involve spatial narrowing of consciousness and, simultaneously, its functional extension.

In the holotropic mode, it is possible to enter various parts of one's body and witness the activities occurring there, or even to identify experientially with specific organs and tissues. One can literally become one's heart and experience the work of the cardiac musculature, the opening and closing of the valves, the biodynamic flow of blood, and the action of the pacemaker. While identifying with the liver, it is possible to experience the drama of its detoxifying activities, or the production, collection, and excretion of gall. In a similar way, one can become one's reproductive system, various parts of the gastrointestinal tract or, for that matter, any other organ or tissue.

In these states, consciousness often seems to regress all the way to the cellular level and even to subcellular structures and processes. On many occasions, subjects under the influence of psychedelic substances or in the sessions of holotropic breathing have reported that they experienced themselves as red or white blood corpuscles, cells in the gastrointestinal epithelium or in the uterine mucous membrane, sperms and ova, or as neurons in their own brains. Another interesting phenomenon is conscious exploration of the cellular nucleus and of the chromosomes, associated with insights into the physiochemical code of the genes and a sense of "reading one's DNA." Experiences of this group bear close resemblance to various scenes from Isaac Asimov's movie *The Fantastic Voyage*.

This phenomenon is of particular interest for researchers trying to combine traditional medical therapy with psychological healing; this approach was pioneered by the oncologist and radiologist Carl Simonton (Simonton, Matthews-Simonton and Creighton 1978). In our program of LSD therapy for cancer patients, we have repeatedly observed that individuals suffering from various forms of malignancy were able to connect experientially with their tumors on a tissue and cellular level. They have often made spontaneous attempts to use this experience for healing by creating psychologically positive energy fields, confronting negative emotions they felt were associated with the disease process, mobilizing the defenses of the organism, or attacking mentally the tumors. Several instances of surprising temporary remissions which occurred in this context suggest that this possibility should be systematically explored. (Grof and Halifax 1977).

Many aspects of the organ, tissue, and cell consciousness are illustrated in the following account of a session with 125 milligrams of MDA (methylene-dioxy-amphetamine), a psychedelic substance which belongs to a group that in terms of its chemical structure bridges between mescaline and amphetamine.

Now my attention shifted from my mouth to the *oesophagus*. I started a slow journey down my gastrointestinal tract, connecting with all the digestive processes on a cellular and even biochemical level. I literally became the cells of the epithelium lining my stomach and participated in the resorption of food and in the incredible alchemy of digestion. The distinct smell and taste of the gastric content entirely filled my consciousness. At first, I brought in my human value system and shuddered in disgust. Gradually, I was able to leave the human behind and respond on the level of biology.

From there, the process continued to the duodenum, jejunum, and ileum. As the focus of my awareness was gradually shifting downwards, I explored all the nuances of the "bouquet" of the intestinal juices, enzymes, and gall and their respective combinations. While I was becoming all the villi, membranes, and cells, I was astonished by the miracle of this incredible laboratory of life. Although I had studied all this from many different aspects during my medical studies, I have never fully appreciated what was involved.

In the final stages of this "fantastic journey", I encountered the complexity of feelings and attitudes our culture has developed toward feces. In addition to disgust and revulsion, I had to confront an incredible amount of disowned, repressed, and unacceptable emotions of greed, avarice, envy, and malice. At one point they took on the personified form of grotesque, gnomelike, mythological creatures.

I started to understand the process I was going through. It seemed essential that I accept the entire gastrointestinal tract with all its products and contents as part of myself and befriend it. To overcome the repression and denial appeared to be critical for genuine and unconditional self-acceptance and personal integration. And I could not help feeling that this peculiar sequence of experiences was in its essence healing.

EXPERIENTIAL EXTENSION BEYOND CONSENSUS REALITY AND SPACE-TIME

In a large group of transpersonal experiences, the extension of consciousness seems to go beyond the phenomenal world and the time-space continuum as we perceive it in our everyday life. Here belong certain astral-psychic phenomena, such as apparitions of and communication with deceased people or experiences of the chakras, auras, meridians, and other subtle energetic manifestations. Other important experiences of this category involve spirit guides in animal or human form and various superhuman entities. On occasion, subjects have reported fantastic adventures that seemed to be happening in universes other than our own.

In nonordinary states of consciousness, the world of primordial images of the collective unconscious as described by Carl Gustav Jung (Jung 1959) can come alive and take the form of various mythological and legendary beings and sequences, fairy tale scenes, blissful and wrathful deities from different cultures, or transcultural archetypes and universal symbols. In its furthest reaches, individual consciousness can identify with the Creator and tap sources of cosmic creativity, or merge with the Universal Mind, with the Supracosmic and Metacosmic Void, or with the Absolute.

a.   Spiritistic and Mediumistic Experiences

Experiences that belong to this category have been the primary focus of interest of the participants of spiritistic seances, researchers in the area of survival after death, and writers of occult literature. They involve encounters and telepathic communication with deceased relatives and friends, contacts with discarnate entities in general, and the experiences of the astral realm. In the simplest form of this experience, subjects see apparitions of deceased people and receive from them various messages. The content of these messages can be addressed to the experiencer, or the recipient is used as a channel to deliver them to other people. Experiences of this kind have been reported by psychedelic subjects, clients in experiential psychotherapies, and individuals who had near-death experiences (NDEs).

Sometimes the subject does not perceive an individual discarnate entity, but an entire astral realm with various ghostly apparitions. Raymond Moody's description of the "realm of confused spirits" can be mentioned here as an example (Moody 1977). In a more complex form of this phenomenon, the subject actually enters a trance state and appears to be taken over by an alien entity or energy form. Events of this kind bear a striking resemblance to mediumistic trances occurring in spiritistic seances.

In such a mediumistic trance, the subject's facial expression can be grotesquely transformed, his or her postures and gestures appear bizarre and alien, and the voice is dramatically changed. I have seen individuals in this state talk in languages they did *not* know, speak in tongues, write automatic texts, paint elaborate pictures, produce obscure hieroglyphic designs, and draw intricate unintelligible squiggles. These manifestations are, again, reminiscent of those described in spiritistic and occult literature. Most fascinating examples of this phenomenon can be observed in the Spiritist Church in the Philippines and in Brazil, inspired by the teachings of Allan Kardec (Kardec 1975ab).

> The Brazilian psychologist and psychic Luiz Antonio Gasparetto, closely related to the Spiritist Church, is capable of painting in a light trance in the style of a wide variety of painters of different countries of the world. During the time when he participated as an invited guest in our monthlong seminars at the Esalen Institute, we had the opportunity to witness the remarkable speed of his work when he was subjectively experiencing channeling of dead masters (up to 25 canvasses in an hour). He was able to work in complete darkness or with red light that makes it virtually impossible to discriminate colors, could work on two paintings at a time, and occasionally painted with his feet while they were under the table where he could not see them. A selection of his mediumistic paintings has been reproduced in a special monograph (Marçalo Gaetani 1986). The phenomenon of psychic surgery, practiced in Brazil and in the Philippines, is also closely related to the teachings of Allan Kardec and to the Spiritist Church.

If the experiences of communication with discarnate entities and spirits of dead friends and relatives involved only visions of these persons and a subjective sense of interaction, the situation would be relatively simple. In that case, these phenomena could be easily discounted as figments of imagination combining elements of memory, human fantasy, and wishful thinking. However, the situation is much more complex than that. Before we discard these phenomena as being absurd and not worth the interest of reputable researchers, let me mention some observations that deserve serious attention.

As the following two examples indicate, experiences of this kind sometimes have certain extraordinary aspects that are not easy to explain. I have personally observed several instances where sequences involving discarnate relatives and friends provided some unusual and verifiable information that the recipients could not have possibly obtained through the ordinary means and channels. Similarly, individuals who receive messages from deceased strangers find sometimes to their great surprise that they have been given an existing address and correct name of the relatives of a person who actually recently died.

Personal survival of physical death is not necessarily the only explanatory framework for these findings, and it is certainly possible to conceive of other interpretations than actual communication with objectively existing astral realms of discarnate beings. However, one thing is certain: none of the alternative explanations will be compatible with the traditional Newtonian-Cartesian thinking. In any case, we are dealing here with fascinating phenomena of their own right that should be systematically studied.

To discard the extraordinary features of these experiences and the conceptual challenges associated with them just because they do not fit the current paradigms in science certainly is not the best example of a scientific approach. We must accept the universe as it is, rather than imposing on it what we believe it is or think it should be. Our theories must deal with the facts in their totality, rather than with a convenient selection of them that fits our worldview and belief system. Until modern Western science is able to offer plausible explanation of all the observations surrounding such phenomena as spiritistic experiences and past incarnation memories, the concepts found in mystical and occult literature have to be seen as superior to the present approach of most Western scientists, who either do not know the facts or ignore them.

The first illustrative example is from psycholytic treatment of a young depressed patient, whose history was briefly described in my book *Realms of the Human Unconscious* (pp. 57–60) under the name Richard.

> In one of his LSD sessions, Richard had a very unusual experience involving a strange and uncanny astral realm. It had an eery luminescence and was filled with discarnate beings that were trying to communicate with him in a very urgent and demanding manner. He could not see or hear them; however, he sensed their almost tangible

presence and was receiving telepathic messages from them. I wrote down one of these messages that was very specific and could be subjected to subsequent verification.

It was a request for Richard to connect with a couple in the Moravian city of Kroměříž and let them know that their son Ladislav was doing all right and was well taken care of. The message included the couple's name, street address, and telephone number; all of these data were unknown to me and the patient. This experience was extremely puzzling; it seemed to be an alien enclave in Richard's experience, totally unrelated to his problems and the rest of his treatment.

After some hesitation and with mixed feelings, I finally decided to do what certainly would have made me the target of my colleagues' jokes, had they found out. I went to the telephone, dialed the number in Kroměříž, and asked if I could speak with Ladislav. To my astonishment, the woman on the other side of the line started to cry. When she calmed down, she told me with a broken voice: "Our son is not with us any more; he passed away, we lost him three weeks ago."

The second illustrative example involves a close friend and former colleague of mine, Walter N. Pahnke, who was a member of our psychedelic research team at the Maryland Psychiatric Research Center in Baltimore. He had deep interest in parapsychology, particularly in the problem of consciousness after death, and worked with many famous mediums and psychics, including his friend Eileen Garrett, president of the American Parapsychological Association. In addition, he was also the initiator of the LSD program for patients dying of cancer.

In summer 1971, Walter went with his wife Eva and his children for a vacation in a cabin in Maine, situated right on the ocean. One day, he went scuba-diving all by himself and did not return from the ocean. An extensive and well-organized search failed to find his body or any part of his diving gear. Under these circumstances, Eva found it very difficult to accept and integrate his death. Her last memory of Walter when he was leaving the cabin involved him full of energy and in perfect health. It was hard for her to believe that he was not part of her life any more and to start a new chapter of her existence without a sense of closure of the preceding one.

Being a psychologist herself, she qualified for an LSD training session for mental health professionals offered through a special program in our institute. She decided to have a psychedelic experience with the hope of gettimg some more insights and asked me to be her sitter. In the second half of the session, she had a very powerful vision of Walter and carried on a long and meaningful dialogue with him. He gave her specific instructions concerning each of their three children and released her to start a new life of her own, unencumbered and unrestricted by a sense of commitment to his memory. It was a very profound and liberating experience.

Just as Eva was questioning whether the entire episode was just a wishful fabrication of her own mind, Walter appeared once more for a brief period of time with the following request: "I forgot one thing. Would you please do me a favor and return a book that I borrowed from a friend of mine. It is in my study in the attic." And he proceeded to give her the name of the friend, the name of the book, the shelf, and the sequential order of the book on this shelf. Following the instructions, Eva was actually able to find and return the book, about the existence of which she had had no previous knowledge.

It would certainly have been completely consistent with Walter's lifelong search for a scientific proof of paranormal phenomena to add a concrete and testable piece of information to his interaction with Eva to dispel her doubts. Earlier during his life, he had made an agreement with Eileen Garrett that she would try to give him after her death an unquestionable proof of the existence of the beyond.

b.   *Energetic Phenomena of the Subtle Body*

In nonordinary states of consciousness, it is possible to see and experience various energy fields and energy flows that have been described by the mystical traditions of ancient and non-Western cultures. These descriptions do not make any sense in the context of the Western medical model, since they do not correspond to any known anatomical structures or physiological processes. However, the esoteric traditions never claimed that these were phenomena in the gross material realm; they have always described them as related to the subtle body. It came as a great surprise for me when Western subjects — even those totally unfamiliar with these esoteric systems — experienced and reported virtually identical experiences in unusual states of consciousness.

A very common experience in the holotropic mode is to see energy fields of various colors around other people that correspond to the traditional descriptions of auras. Occasionally, these are associated with spontaneous specific insights into the health condition of the people involved. I have personally observed phenomena of this kind, not only in subjects in unusual states of consciousness, but also in accomplished psychics who can use their capacity to see auras in a reliable way in their everyday life. The extraordinary ability of one of these psychics, Jack Schwartz, to read the medical history of his clients and diagnose current diseases has been repeatedly tested and documented by medical researchers with impressive credentials.

Another interesting group of phenomena is related to the concept of the Serpent Power, or *Kundalinī*, which plays an important role in the Indian spiritual tradition. According to the Hindu and Buddhist Tantric schools, Kundalini is seen as the creative energy of the universe that is feminine in nature (Muktananda 1979, Mookerjee 1982). In her external aspect, she is manifested in the phenomenal world. In her internal aspect, she lies dormant at the base of the human spine. In this form, she is traditionally symbolically represented as a coiled serpent. Activated by spiritual practice, by contact with a guru, or spontaneously, it rises in the form of active energy, or Shakti, up the conduits in the subtle body called *nādīs*, opening and lighting up the psychic centers, or *chakras*.

Although the concept of Kundalini found its most elaborate expression in India, important parallels exist in many cultures and religious groups — in the Taoist yoga, Korean Zen, Tibetan Vajrayana, Sufism, the freemasonic tradition, the !Kung Bushmen of the African Kalahari Desert, North American Indian tribes, especially the Hopi, and many others. It is of special interest that similar phenomena have been reported repeatedly also in the Christian mystical tradition, particularly in the *hesychasm*. The *hesychasm* is an Eastern Christian monastic practice and way of life, emphasizing prayer that involves the entire human being — the soul, mind, and body. The purpose of this so-called "Jesus prayer" is to achieve divine quietness, or *hesychia* (Matus 1984).

The Tantric schools have developed intricate maps of the *chakras*, have described in detail the physical, emotional, and spiritual manifestations of Kundalini awakening, and have preserved elaborate mythologies related to this process. Although not without dangers and pitfalls, the process of Kundalini rising is seen, in general, as one conducive — at least potentially — to psychosomatic healing, to positive restructuring of the personality, and to consciousness evolution. However, because of its uncanny power, the scriptures treat this process very seriously and recommend the guidance of an experienced teacher for persons involved in it.

The ascent of Kundalini Shakti, as described in the Indian literature, can be accompanied by dramatic physical and psychological manifestations called *kriyas*. The most striking among these are powerful sensations of heat and energy streaming up the spine associated with intense emotions of various kinds, tremors, spasms, violent shaking, and complex twisting movements. Quite common is also involuntary laughing or crying, chanting of mantras or songs, talking in tongues, emitting of vocal noises and animal sounds, and assuming spontaneous yogic gestures (*mudras*) and postures (*asanas*).

Although the descriptions of Kundalini have been known in the West for a long time, they have been considered until recently to be

Figure 8   A nineteeth century gouache from Rajasthan showing the two aspects of Kundalini: in her latent form as a coiled serpent and in her activated form or Shakti as a goddess appearing in an altar of fire (from: Ajit Mookerjee: *Kundalini*, Destiny Books, New York, 1982, plate IV, page 28).

an exclusively Oriental phenomenon. Even Carl Gustav Jung, who showed keen interest in the Kundalini phenomenon (Jung 1975), thought that it rarely, if ever, occurred in the West. He and his colleagues expressed the opinion that it might take a thousand years before Kundalini is set in motion in our culture through the influence of depth psychology. However, future development showed this estimate to be wrong.

Whether this can be attributed to accelerated evolution, popularity and rapid spread of various forms of spiritual practice, pressure of the dangerous global crisis, or the facilitating effect of psychedelic drugs, it is quite clear that unmistakable signs of Kundalini awakening can be observed these days in thousands of Westerners. Gopi Krishna, a world-known pandit from Kashmir, who had himself undergone a profound crisis of a stormy spiritual opening, tried to alert Western audiences to the paramount significance of the phenomenon of Kundalini in a series of articulate popular books (Krishna 1970 and others). The merit of bringing this fact to the attention of the professional circles belongs to the Californian psychiatrist and ophthalmologist Lee Sannella (Sannella 1976).

I have myself observed repeatedly in psychedelic sessions and various nondrug states manifestations that matched closely the descriptions of the arousal of Kundalini, opening of the *chakras**, and flow of the Kundalini energy through the main conduits, Ida and Pingala, and through the intricate network of the *nadis*, fine and ramified channels for pranic energy, as they have been described and depicted in Tantric texts.

However, it is important to emphasize that experiences of this kind — Kundalini-like phenomena that would in traditional Indian literature be described as *pranic* — have to be distinguished from true

---

*Chakras (a Sanskrit term for "wheels") are hypothetical centers of radiation of primal energy (*prāṇa*) roughly corresponding to certain levels of the spinal cord and associated with specific organs of the body. Most systems distinguish seven *chakras*: 1. root *chakra* (*mulādhāra*), 2. genital *chakra* (*svādhiṣṭhāna*), 3. navel *chakra* (*maṇipūra*), 4. heart *chakra* (*anāhata*), 5. throat *chakra* (*viśuddha*), 6. brow *chakra* (*ajñā*), and 7. crown *chakra* (*sahasrāra*). The flow of *prāṇa* is mediated by one central conduit (*suṣumṇā*), and two lateral conduits (Ida and Pingala).

awakening of Kundalini. The latter is an involved process of profound significance and transformative power, the completion of which often requires years. In comparison with isolated pranic experiences, such

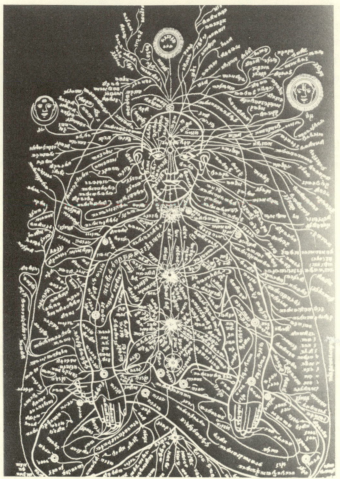

Figure 9 An Indian ink drawing representing a yogic diagram of a complex system of channels for psychic energy or nadis in the subtle body that can be experienced in spiritual practice. It shows clearly that these energetic conduits extend beyond the boundaries of the physical body ((Bihar, 19th century, from: Ajit Mookerjee *Yoga Art*, New York Graphic Society, Little Brown & Co., 1975, plate 9., page 27.).

an awakening of Kundalini occurs only very rarely as a result of psychedelic experiences or experiential psychotherapy and seems to be an independent phenomenon.

The patterns of energy flow in the subtle body described in the literature on Kundalini do not seem to be universal and absolute. In several instances, subjects who tuned into the Chinese archetypal world experienced the energy flow in a way that exactly followed the maps of meridians found in Chinese medicine and became aware of the special significance of the acupuncture points. This was followed by philosophical insights into the Chinese system of five elements (wood, fire, earth, water, and metal), which is distinctly different from the one found in the European tradition. I have also observed subjects who gained deep experiential understanding of the special role of the abdominal center (*hara*) and the dynamics of the *ki* energy underlying the Japanese martial arts.

Various energetic phenomena of the subtle body are extremely frequent in the sessions of holotropic breathing. The energy fields and the streaming of energy can be experienced in a tangible way and can even be visually perceived with the eyes closed. The following holotropic experience of a participant in one of our five-day workshops bore close resemblance to the descriptions from Tantric literature.

As I continued to breathe, I started feeling an incredible upsurge of energy in my pelvis. In my sacral area was a powerful source of light and heat that was radiating in all directions. And then this energy started to stream upward along my spinal cord, following a clearly defined line. On the way, it was lighting up additional sources of energy in the places where the esoteric maps place the different chakras.

As this was happening, I was experiencing very blissful orgiastic feelings. One of the most powerful experiences of this session was when this energy reached the area of my heart. I felt such incredible love toward the world and toward other people that I wanted to get up and give a big hug to everybody in the group. It was strange how close I felt toward people whom I had met last night for the first time and whom I did not really know.

But I stayed with the experience and the energy continued to flow upward. When it reached the top of my head, it exploded into a fantastically beautiful aureole that had a rosy-orange hue, like the pictures of the Thousand Petal Lotus. I felt the need to flex my legs and join the soles of my feet to create a closed circuit of energy. My energetic field was now extended far beyond the boundaries of my physical body; I suddenly understood why the esoteric maps show the subtle energy body as much larger than the material body; one can actually experience it that way in these states.

The energy was flowing upward, leaving through the top of my head and then returning to the lower parts of my body to participate again in the upward flow. I stayed in this state for a long time, drawing a lot of strength and emotional nourishment from this energy.

Figure 10   Channeled paintings of Guenn Eoná Nimüe from Seattle, who has been involved in the last 44 years in a powerful spontaneous inner process. During this time, she has had numerous experiences of direct communication with animals and their guardian spirits, elemental beings representing various forces of nature, extraterrestrial visitors, and archetypal deities. Paintings depicting the animal spirits and guardians of the Bear, Wolf, and Seal.

c. Experience of Animal Spirits

In this type of experience, subjects have the feeling of profound connection with various animals — not their concrete physical forms, but their archetypal essence. This can occasionally be triggered by an actual encounter with a representative of a particular species who is perceived in a deified form by the individual in a nonordinary state of consciousness. Experiences of this kind have been repeatedly reported by people who have taken psychedelics in the wilderness or in the presence of various domesticated animals. More frequently, experiences of this kind occur as independent events in the inner world.

In many instances, animal spirits encountered in unusual states of consciousness are perceived not only as divine in nature, but as teachers and friends offering help and spiritual guidance. This can be associated with deep insights into the sacred function of various animals in certain cultures, such as the cow in India, the cat, crocodile, and falcon in Egypt, or the vulture among the Parsees. Experiences of this kind can also impart unique insights into the psychology of totemistic cultures and the function of the totem animals. However, particularly frequent are references to shamanism and understanding of the role of various animals as spirit helpers of the shaman.

The inner process of a Western subject can occasionally take on the form known from shamanic cultures. This involves powerful death-rebirth sequences with descent into the underworld and ascent to the supernal realms that the anthropologists have described as "shamanic illness". Another important characteristic of this process is a strong sense of special connection with nature and an abundance of experiences of animal identification and of encounters with spirit guides in animal form. Shamanism is the oldest religion of humanity, reaching back tens of thousands of years. It is also a phenomenon that is practically universal. Its different varieties can be found in Siberia and other parts of Asia, in North and South America, Australia, Oceania, Africa, and Europe (Eliade 1964, Harner 1980, Campbell 1984). Shamanic and totemistic experiences thus connect the individual with deep and primordial aspects of the psyche.

Before concluding this section, I would like to compare the experiences of animal spirits with other types of transpersonal phenomena involving animals. They all have specific characteristics that make it possible for experienced subjects to differentiate them from each other. In general, it is important to distinguish experiential identification with various animals who are part of the phenomenal world from symbolic representations of the individual unconscious and from archetypal images of the psyche.

Subjects who work on various biographical issues in experiential psychotherapy often report visions of various animals or even identification with them. Analysis of these phenomena makes it clear that they are complex formations with a dynamic structure that is similar to Freudian dream images. On this level, *animal autosymbolic visions* or *transformations* represent a more or less cryptic message about the subject's personality or life situation and can be easily recognized as such. An autosymbolic identification with a predator, such as a tiger, lion, or black panther, can be deciphered as an expression of the person's intense aggressive feelings. A strong sexual drive can be symbolized by a stallion or a bull; if it has the objectionable form of sheer lust and base instincts, it might be symbolized by a wild boar or sow. Masculine vanity and sexually tainted exhibitionism can be ridiculed by an autosymbolic identification with a noisy cock on the dunghill. Similarly, a hog can represent self-neglect, sloppiness, and moral flaws; a monkey, polymorphous perversion and indulgence in genital and pregenital pleasures; a mule, hard-headedness and stubbornness; and an ass, stupidity.

In comparison with autosymbolic transformation, true *animal identification* is a clearly transpersonal phenomenon that cannot be derived from other unconscious contents or interpreted symbolically. The same subjects who earlier readily cooperated in deciphering symbolic animal experiences will refuse to approach genuine identifications in that way. I have heard in this context repeatedly statements like: "No, you do not understand; there is nothing to analyze here, I really was an elephant. I knew what an elephant feels like when he is angry or sexually aroused, and what it is like when water enters his trunk. An elephant does not stand for anything; an elephant is an elephant." Phylogenetic experiences have all the characteristics of true animal identification but are associated, in addition, with a sense of historical regression in the evolutionary pedigree. An interesting phenomenon that seems to represent a transition between autosymbolic transformation and true animal identification is the experience of being a werewolf or a vampire. It is clearly related to Transsylvanian folklore, the stories about lykanthropy, and its Malaysian parallel of tigeranthropy.

Instead of identifying with one particular member of a species, it is also possible to experience something like the "animal soul" *of a species*, which seems to be a composite experience of all its members in a historical perspective — all the learning of the species, its instinctive behaviors, intraspecies communication patterns, habits, etc. Experiences of this kind seem to be closely related to the concept of morphic resonance described by Rupert Sheldrake (Sheldrake 1981) and Gregory Bateson's understanding of mind in nature (Bateson 1972, 1979). This suggests that this phenomenon can be discussed in the context of natural sciences.

The *animal spirits* and *spirit guides* as they are experienced in various nonordinary states, while clearly related to and supraordinated to specific species, belong to the world of mythical and archetypal forms. However, their immediate connection with nature distinguishes them from various *theriomorphic deities* who have an animal form but are not intimately anchored in nature, or those who combine animal and human elements. The elephant god, Ganesha, of the Hindu pantheon has much less in common with the actual Indian elephant than, for example, the Deer Spirit of the Mexican Huichol Indians has with the forest deer. The symbolic meanings related to his function as a deity by far supersede his connections to the elephant species.

This is even more evident when the deity involved is an *animal-human composite image*, such as the Egyptian ibis-headed Thoth and jackal-headed Anubis, or the Indian Narasimha, who combines human and leonine characteristics. These deities do not even share the full physical form of the animal they are connected with. A separate interesting group of animals appears in the role of *vehicles for divine beings*. Here belong, for example, the mouse that carries the Hindu god Ganesha, Shiva's bull Nandi, the lion or tiger who serves the goddess Durga, the peacock who supports Brahma's consort Sarasvati, and the Tibetan lamaistic deities, the stallions of the sun chariot of the Greek god Helios, or the rams of the Nordic Goddess Fricka.

An excellent example of the experience of animal spirits can be found in the account of a visionary state of the shaman of the Jivaro, a head-hunting tribe in Ecuador; it was induced by the ingestion of *ayahuasca* (Harner 1973).

> He had drunk and now he softly sang. Gradually, faint lines and forms began to appear in the darkness, and the shrill music of the *tsentsak*, the spirit helpers, arose around him. The power of the drink fed them. He called and they came. First, *pangi*, the anaconda, coiled about his head, transmuted into a crown of gold. Then *wampang*, the giant butterfly, hovered above his shoulder and sang to him with his wings. Snakes, spiders, birds, and bats danced in the air above him. On his arms appeared a thousand eyes as his demon helpers emerged to search the night for enemies.
>
> The sound of rushing water filled his ears, and listening to its roar, he knew he possessed the power of Tsungi, the first shaman. Now he could see.

d.   *Encounters with Spirit Guides and Suprahuman Beings*

Experiences of encounters with guides, teachers, and protectors from the spiritual world belong to the most valuable and rewarding phenomena of the transpersonal domain. The subjects perceive these beings as suprahuman entities existing on higher planes of consciousness and higher energy levels. Sometimes they appear quite spontaneously at a certain stage of the spiritual development of the individual; other times they suddenly emerge during an inner crisis, responding to an urgent call for help. In many instances, they continue appearing to the subject either on their own terms or at the request of their protégé.

Sometimes the spirit guides have a human form with a distinctly numinous quality. Other times they appear as a source of radiant light or a powerful energy field. Many subjects explain that they do not actually have any sensory perceptions of their guides; they simply sense their presence. Only exceptionally do the guides communicate with the subject verbally. In most instances, the messages, explanations, and instructions are conveyed by telepathic transfer of thoughts or through other extrasensory means.

The assistance that the spirit guides offer has many different forms and degrees. Sometimes they intervene in difficult and dangerous experiences on the subject's behalf. Other times they accompany him or her through various critical situations on the inner plane, as Vergil guided Dante in the *Divine Comedy*. They give intellectual, moral and spiritual support, help to combat evil and destructive forces, or create protective shields of positive energy. They can also occasionally give specific directives and suggestions concerning the subject's problems or the general direction of his or her life. Some spiritual guides remain anonymous and unrecognized; others introduce themselves by name, or the subject is able to identify them by some clues.

On occasion, persons in nonordinary states of consciousness report direct experiences of great religious personages of the stature of Jesus Christ, Buddha, Mohammed, Zoroaster, Sri Ramana Maharshi, or Moses. These are usually one-time appearances; it is uncommon for personalities of this rank to be claimed as personal guides, except in a metaphorical sense.

The most interesting aspect of the experiences involving guides from other planes is that they occasionally mediate access to information that the subject did not possess in the conventional sense before the event. A good example is the famous parapsychologist Thelma Moss, who connected in one of her psychedelic sessions with an entity who introduced himself as Benjamin Franklin; she prefers to think about him as the Old Wise Man archetype. For about one year following this session, she was able to evoke his presence in a meditative state, conduct conversations with him, and ask him for information and guidance. At one time, when she was in an impasse in her research of bioenergies, "Benjamin Franklin" directed her to get a specific book by the researcher Becker, where she found the critical information she needed.

It seems appropriate to mention in this context a phenomenon that has been recently receiving increasing popularity. It is channeling, which is a contemporary term for the process where a person transmits through automatic writing, speaking in trance, or mental dictation messages from a source external to his or her consciousness. The source often identifies itself as a being from a nonphysical reality; the hierarchical rank of this entity can range from a deity or angel to a superhuman advanced being or a discarnate individual.

Historical examples of channeled spiritual teachings include the Koran (Mohammed) and the Book of Mormon (Smith). An entity who called himself the Tibetan was acknowledged by Alice Bailey as the real author of a large series of her spiritual writings. Roberto Assagioli credited the same entity as the source of his psychological system of psychosynthesis. Among the most popular modern texts are *Seth Speaks* (Roberts), *Messages from Michael* (Yarbro), *Course in Miracles* (Schucman), *New Age Transformation: Revelations* (Spangler), *Starseed Transmissions* (Rafael), *Urantia Book* (Anonymous), *Emmanuel's Book* (Rodegast), and *Ramtha* (Knight). Channeling as a phenomenon and its specific manifestations in religion, philosophy, art, and science will be explored in the forthcoming comprehensive book by Arthur Hastings.

e.   *Visits to Other Universes and Meetings with Their Inhabitants*

In this type of experience, subjects get involved in wild adventures in strange, alien worlds that have reality of their own, although not within the range of our cosmos. These universes seem to exist on other levels of reality or in other dimensions, parallel with and coexistent with ours. The entities inhabiting them possess bizarre physical forms, have physiologial and metabolic processes completely different from our own, and operate on the basis of some incomprehensible laws. Many of them are obviously intelligent creatures, but their emotional and ideational characteristics do not resemble anything known to humans.

These alien universes can be much smaller or infinitely bigger than ours, and their inhabitants can be friendly, neutral, or hostile to visitors from other dimensions. Experiences of this kind are usually perceived as dangerous; sometimes this is due to the obvious hostility of the creatures involved, other times to uncertainty in facing the unknown. In some instances, the danger seems to stem from the fact that the visitor appears to be so insignificant in the alien world that he or she could be destroyed by negligence or by an unfortunate accident. People describing these extraordinary cosmic adventures often liken them to the most ingenious science fiction stories ever written.

I should mention, in this context, experiences with alien aircrafts, spaceships, and flying saucers. According to the descriptions by subjects who have seen them, have experienced meetings with their

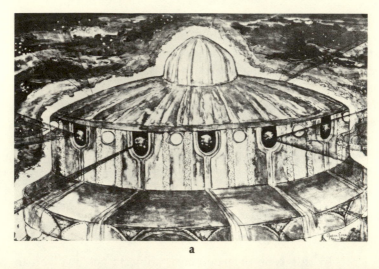

a

b

c

Figures 11a–e A series of paintings by Guenn Eoná Nimüe representing experiences with extraterrestrial and archetypal interstellar beings. **a.** An enormous extraterrestrial mothership, "Halcyon House of Light." **b.** HAMAL-LODKHEANNH, Creator of the Milky Way Galaxy or Great Fisher of the Ocean of Love, a cosmic being who has within his core memory banks the stories of creation's beginning, **c.** KAMIKSTEKAL OHLAHANDRA DOOREESHAMH, Lord of the Firey Cross, a consular advocate for a large number of constellations.

d   e

d. An extraterrestrial being from a star system that lies beyond our galaxy; his picture was perceived as sent by solar transmitters aboard a lightship. **e.** A drawing representing two beautiful quasar soulmate deities expressing for each other since time immemorial their eternal love.

crews, or have reported that they had been taken for a ride or had visited their interiors, these experiences have a strange quality that puts them in the twilight zone between physical reality and the archetypal world. In some instances, the experients were more inclined to see them as actual extraterrestrial spacecraft from another part of our universe; in others, as visitors from a different dimension or as intrapsychic phenomena. I will return to this subject later in connection with transpersonal experiences of psychoid nature (p. 156).

These reports often involve descriptions of physical examinations and operations using various mysterious gadgets, mental communications with the aliens and their intelligent machines, lessons in higher-dimensional thinking, and the like. Systematic analysis of the content of abduction experiences conducted by Alvin Lawson (Lawson 1984) has shown a surprising abundance of perinatal elements and themes. Although this is certainly not a proof that these phenomena are nothing but fantasies derived from the memory of the birth trauma, this fact deserves further attention.

Particularly good examples of extraterrestrial contacts and visits to other universes can be found in the writings of the famous researcher and unrelenting psychedelic self-explorer John Lilly, in whose nonordinary states of consciousness they seem to be unusually rich and frequent (Lilly 1972, 1978).

The following example is the experience of a thirty-five-year-old writer who took in an exploratory group setting two empathogenic amphetamine derivatives — first 150 milligrams of MDMA (Adam or Ecstasy) and four hours later 20 milligrams of 2CB (Adamson 1986).

> About an hour and a half into the trip I was seeing my visions with my eyes open or closed; and I was traveling to other planets and dimensions. In each realm a religious ceremony was in progress. On one plane, there were huge, mantis-like beings that were wise, sepulchrally dignified, welcoming me with their ritual. On another plane, green, gold, blue, and purple beings that looked like small, crystalline insects shaped and reshaped in kaleidoscopic formations, sending me urgent messages of mute support.
>
> Finally, a dimension appeared where all was crystal life forms; all were incredibly beautiful energy beings, on both micro and megascopic scales.

f. Experiences of Mythological and Fairy Tale Sequences

In this type of transpersonal experience, the world of myths, legends, and fairy tales literally comes to life. The subject can witness numerous scenes from the mythology and folklore of any culture in the world and visit any number of mythical landscapes. He or she can also experientially identify with legendary and mythical heroes and heroines, or fantastic mythological creatures. It is possible to experience the labors of Hercules or the adventures of Theseus and Jason. One can become the legendary Polynesian hero Maui, or suffer through the ordeals of the twins in the Mayan Popol Vuh. Among the archetypal creatures that subjects have identified with in psychedelic sessions and during holotropic breathing were Uroboros, Typhon, Centaurus, Cerberus, Sphinx, various European, oriental, and pre-Columbian dragons, Snow White, Sleeping Beauty, legendary knights, mermaids, fairies, elves, gnomes, Scandinavian trolls, and others.

Such sequences can emerge as independent transpersonal themes or in meaningful connection with personal problems of the subject. Among the motifs that often associate with biographical issues are that of the evil stepmother and battered stepdaughter (Cinderella), the good brother and the bad brother (Cain and Abel), love for one's mother and aggression toward one's father (Oedipus), love for one's father and hatred toward one's mother (Electra), loving siblings endangered by evil adults (Hansel and Gretel), conflict between love and power (Alberich), and the great love endangered by circumstances (Tristan and Isolde). All these can appear in a specific cultural form or in a more abstract archetypal form.

I have already mentioned earlier some specific associations between certain mythological themes and the basic perinatal matrices. For BPM I, these are images of heavens or paradises of different cultures; for BPM II, images of hells; BPM III is similarly connected with experiences involving purgatories. In addition, sequences of BPM II often involve mythological scenes of eternal damnation and the figures of tragic heroes that embody suffering without redemption — Prometheus, Tantalus, Sisyphus, Ixion, the wandering Jew Ahasuerus, and others. Mythological motifs characteristic of BPM III and BPM IV portray labors, ordeals, and struggles of heroes that have a positive resolution — killing of monsters, victory over evil, overcoming of death, personal liberation or redemption, and sacred marriage.

In principle, every individual seems to have experiential access to mythological themes of all times and all cultures. On many occasions, unsophisticated subjects have described in detail complex mythological images and even entire scenes from Central or South America, Polynesia, Mesopotamia, India, Egypt, Japan, and other areas that they definitely did not know intellectually. These observations clearly support Carl Gustav Jung's concept of the collective unconscious based on emergence of often obscure and unknown mythological motifs in dreams, even those of children and uneducated persons, and in the manifest symptoms of neurotic and psychotic patients (Jung 1959).

To illustrate this category of transpersonal experience, I will use the description of a session of holotropic breathing conducted in the

a   b

c   d

Figures 12a–g A series of paintings by Guenn Eoná Nimüe representing the world of the "Little People," elemental beings connected with various forces and aspects of nature. **a.** Mentifil, the powerful ruler of the Kingdom of Gnomes under the Earth. **b.** Orova, great guardian of all the precious stones found in the Earth. **c.** Ordaphe, powerful gnome ruler of the kingdoms of gold, silver, and other ores found under the surface of the Earth. **d.** Hadrian of the House of Ascher, the oldest of the gnome people.

e. A painting showing from the left TOH-PHUT-ET, Guardian to the Little People of all the waters on this planet, KA-MO-PANSET, ruler to the elven House of Orange, and PUTARCH-RHIANNHAN-AKAL, Lord of Clowns and Jesters.

f. A painting showing what a person with inner sight can see at "power spots," where sacred edifices were often positioned in the past: here are two Water Serpents linking their heads and a dragon with its companion/guardian who have been lying there for countless eons.

g. Earth Mirror, a magical hologram produced by the "Little People" when they designed King Arthur's sword Excalibur.

context of one of our five-day experiential seminars. The participant was a woman of Japanese origin.

> At the beginning of the session I experienced deep grief which was so overwhelming that I could not cry. I thought about the possible cause of my grief. Then I remembered that there existed a formless darkness which had taken my baby out of my hands. I had felt powerless against the darkness.
>
> When I remembered the reason for my grief, intense anger arose. I felt powerful and strong, and the anger showed itself as fiery extensions to my body. I fought against the darkness and took back my child, but the child was dead. It made me sad to see the body of my own child being burnt by my fiery hands. The burnt body turned to ashes and spread on the soil.
>
> I became a very quiet goddess-like figure walking around the place where the ashes had fallen to the ground. My tears nurtured seedlings which sprouted where the ashes lay. One plant grew and a flower bloomed. In the middle of the blossom a glowing sphere appeared. The sphere turned into a precious baby. At that time I felt that the circle had closed. I realized it would repeat itself again and again. I felt I had completed the work.
>
> Then I felt my body and had three more experiences, although I am not certain in which order they occurred. 1. My left side turned into mountains and I experienced the geological cycle of mountain-building and erosion. 2. My right side turned into a forest. 3. Between my legs I felt the ocean with the ebb and flow of the tides. I felt that the cycle I had experienced was endless; if I were caught in it, it would continue forever. But I found that there was a direct path from each of the stages to the center which would allow me to break the cycle.

8. Experiences of Specific Blissful and Wrathful Deities

This category is closely related to the previous one and could be considered its special subgroup. Mythological images belonging here are endowed with special power and numinosity that gives them divine status. They are also very specific and can be clearly identified as deities from the pantheons of different cultures. In some instances, the subjects are familiar with the deities they are experiencing and can give their names and the cultural areas they belong to. However, the experience often conveys much new information that is far beyond the previous knowledge of the person involved. Other times, the deities are entirely unknown to the experient, but he or she is able to draw their pictures, describe in great detail their functions, and identify the general cultural area from which they come. This information then makes it possible to consult the appropriate sources and assess its accuracy. There also exist situations where the identity of the experienced deities remains obscure or uncertain in spite of combined research efforts of the client and the therapist.

Most deities encountered in nonordinary states of consciousness fall into two clearly dichotomized groups: the blissful and beneficent divinities associated with the forces of light and good and the wrathful and malific ones representing the forces of darkness and evil. However, this distinction is in no way absolute; there exist deities that seem to fall in between and there are others that are encompassing and have beatific and horrific aspects. A typical example of the last group are the Dhyani-Buddhas of the *Tibetan Book of the Dead* (*Bardo Thötröl* or *Thödöl*) who first appear to the dying person in their radiant forms and later in their demonic aspects.

For many individuals on the spiritual path, the first encounter with archetypal deities occurs in the context of the death-rebirth process. The dark deities, such as Satan, Lucifer, Hades, Ahriman, Huitzilopochtli, Kali, Lilith, Rangda, Coatlicue, or Moloch, would typically appear in connection with BPM II, BPM III and with the ego death. Deities symbolizing death and rebirth (Osiris, Pluto and Persephone, Attis, Adonis, Quetzalcoatl, Dionysos, Wotan, Balder, Christ) have a specific affiliation with BPM III and with the transition to BPM IV. The blissful deities — the Virgin Mary, Aphrodite, Apollo, Isis, Ahura Mazda, Lakshmi, or Kuan-yin (Kannon) — appear in ecstatic episodes related to BPM IV or BPM I.

Archetypal images of specific deities can also be encountered quite independently in the context of psychedelic or holotropic experiences that are purely transpersonal in nature. They typically appear in the form of powerful visions that the subject is witnessing; however, an important alternative is full experiential identification with these deities. In addition to separate individual appearances, various deities can also participate in complex cosmic dramas, such as the battle between the forces of Ahriman and Ahura Mazda of the Zoroastrian pantheon, the war between the Olympian gods and the Titans, the fall of Lucifer and his peer angels, the churning of the

Figure 13 A painting depicting a powerful experience from a holotropic breathing session. It involved identification with a sensuous female deity appearing in fire and representing creative forces of nature. The subject contrasted this experience with the death-oriented Christian religion that had been an important part of her upbringing.

ocean by the Hindu gods and demons to obtain the nectar amrita, and Ragnarok, or the twilight of the gods of the Nordic mythology.

Subjects experiencing encounters with various blissful and wrathful deities usually have very powerful emotional reactions, ranging from ecstatic rapture and extreme bliss to metaphysical terror, abysmal pain, and feelings of insanity. However, as powerful as these images can be, the experient does not have the sense of confrontation with the Supreme Being, or the ultimate force in the universe. This feeling is reserved for experiences of a higher order that will be described later.

The example I have chosen as an illustration for this category of experiences, is an excerpt from a high-dose LSD session. It describes an encounter and identification with the twin figures of Christ and Antichrist.

Figure 14 A painting symbolizing the union of Heaven and Earth experienced in a holotropic breathing session. The combination of an exotic bird representing the celestial element and of a snake representing the earthly dimension is reminiscent of the Pre-Columbian diety Quetzalcoatl.

The most difficult part of the experience was the identification with the devil, with the evil principle in the universe. Somewhere across from me was a most vile and nasty creature squatting down and overlooking the entire region. I had to become him, identify with this most despicable entity. I became Hitler, a General of Death. I was feeling pure hate; all I wanted to do was to kill, to inflict pain, to make people suffer. It was very painful, but I had to do it. I could not believe there was so much hate in me. I could perceive hate as something tangible — as black evil substance, or dark thick kind of energy.

I felt the presence of a demonic existence right next to Christ; this was the Antichrist! He too was part of the cosmic journey. All the Hitlers of the world, all the despotic rulers and tyrants were manifestations or personifications of this evil principle. The difficult realization was how close Christ and Antichrist were to each other. It was very confusing; how could one know which was which? I understood how difficult it would be on earth to find the right spiritual teacher to follow. How could one know whether a particular spiritual leader was emanating from Christ or from Antichrist? Spiritual goodness and evil were just two sides of the same coin. In a way, this close paradoxical association of the two opposite cosmic energies explained seemingly confusing human events, such as the rise of tne Nazi party in Germany or the problematic developments in certain religious cults.

(This encounter with archetypal evil continued in the next LSD session of the same subject.) At another point, I had a brief, but extremely powerful experience which I will never forget. I felt the presence of Lucifer and then saw him clearly. He was a huge dark creature, partly human and partly animal, with a hairy body, large claws, and the wings of a dragon. He was coming out of a dark cave, flying through the pitch black sky in the middle of the night like a gigantic bat. As I was looking at him from a distance, I noticed to my astonishment that his head was on fire. The Devil, Lucifer himself, was being transmuted by the Light into the Light. I understood now why Lucifer means literally "the carrier of light." He was being consumed by the Purifying Fire right in front of my eyes. I knew that I would no longer be afraid of evil or of the Devil himself.

h.   Experiences of Universal Archetypes

The term "archetype" was introduced into psychology by Carl Gustav Jung; he used this name alternately with the terms "primordial image" and "dominant of the collective unconscious." In its broadest sense, an archetype can be described as any static pattern and configuration, as well as dynamic happening in the psyche that is transindividual and has a universal quality (Jung 1959). Such a definition is extremely general and would apply to many trans- personal phenomena described in this section. In the Jungian liter- ature, one can find hierarchical descriptions of various orders of archetypes (see figure 16). I will take the liberty to narrow the term here to those archetypes that represent truly universal patterns, rather than their specific cultural manifestations, variations, and inflections.

Some of such universal archetypes represent generalized bio- logical, psychological, social, and professional roles. Examples of biologically defined universal archetypes would be the Woman, Man, Mother, Father, Child, the Jew, and the Member of the White, Black or Yellow Race. Additional psychological characteristics would then define the archetypes of the Good or Terrible Mother, Tyrant Father,

Lover, Martyr, Fugitive, Outcast, Avarice, Despot, Vicious Spoiler, Trickster, Wise Old Man and Woman, Ascetic, Hermit, and many others. In some of these, the archetype reaches mythological dimensions and has a special numinous power. This is true for the images of the Great and Terrible Mother Goddess, the Great Hermaphrodite, or the Cosmic Man.

Figure 15   A painting by Guenn Eoná Nimüe representing the archetypal figure of the Earth Mother Goddess.

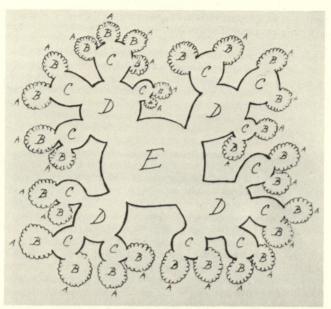

Figure 16 A diagram used by Marie-Louise von Franz to illustrate the hierarchical structure of the unconscious. The outermost small circles (A) represent the ego consciousness of human beings. The deeper layers (B) depict the spheres of the personal unconscious discovered by Freud. Below lie the domains of the group unconscious of families, groups, clans, and tribes (C) and further the large spheres of the common unconscious of wide national units that share important mythological motifs, such as the Australian Aborigines or South American Indians (D). Finally, the central area constitutes the universal pool of archetypal structures shared by all of humanity (E); to this latter group belong such archetypal ideas as that of the Cosmic God-Man, Mother Earth, the Hero, the Helpful Animal, the Trickster, or Mana that are found in all mythologies and religious systems.

Examples of archetypes representing certain professional and social types and roles would be the Scientist, the Healer, the Enlightened Ruler, the Dictator, the Worker, the Revolutionary, or the Capitalist. These experiences are closely related to, but not identical with, the experiences of group consciousness described earlier. In the latter, the subject feels simultaneously identified with all individual members of a particular group; the former represent personified concepts of the roles involved, something like the Platonic ideas.

An example of these two types of phenomena would be the experience of the group consciousness of all the revolutionaries of the world, as compared with the experience of becoming the archetypal

Revolutionary. Archetypal images of this kind can be beautifully illustrated by holographic pictures created by sequential exposure of a number of people of the same category without changing the angle of the laser. At a holographic exhibition that took place several years ago in Honolulu, one of the holograms with the title *The Child of Hawaii* consisted of a large number of three-dimensional images of Hawaiian children occupying the same space. It was an amazing illustration of the type of experience I am discussing here. A less dramatic simulation of this phenomenon can be achieved by cumulative exposure in conventional photography, as exemplified by Francis Galton's composite photographs used by Rupert Sheldrake to illustrate his concept of morphic resonance (Sheldrake 1981). Another special category of archetypes represents certain personified aspects of human personality; these are C. G. Jung's famous Animus, Anima, and the Shadow.

The example I would like to use here is an experiential sequence from my own session with 200 milligrams of MDMA (Adam or Ecstasy). It combines the archetype of the Apocalypse with personified archetypes of the universal principles.

I started experiencing strong activation in the lower part of my body. My pelvis was vibrating as enormous amounts of energy were being released in ecstatic jolts. At one point, this streaming energy swept me along in an intoxicating frenzy into a whirling cosmic vortex of creation and destruction.

In the center of this monstrous hurricane of primordial forces were four giant herculean figures performing what seemed to be the ultimate cosmic saber dance. They had strong Mongolian features with protruding cheekbones, oblique eyes, and clean-shaven heads decorated by large braided ponytails. Whirling around in a frantic dance craze, they were swinging large weapons that looked like scythes or L-shaped scimitars; all four of these combined formed a rapidly rotating swastika. I joined the dance, becoming one of them, or possibly all four of them at once, leaving my own identity behind.

Then the experience opened up into an unimaginable panorama of scenes of destruction. In these visions, natural disasters, such as volcanic eruptions, earthquakes, crashing meteors, forest fires, floods and tidal waves, were combined with images of burning cities, entire blocks of collapsing highrise buildings, mass death, and horror of wars. Heading this wave of total annihilation were four archetypal images of macabre riders symbolizing the end of the world. I realized these were the Four Horsemen of the Apocalypse. The continuing vibrations and jolts of my pelvis now became synchronized with the movements of this ominous horseback riding and I became one of them.

The above descriptions might create the impression that the experience was unpleasant and frightening. However, possibly due to the generally benevolent nature of the amphetamine-related empathogens, the dominant feeling was ecstatic merging with the unleashed energies and fascination by the incredible philosophical and spiritual insights associated with this session. I realized that the concept of the Apocalypse should not be taken literally, as it is the case in the concretistic interpretations of mainstream Christianity.

Although it is possible that the Apocalypse will in the future be actually manifested on a planetary scale as a historical event, it is above all an archetype. As such it seems to reflect the stage in consciousness development where the individual recognizes the illusory nature of the material world. As the universe reveals its true essence as a cosmic play of consciousness, the world of matter is destroyed in the psyche of the individual. The situation here resembles an earlier stage, in which identification with the archetype of crucifixion and resurrection of Christ terminates one's philosophical identification with the body.

The apocalyptic visions were interspersed with archetypal images from various cultures, symbolizing the unreality of the phenomenal world. Probably the most impressive of these was the image of Plato's cave. The final major sequence of the session was a magnificent parade of personified universal principles, archetypes that, through a complex interplay, create the illusion of the phenomenal world, the divine play that the Hindus call *lila*.

They were protean personages with many facets, levels, and dimensions of meaning that kept changing their forms in extremely intricate holographic interpenetration as I was observing them. Each of them seemed to represent simultaneously the essence of his or her function and all the concrete manifestations of this element in the world of matter. There was Maya, a mysterious ethereal principle symbolizing the world illusion; Anima, embodying the eternal Female; a Mars-like personification of war and aggression; the Lovers, representing all the sexual dramas and romances throughout ages; the royal figure of the Ruler; the withdrawn Hermit; the elusive Trickster; and many others. As they were passing across the stage, they bowed in my direction, as if expecting appreciation for the stellar performance in the divine play of the universe.

i.   Intuitive Understanding of Universal Symbols

Among the most interesting archetypal experiences are

found insights into their esoteric meaning. Experiences of this kind support the understanding of symbols suggested by Carl Gustav Jung (Jung 1971, p. 473). In contrast to Sigmund Freud's interpretation of symbols as representing something already known but objectionable, Jung saw symbols as the best possible representations of something that belongs to a higher level of consciousness and cannot be in principle expressed in any other way. Far from being cryptic statements about simple biological functions, universal symbols refer to complex transcendental realities. What Freud described as symbols — cryptic allusions to elements on the same level of consciousness — can best be referred to as signs.

In nonordinary states of consciousness, visions of various universal symbols can play a significant role even in experiences of individuals who previously had no interest in mysticism or were strongly opposed to anything esoteric. These visions tend to convey instant intuitive understanding of the various levels of meaning of these symbols and generate a deep interest in the spiritual path. The most frequent of these symbols that I have observed in my research were the cross, the quadrated circle, the Indo-Iranian swastika in both its ominous and peace-bestowing form, the ancient Egyptian ankh (Nile cross or *crux ansata*), the lotus blossom, the Taoist yin-yang, the Hindu sacred phallus (*Shiva lingam*) and vulva (*yoni*), the diamond and other precious stones, the Buddhist wheel, and the six-pointed star, both in its Hebrew form of the Star of David and its Tantric form as the symbol of the union of the male and female energy.

As a result of experiences of this kind, subjects can develop accurate understanding of various complex esoteric teachings. In some instances, persons unfamiliar with the Kabbalah had experiences described in the Zohar and Sepher Yetzirah and obtained surprising insights into Kabbalistic symbols. Others were able to describe the meaning and function of intricate mandalas used in the Tibetan Vajrayana and other Tantric systems. Subjects who had previously ridiculed astrology, alchemy, and the ancient forms of divination, such as the I Ching and Tarot, suddenly discovered their deeper meaning and found genuine appreciation of their metaphysical relevance. Similarly, such illuminating insights can suddenly open skeptical individuals to Gnostic teachings or the Pythagorean theories of geometrical solids and of the numerical order in the universe.

An interesting example of an entire series of images and insights related to the universal symbol of the cross can be found in the book *Varieties of Psychedelic Experience* by Robert Masters and Jean Houston (Masters and Houston 1966, p. 222). It comes from a psychedelic session (100 micrograms of LSD-25) of an attorney and former divinity student who had left the seminary because of religious doubts. This experience was triggered by looking at an ornate cross offered to the subject by the experimenters.

> I saw Jesus crucified and Peter martyred. I watched the early Christians die in the arena, while others moved hurriedly through the Roman back streets, spreading Christ's doctrine. I stood by when Constantine gaped at the vision of the cross in the sky. I saw Rome fall and the Dark Ages begin and observed as little crossed twigs were tacked up as the only hope in ten thousand wretched hovels. I watched peasants trample it under their feet in some obscene forest rite, while, across the sea in Byzantium, they glorified it in jeweled mosaics and great domed cathedrals.
>
> My hand trembled, the cross glimmered, and history became confused. Martin Luther walked arm in arm with Billy Graham, followed by Thomas Aquinas and the armies of the Crusades. Inquisitorial figures leveled bony fingers at demented witches and a great gout of blood poured forth to congeal in a huge, clotted cross. Pope John XXIII called out "good cheer" to a burning, grinning Joan of Arc, and Savonarola saluted a red-necked hell-fire and brimstone Texas preacher. Bombers flew in cross formation and St. Francis preached to the birds.
>
> A hundred thousand episodes erupted from the glinting facets of that cross and I knew that a hundred thousand more were waiting for their turn. But then, and I don't know when or how it happened, I was immersed in it; my substance — physical, mental, and spiritual — was totally absorbed in the substance of the cross. My life became the glinting, sparkling episodes of the history of the cross, and the hundred thousand remaining events were those of my own life's history. The shame and victory of the cross was endlessly repeated in the minutiae of my own life. Mine was the shame and mine was the victory. I had been inquisitor and saint, had falsely damned and sublimely reasoned. And, like the cross, I too had died, and lived, and died, and lived and died to live again and again. And perhaps once more I would die. But now I knew (and now I know) that redemption is a constant thing and guilt is only transitory.

j.   *Creative Inspiration and the Promethean Impulse*

Even a cursory study of the literature on creativity clearly indicates that true artistic, scientific, philosophical, and religious inspiration is mediated by nonordinary states of consciousness and comes from transpersonal sources. The mechanisms related to the dynamics of the creative process seem to fall into three large categories.

The first one relates to situations in which the individual has struggled for years with a problem, unable to find the solution. This preparation period includes typically numerous observations, study of all the pertinent literature, and repeated unsuccessful attempts to tackle the problem with ordinary logic. The solution then comes in a nonordinary state of consciousness — in a dream, during a time of exhaustion, as in a hallucination due to a febrile disease, or in meditation. This mechanism can be illustrated by many famous examples.

The chemist Friedrich August von Kekule arrived at the final solution of the formula of benzene — the basis of organic chemistry — in a dream in which he saw the benzene ring as a little Uroboros snake biting its tail. The design for the crucial experiment leading to the Nobel Prize-winning discovery of the chemical transmission of neuronal impulses occurred to the physiologist Otto Loewi while he was asleep. Werner Heisenberg found the mathematical solution for the problem in quantum physics during his stay in Helgoland, when his consciousness was altered by severe hay fever. In all these instances, the nonordinary state of consciousness seemed to suspend the traditional ways of thinking that prevent a solution and allow a new creative synthesis.

In the second category, the general form of an idea or a system of thought comes as a sudden inspiration from the transpersonal domain, often long before the development in the field would justify it. It then might require years, decades, or even centuries to amass sufficient evidence to support it. Ancient examples for this mechanism would be the atomistic theory of Leukippos and Demokritos, or the idea that life evolved from the ocean, formulated by the Ionic philosopher Anaxagoras. The concept of distribution of information about the universe through all its parts found in the ancient Jainist theory of the jivas, or the idea of mutual interpenetration of all things that forms the basis of Avatamsaka Buddhism (the Chinese *Hwa Yen* and Japanese *Kegon*) seemed bizarre and preposterous before the discovery of the vibratory nature of the universe and of the holonomic principles. Similarly, the ancient cosmogenetic systems that saw light as the creative principle in the universe received recently unexpected independent confirmation from science with the discovery of the special role of photons among subatomic particles and in the context of Arthur Young's theory of process (Young 1976).

In the third category are instances of a true Promethean creative impulse, where the inspiration comes in the form of a finished product ready to be communicated to others. Nikola Tesla constructed the electric generator, an invention that revolutionized industry, after its complete design and a prototype in full function appeared to him in great detail in a vision. Albert Einstein discovered the basic principles of his theory of relativity in an unusual state of consciousness; according to his description, most of the insights came to him in the form of kinaesthetic sensations in his muscles. Richard Wagner allegedly hallucinated much of his music when he was composing, and Wolfgang Amadeus Mozart claimed that he often found his symphonies in their final form in his head before he wrote them down. The articles of the Moslem faith were communicated to Mohammed in a visionary state when he felt the presence of Allah and was in a state of "ecstasy approaching annihilation."

k.   *Experience of the Demiurg and of Cosmic Creation*

In this type of experience, the subject has the feeling of encountering the *Creator* of the universe, or even of full identification with him. This can be accompanied by extraordinary insights into the process of creation, its motives, specific mechanisms, purpose, and problems. On this level, the Creator usually has many personal characteristics, although not necessarily an anthropomorphic form. It is possible to sense the forces that underlie and initiate the process of creation. Various subjects identified them as overabundance of generative energy, irresistable artistic impulse, boundless curiosity, passion for experimentation, thirst for knowledge or self-knowledge, pursuit of experience, immense love that wants to be expressed, or even flight from monotony and boredom.

Experiences of this kind can lead the subject to serious questions about his or her role in the universe. Some feel exalted by discovering that they can experientially identify with the Creator and gain an entirely new metaperspective on their daily problems. They find it difficult to feel victimized by adverse circumstances in the universe after the realization that, on another level, they are identical with the force that created it.

Others are still strongly attached to their everyday identity and feel the need to find a specific purpose for their existence in that form. The idea that human beings are actors in a predetermined cosmic play can be elevating or discouraging. Different individuals tend to experience in this respect different scenarios and find their own answers. In some of them, the phenomenal world is an illusion and the highest purpose is to awaken to this fact. In others, humans have a genuine role to play as intelligent agents helping to facilitate evolution or remove from the universal scheme elements that are undesirable but unavoidable side-products of creation.

The Demiurg can be seen as the supreme force of existence, comparable to the concept of God in different religions. However, in some instances, it is one of the creators of many universes, or the creator of many universes. Some subjects even reported experiences in which there was a male-female *dyad* of creators similar to the cosmologies of some non-Western cultures, or a situation where this universe was created in the process of a game involving several superior entities.

The account that I will use here as illustration of this type of experience comes from a psychedelic session with a high dose of LSD-25.

> What followed was a tremendous expansion of consciousness. I was out in interstellar space witnessing galaxies upon galaxies being created right in front of my eyes. I felt that I was moving faster than the speed of light. There were galaxies passing by me one after the other. I was approaching a central explosion of energy from which everything in the universe seemed to originate. It was the very Source of all that was created. As I moved closer and closer to this area, I felt the incandescent heat emanating from it. It was a gigantic furnace, the furnace of the universe.
>
> The sensation of heat was growing to unbelievable proportions, as was the intensity of the light. I recognized that the burning I was experiencing was the burning of the Purifying Fire. As I moved closer, I sensed that my identity was shifting from being the manifestation of this Energy to being the Energy itself. It seemed that I momentarily entered the very core of this Universal Furnace of cosmic creation. The experience was ecstatic and filled me with a sense of Infinite Power.

I suddenly understood the principle underlying the organization of the cosmos. It was the Universal Consciousness playing out an endless series of dramas in a way we can see represented on the theater stage or in the movies. In this drama it plays a game of losing itself for the purpose of finding itself again. This Universal Consciousness would plunge into separation, rejection, pain, evil, agony, and darkness to experience the infinite joy of rediscovering its original pristine, safe, and blissful state. Its true identity is indivisible oneness, beyond negativity and dualities of any kind. To make the journey, it had to create the illusion of space, matter, and time and, together with it, the categories of evil, darkness, pain, and destruction.

I continued to think about the analogy to the movies; it seemed particularly fitting as a metaphor for the process of creation. What I was experiencing in my psychedelic sessions was like turning my back to the various images projected on the screen and looking directly into the light of the projector. A single source of light creating an infinite number of pictures and scenes projected on the screen! It is also possible to follow the beam of light all the way into the interior of the projector. There is the emptiness from which the light comes. The film itself then would be an equivalent of the archetypes determining the type of experiences created by projection as a four-dimensional space-time continuum.

1. Experience of Cosmic Consciousness

Individuals experiencing identification with Cosmic Consciousness have the feeling of encompassing the totality of existence and reaching the Reality underlying all realities. They sense beyond any doubt that they are in connection with the supreme and ultimate principle of Being. This principle is the only real mystery; once its existence is accepted, everything else can be explained from it and understood. The illusions of matter, space, and time, as well as an infinite number of other forms and levels of reality, have been completely transcended and reduced to this one mysterious principle as their common source and denominator.

This experience is boundless, unfathomable, and ineffable. Verbal communication and the very symbolic structure of our language appear to be a ridiculously inadequate means to capture it and convey its qualities. Our phenomenal world and everything that we experience in the ordinary states of consciousness fades away in the light of this supreme awareness as limited, illusory, and idiosyncratic aspects of this one Reality. This principle is clearly beyond any rational comprehension, and yet even a short experiential exposure to it satisfies all the subject's intellectual and philosophical craving. All the questions that have ever been asked seem to be answered, or there is no need to ask any questions at all.

The best approximation to the nature of this experience is to describe it in terms of the concept of *saccidānanda* that occurs in Indian religious and philosophical scriptures. This composite Sanskrit word consists of three separate roots: *sat*, meaning existence or being; *chit*, usually translated as awareness or knowledge; and *ānanda*, which stands for bliss. The formless, dimensionless and intangible cosmic consciousness can best be described as Infinite Existence, Infinite Awareness and Knowledge, and Infinite Bliss. However, any words refer primarily to phenomena and processes of the material reality and are, therefore, only pitiful attempts to convey the essence of this transcendental principle.

The only means one has to express this is to capitalize the first letters of the words used, a practice known from the writings of psychotic patients desperately trying to communicate about their ineffable world. Individuals who had experiences of this kind frequently commented on the fact that the language of poets, although still highly imperfect, seems to be a more appropriate and adequate tool for this purpose. The immortal art of transcendental writers like Hildegard von Bingen, Rumi, Kabir, Mirabai, Omar Khayyam, Kahlil Gibran, Rabindranath Thakur, or Sri Aurobindo deserves to be mentioned in this context.

The following experience from a session with 150 milligrams of Ketalar (ketamine) combines the elements of cosmic consciousness, identification with other persons, and the archetypal celestial realm or Heaven.

> I had a sense of presence of many of my friends with whom I share interests, a system of values, and a certain direction or purpose in life. I was not seeing them, but was somehow perceiving them in their totality through extrasensory means. We were going through a complex process of identifying areas of agreements and differences among us, trying to eliminate friction points by an almost alchemical procedure of neutralizing them.
>
> At a certain point, it seemed that we got it all together and became

a completely unified network, one entity with a clear purpose and no inner contradictions. And then this organism became what I called for myself a "spaceship in consciousness." We started going through a movement that combined the elements of spatial flight, with a highly abstract representation of consciousness evolution.

In my previous psychedelic sessions, I had experienced and accepted philosophically the Hindu image of the universe as *lila*, or Divine Play. In this kind of cosmic game of hide and seek everything is on some level already known and has already happened. The only task for the individual is to lift the veil of ignorance and catch up. What I was experiencing now was new and very exciting. It seemed that true evolution was a real possibility and that each of us could play an important part in it. This evolution would lead into dimensions that I was not aware of in my everyday life and that I had not discovered in my previous nonordinary states of consciousness.

The movement was becoming faster and faster, until it reached what seemed to be some absolute limit, something like what the velocity of light is in the Einsteinian universe. We all felt that it was possible to push beyond this limit, but that the result would be absolutely unpredictable and potentially dangerous. In a highly adventurous spirit that characterizes the group of the individuals involved, we decided to go ahead and face the Unknown.

When the limit was transcended, the experience shifted dimensions in a way that is difficult to describe. Instead of movement in space, there seemed to be immense extension of consciousness. Time stopped and we entered a state that I identified as consciousness of amber. The external manifestation of this state where time is frozen is the fact that life forms, such as plants and insects, are preserved in amber in an unchanged state for millions of years and amber itself is mineralized organic substance-resin.

We underwent a process of purification, through which any reference to organic life was eliminated from the experience. I realized that the state of consciousness I was in was that of a diamond. It seemed very important that diamond is pure carbon, an element on which all life is based, and that it originates in conditions of extreme temperatures and pressures. It was as if the diamond contained all the information about life and nature in an absolutely pure and condensed form, like the ultimate computer.

All the other physical properties of the diamond seemed to be pointing to its metaphysical significance — beauty, transparence, luster, permanence, unchangeability, and the capacity to bring out of white light a rich spectrum of colors. I felt that I understood why the Tibetan Buddhism is called Vajrayana; the only way I could describe this state of ultimate cosmic ecstasy was to refer to it as "diamond consciousness". Here seemed to be all the creative energy and intelligence of the universe as pure consciousness existing beyond time and space. It was entirely abstract, yet containing all the forms and secrets of creation.

I was floating in this energy as a dimensionless point of consciousness, totally dissolved, yet maintaining some sense of separate identity. I was aware of the presence of my friends who made the journey with me; they were formless, but distinctly present. We all felt that we have achieved the state of ultimate fulfillment; we have reached the source and the final destination, as close to Heaven as I could imagine.

m.   *The Supracosmic and Metacosmic Void*

The experience of the Void is the most enigmatic and paradoxical of all the transpersonal experiences. It is experiential identification with the primordial Emptiness, Nothingness, and Silence, which seem to be the ultimate cradle of all existence. While it is the source of everything, it cannot be derived from anything else; it is the uncreated and ineffable Supreme. The terms supracosmic and metacosmic used by sophisticated subjects to describe this experience refer to the fact that this Void seems to be both supraordinated to and underlying the phenomenal cosmos as we know it.

The Void is beyond space and time, beyond form of any kind, and beyond polarities, such as light and darkness, good and evil, stability and motion, and ecstasy or agony. While nothing concrete exists in this state, nothing that is part of existence seems to be missing there either. This emptiness is thus, in a sense, pregnant with all of existence, since it contains everything in a potential form. This experience has a certain similarity with the experience of the interstellar space and with the concept of the dynamic void known from quantum-relativistic physics, although it is obviously on a much higher metaphysical level than either of the above.

The experience of the Void also transcends our ordinary concepts of causality. Subjects who are having this experience accept as self-evident that various forms of phenomenal worlds can emerge into existence out of this void without any obvious cause. The possibility of something originating out of nothing or of something vanishing without any traces does not appear absurd, as it would in everyday consciousness. The idea of something happening without a tangible precedent, sufficient cause, or initiating impulse simply is not questioned on this level of experience. Paradoxical and enigmatic passages from the Buddhist texts equating form with emptiness and emptiness with form suddenly appear crystal clear. The Void is emptiness that is pregnant with form, and the many forms on various levels of existence are essentially empty.

TRANSPERSONAL EXPERIENCES OF PSYCHOID NATURE

Transpersonal phenomena of psychoid nature have peculiar characteristics. On the one hand, they are clearly subjective intrapsychic events; on the other, they are meaningfully connected with specific physical changes in the world of consensus reality. The latter aspect can be observed, shared, and even measured by others. The term *psychoid* that I am using here suggests that these phenomena are strange hybrids that lie in the twilight zone between consciousness and matter. Carl Gustav Jung used the term *psychoid* in relation to certain properties of the archetypes and to synchronistic events involving the psyche, as well as elements of the material world (Jung 1964). I have taken the liberty to extend it to other types of phenomena discussed in this section.

The descriptions of all the transpersonal phenomena discussed earlier are based on firsthand experience. I have observed them repeatedly in psychedelic sessions of my clients and during workshops that included holotropic breathing. In addition, I have experienced most of them personally in my own nonordinary states of consciousness of various kinds. In comparison, I have had only limited experience with psychoid phenomena described in this section, with the exception of synchronicities — a common occurrence in the work of every researcher of nonordinary states of consciousness. However, I feel strongly that psychoid events should be at least briefly mentioned in this context, in spite of their highly controversial nature. There are several reasons to include them in a comprehensive discussion of transpersonal experiences.

The first reason is that psychoid phenomena have been described in mystical literature of different cultures all through ages, with sufficient consistency to deserve serious attention. They are typically discussed in connection with many other types of transpersonal experiences, the existence of which has been confirmed by modern consciousness research. In addition, there exists direct supportive evidence for some of the psychoid phenomena in Jungian psychology, experimental psychiatry, and contemporary parapsychology. And finally, the scientific climate is becoming gradually more open for an unbiased study of this realm.

The main obstacle for serious research of psychoid manifestations has been a mechanistic understanding of consciousness and its relationship to matter characteristic of Newtonian-Cartesian science. The authoritative assumption that consciousness is an accidental product of matter and an epiphenomenon of physiological processes in the brain made their existence, in principle, impossible and absurd. Modern developments in a variety of scientific disciplines, including quantum-relativistic physics, information and system theory, biology, thanatology, neurophysiology, and psychedelic research suggest that mind and possibly consciousness are inherent properties of nature and the cosmos. In the context of the emerging paradigm in science, the existence of various psychoid phenomena appears possible and, in a sense, plausible. The future task for serious research remains unbiased scientific scrutiny of the mostly anecdotal claims and modern reformulation of the underlying theories.

Some aspects of psychoid events can be discussed in psychological terms, others in strictly physical terms. The proportion of these two components varies from one type of psychoid experience to another and also varies for different events of the same category. Even in relation to the same event, it can often be influenced by circumstances and by the point of view of the individuals involved. In many instances, psychoid events are sufficiently protean to allow for either psychological or physical interpretation, depending on the approach of the investigator. The strikingly frequent failures of electronic equipment occurring in critical moments of parapsychological experiments, strange coincidences interfering with recording what would be the most convincing evidence, or the ambiguity of various pieces of information in the investigation of the UFO phenomena can be mentioned here as examples. There are strong indications that this elusiveness might be an inherent characteristic of psychoid events rather than a reason to question their existence and validity.

Psychoid phenomena can be divided into three large categories. The first of these includes unusual synchronicities linking various types of transpersonal experiences to physical events in the phenomenal world. Here consciousness interacts in a peculiar way with the world of matter to create meaningful gestalts. However, it is not necessary to assume that consciousness actively intervenes in material reality and produces physical changes. The material events, in and of themselves, are firmly imbedded in the Newtonian world; they follow the principle of cause and effect and are not in conflict with traditionally accepted natural laws.

In the second category are spontaneous psychoid events in which psychological processes seem to influence physical reality and change the laws that mechanistic science sees as mandatory. However, these events occur in an elemental fashion and not as a result of specific conscious intention. The individuals might deliberately create a context for their occurrence, as it is the case for psychoid events that happen during various goal-oriented sport activities or during spiritistic seances (physical mediumship), but they do not consciously will the specific events to happen. Additional examples of psychoid experiences of this type are stigmata, Poltergeist, experiences of "flying saucers" (UFOs), and luminosity of the body of saints and spiritual teachers.

Finally, the third category contains instances of intentional psychokinesis, or specific and deliberate intervention in the physical world by psychological means. Here belong the many forms of spiritual healing and hexing, rituals of aboriginal cultures conducted for the purpose of making rain or for other pragmatic reasons, various forms of magic, voluntary control of autonomous functions, supernormal powers (*siddhis*) of the yogis, trance phenomena, moving objects at will, hypnosis at a distance, laboratory experiments with psychokinesis, and others.

1   Synchronistic Links between
     Consciousness and Matter

The principle of synchronicity as a significant alternative to linear causality that dominates the thinking of Newtonian-Cartesian science was first described by Carl Gustav Jung. According to him, synchronicity is an acausal connecting principle that refers to meaningful coincidences of events separated in time and/or space (Jung 1960). Synchronicity can take many different forms; some of them connect individuals and events in separate locations, others across time. In this context, I will focus on the most interesting form of synchronicity — one that connects intrapsychic events of a particular individual, such as dreams, spontaneous visions, meditative states, psychedelic phenomena, or near-death experiences, with physical events in his or her own life.

Synchronistic events of this kind can be associated with all forms of transpersonal experiences and, occasionally, with various aspects of the perinatal process. One of Jung's own examples is the famous story of a rare specimen of goldchafer beetle that hit the windowsill of his office just at the time when he was discussing the symbolism of the Egyptian scarab in the dream of a patient who was particularly resistant to any notion of the transpersonal domain (Jung 1961). I have already described the particularly important synchronistic events that often surround reliving of past incarnation memories. Another typical example is the frequent accumulation of dangerous situations and accidents — even those caused by others or by independent external factors — in the lives of persons who have come in their inner exploration close to the experience of the ego death. When these people face the ego death in their inner process and experience rebirth, such situations tend to clear up as magically as they developed.

Similarly, when the individual has a powerful experience of a shamanic type that involves an animal spirit guide, this animal can suddenly appear in this person's life in various forms, with a frequency that is beyond any reasonable probability. At the time of inner confrontation with the archetypal images of the Animus, Anima, Wise Old Man, or Terrible Mother Goddess, ideal examples of these figures will emerge in the everyday life of the individual involved. It has been the experience of many people that when they become involved unselfishly in a project that has been inspired from the transpersonal realms of the psyche, incredible synchronicities tend to occur and make their work surprisingly easy.

It is important to know that extraordinary synchronicities can appear in the lives of people who get involved in experiential exploration of the transpersonal domain. Traditional psychiatry does not distinguish between true synchronicities and psychotic misinterpretation of the world. Any intimation of extraordinary coincidences in the patient's narrative will be automatically labeled as delusions of reference and be considered a symptom of mental disease. However, an open-minded researcher will find that in the case of true synchronicities, any person who has access to the facts has to admit that the coincidences involved are beyond any statistical probabilities.

Jung was aware of the fact that the phenomenon of synchronicity was incompatible with traditional thinking in science. He became very interested in the developments in quantum-relativistic physics and in the alternative worldview that it was suggesting. It was Albert Einstein who, during a personal visit, encouraged Jung to pursue his idea of synchronicity as fully compatible with the new thinking in physics (Jung 1973). Jung also developed friendship with Wolfgang Pauli, one of the founders of quantum physics; his essay on synchronicity has been for years traditionally published jointly with Pauli's work on the role of the archetypes in the thinking of the astronomer Johannes Kepler (Pauli 1955). The synchronistic phenomena in transpersonal psychology seem to bear some similarity to the problems in modern physics related to Bell's theorem (Bell 1966, Capra 1982).

I have seen many remarkable examples of synchronicities in my work with psychedelic and holotropic therapy, and also around the late Swami Muktananda, head of the Siddha Yoga lineage. However, I would like to use here as an illustration an extraordinary story told by the world-famous mythologist Joseph Campbell in a seminar at the Esalen Institute that my wife Christina and I attended. He used it while answering a question of one of the participants about Jung and the acausal connections in the universe:

> I will tell you an example of synchronicity in my own life. We happen to live in New York City, on the fourteenth floor in an apartment on Waverly Place and Sixth Avenue. The last thing you would expect to see in New York City is a praying mantis. The praying mantis plays the role of the hero in the Bushman folklore. I was reading the Bushman mythology — all about the praying mantis. The room in which I was doing this reading has two windows; one window faces up Sixth Avenue, the other window faces toward the Hudson river. This is the window I look out of all the time: the window on Sixth Avenue, I do not think I have opened more than twice during the forty-odd years we have lived there.

I was reading about the praying mantis — the hero — and suddenly I felt an impulse to open the window facing Sixth Avenue. I opened the window and looked out to the right and there was a praying mantis walking up the building. He was there, right on the rim of my window! He was this big [showing the size]; he looked at me and his face looked just like a Bushman's face. This gave me the creeps! You might say this was a coincidence, but what are the odds for something like this to happen by chance?

2 Spontaneous Psychoid Events

a. *Supernormal Physical Feats*

In the spiritual and mystical literature of all ages, one can find numerous descriptions of spectacular physiological changes in the body or seemingly impossible achievements of people in various extraordinary states of mind. The somatic changes range from stigmata appearing during ecstatic raptures, for which one might try to find some traditional explanations, to such extreme situations as luminosity of the body of various saints, or occasional reports of spontaneous combustion of the entire body.

Similarly, many events occurring in the context of various martial arts might appear supernatural. Some of them happen in a spontaneous and elemental fashion, others involve concentration and intention and would thus belong to the next category. In their book *Psychic Side of Sports*, Michael Murphy and Rhea White (Murphy and White 1978) collected anecdotal evidence on fascinating feats of athletes that bordered on the impossible and suggested participation of psychoid mechanisms. Murphy and his team are also conducting, in connection with the Esalen Institute in Big Sur, California, the so-called Body Transformation Project — an extensive historical research of all extraordinary manifestations involving mind and body as they have been documented through ages.

b. *Spiritistic Phenomena and Physical Mediumship*

Another group of phenomena belonging to this category has been traditionally studied by parapsychologists. In a number of "haunted" castles, houses, and other locations, a large number of people have had strange experiences. These were often strikingly similar, or even the same, in independent individuals who had had no previous knowledge of the phenomenon. In some instances, the same things were perceived simultaneously by several witnesses; in others, this was associated with certain objectively detectable changes. A modern example of this phenomenon is the episode that Carl Gustav Jung described in his autobiography (Jung 1961). At a certain time of his life, he felt presences of spirits in his house and heard their voices. These experiences were shared and confirmed by other members of his family. He agreed to write down their communications and produced his famous *Septem Sermones Ad Mortuos (Seven Sermons to the Dead)*, a Gnostic text signed by the name Basilides (Jung 1982).

Similarly, in certain spiritistic seances that involved what J. B. Rhine called physical mediumship, participants shared certain experiences, such as raps and bangs on floors and walls, touches from invisible hands, voices speaking from nowhere, playing of musical instruments, and gusts of cold air. In some cases, this was combined with apparitions of deceased persons, or voices of such persons heard independently or through a medium. In the extremes, this allegedly involved telekinesis and materializations — upward levitation of objects and people, projection of objects through the air, manifestation of ectoplasmic formations, and appearance of writings or objects without explanation (so-called "apports").

Even famous mediums like Eusapia Palladino were occasionally caught cheating, and fraud and serious scholarship form a strange amalgam in the history of parapsychology. Yet, it is hard to imagine that so much attention would have been given to a field with no real phenomena to observe. In any case, one can safely conclude that in no other area of study has unequivocal testimony of so many witnesses of the highest caliber been discounted as stupidity and written off. Among the researchers who shared this fate, some had the highest credentials, such as the Nobel Prize-winning physician and physiologist Charles Richet and Sir Oliver Lodge, a Fellow of the Royal Society in England.

c. *Recurrent Spontaneous Psychokinesis (Poltergeist)*

Recurrent spontaneous psychokinesis (RSPK), for which the parapsychologists have adopted the German term Poltergeist (literally, the tapping sprite) includes a remarkable variety of happenings: movements and destruction of domestic objects, flinging of mud and stones, production of various sounds (raps, bangs, scratchings, whistling, singing, or talking), and even teleportation — mysterious conveyance of various articles in and out of locked rooms and closed drawers or cabinets. While physical mediumship of the extreme form seems to have almost disappeared in modern times, many Poltergeist cases have been studied by contemporary researchers.

The most extensive modern series of investigations of the Poltergeist (*Spuck*) phenomena has been conducted in West Germany under the meticulous scientific guidance of the world-famous parapsychological researcher Hans Bender. During the last 35 years, the team of the Institute for the Study of the Frontiers of Psychology and Psychohygiene in Freiburg (*Freiburg Institut fuer Grenzgebiete der Psychologie und Psychohygiene*) examined 65 cases and amassed remarkable evidence for this phenomenon. Some of these cases have been reported in Hans Bender's books, together with other fascinating parapsychological material on telepathy, precognitive dreams, psychokinetic bending of metals, occult material related to the war, and UFOs (Bender 1984ab, 1985). The most famous modern case of RSPK in California was the Oakland Poltergeist, studied by Arthur Hastings (Hastings 1978). There seems to be general agreement that the Poltergeist phenomena are related to repressed instinctual feelings of a particular (usually adolescent or retarded) person.

I would like to illustrate this category by a case reported by Hans Bender (Bender 1984b). It is of special interest because at least forty persons directly witnessed the phenomena involved or their consequences. Among them were highly qualified technicians, physicists, physicians, psychologists, and policemen. The case was also widely publicized by the television and newspapers.

> At the end of November 1967, a series of enigmatic events occurred in Adam's law firm in the Bavarian town Rosenheim. Fluorescent tubes attached to an eight-foot high ceiling were repeatedly turning off. The electricians established that they were rotated 90 degrees from their original position. There were reports about loud sounds, spontaneous disconnecting of circuit-breakers, and dissipation of the fluid in the copying machine. The four telephones (Siemens units)

were often ringing simultaneously, the telephone discussions were interrupted and connections lost. The equipment was registering non-existing phonecalls and the telephone bill rose to an unprecedented height. To all these events were later added spontaneous movements of pictures that included rotations 360 degrees. Several fluorescent tubes fell off the ceiling, endangering people. The technicians who were called for help replaced the fluorescent lights by regular bulbs. When that happened, the lamps were swinging and bulbs exploding. Specially installed measuring and recording devices were registering discharges up to 50 A during which the circuit-breakers did not interrupt the circuit. Hans Bender called two experts from the Institute for Plasma Physics in Munich-Garching, who conducted complex oscillographic measurements. The electric disturbances continued, although they have eliminated all the conceivable physical causes. The disturbances were so serious that the Adam law firm filed a suit with the criminal police against "Unknown" ("Unbekannt").

Hans Bender was able to trace these phenomena to a 19-year-old girl, Annemarie Sch. He concluded that the necessary "affective field" was created by her strong emotional interest in her boss, a specific situation in the bureau, and the extraordinary public interest in the case. All the phenomena stopped instantly when Annemarie was transferred to another job. One of the results of the analysis of the physicists is worth mentioning. They concluded that to achieve recording of phonecalls without mechanical movement of the dial-ring would require an intelligence that has accurate technical knowledge and is capable to estimate time intervals in the range of milliseconds.

d.   Unidentified Flying Objects

The last phenomenon of this category I would like to discuss, is that of the UFOs (unidentified flying objects), popularly known as "flying saucers". I have already described earlier that subjective experiences of seeing physical or metaphysical spacecrafts, being in contact with their crews or gadgets, and even personally meeting the aliens are common in nonordinary states of consciousness. In this context, I will narrow the discussion to those cases where subjective reports are combined with some physical evidence. There is reason to believe that the conclusions drawn from the US Air Force projects Grudge and Blue Book were politically motivated. The same seems to be true for a special committee of the University of Colorado that attributed virtually all physical evidence to natural causes — balloons, meteors, birds, reflections of light, and others.

As in the case of parapsychological phenomena, many of the UFO reports came from people who were emotionally stable, well-educated and trained, intelligent, and articulate. There are good reasons to assume that the UFO phenomena are psychoid events, in which psychological and physical manifestations can be combined in various proportions. This characteristic would make it very difficult to study them in the context of mechanistic science with its sharp dichotomy: material or psychological. A detailed discussion of the UFO material, historical and modern, which is fraught with many controversies would be clearly beyond the scope of this discussion. I will refer interested readers to Carl Gustav Jung's fascinating book *Flying Saucers: A Modern Myth of Things Seen in the Skies* (Jung 1964) and to the writings of Jacques Vallée, who has dedicated many years of his life to intense and systematic study of the UFO phenomenon (Vallée 1965).

3 Intentional Psychokinesis

Intentional psychokinesis can be defined as the ability to influence the material environment without the physical intervention of the body (muscles and glands) by simply wishing events to happen or by performing acts that have no ordinary cause-and-effect relationship to the outcome.

a. Ceremonial Magic

Many ancient and non-Western cultures have performed elaborate ceremonies to bring rain, good harvest, successful hunt, or to gain some other practical advantage. The four oracles in Buddhist Tibet who had roots in the ancient Bon tradition had the reputation of being able to control the weather. Instances of many other forms of magic have been described in mystical and occult literature throughout ages. As bizarre as all this might appear to a modern mind brought up in the tradition of materialistic science, phenomena of this kind deserve serious interest of open-minded scientists. There are good reasons to believe that these activities belong to the psychoid category and are often associated with corresponding events in the physical world. It is inconceivable that such procedures as healing rituals and rain-making ceremonies could be conducted repeatedly over centuries without effect. It would be difficult for a shaman to retain his or her image and reputation against such a series of failures. We have ourselves witnessed a profuse rain lasting several hours following a ceremony of the centennerian shaman Don José Matsuwa of the Mexican Huichol Indians in the middle of a two-year period of catastrophic drought in California. The Tibetan culture is known for its most sophisticated achievements in the study of the human psyche and consciousness. The reputation of the Tibetan oracles must have been based at least on a series of remarkable synchronicities and cannot be attributed simply to superstition and self-deception of a primitive people.

b.   Healing and Hexing

Historical and anthropological literature abounds in reports about various forms of spiritual healing and hexing performed by special individuals or entire groups and about complex rituals carried out for that purpose. Studies conducted by medical anthropologists have shown that the therapeutic results of the healing procedures and ceremonies of such systems as *santeria, palerismo,* or *umbanda* in groups of Latin American immigrants are in many cases superior to those achieved by Western psychiatry and medicine. Whether this applies only to emotional and psychosomatic disorders or extends to some categories of medical problems remains to be found. Research of psychedelic substances has shown that many shamans have at their disposal tools which are much more effective than the verbal techniques of Western psychotherapists. Sophisticated researchers with good academic credentials, such as Walter Pahnke, Andrija Puharich, or Stanley Krippner, were deeply impressed by the phenomena surrounding the work of the spiritist psychic surgeon Arrigo in Brazil or of Tony Agpoa and others in the Philippines.

c.   Siddhis

The literature on the Indian yogis contains countless reports about their astonishing abilities to control various autonomous functions of the body: they can stop bleeding, arrest the heart, live without food and even without oxygen. Many of these claims, long considered by the scientific community to be fairy-tale nonsense, have been confirmed by modern science. Systematic exploration of these phenomena led to the development of biofeedback techniques that make it possible for ordinary people to achieve voluntary control of the heart beat, blood pressure, body temperature and other autonomic functions. The reports about the Tibetan practice referred to as *tummo*, which can lead within a short period of time to an astonishing increase of body temperature of many degrees, have been confirmed in a medical study of Benson and Epstein conducted with the permission and help from the Dalai Lama (Benson et al. 1982).

While most of the yogic practices described above can be accounted for within the Western medical model, other supernatural powers, or *siddhis*, that can allegedly be achieved by some individuals during yogic spiritual practice clearly contradict the Western scientific worldview. Here belong the reports about levitation of the body, the ability to project oneself into a distant place, bilocation (physical existence in two places at once), the capacity to materialize and dematerialize various objects or even one's own body. The existence of these phenomena remains to be confirmed or refuted by future research. However, in the light of the new scientific paradigms, they do not seem as absurd and, in principle, impossible as they were in the context of mechanistic science.

Another phenomenon that belongs to the psychoid category is the remarkable ability of subjects in trance to perform things that seem physically impossible, such as rolling around in broken glass or climbing up ladders with swords for rungs. Many remarkable trance events of this kind are still being conducted by various groups in different parts of the world. One of the seemingly impossible performances of this kind — the Indonesian firewalking — was recently brought to California and rapidly became a fad involving tens of thousands of people. Whether crossing glowing embers with a temperature of $1400°$ F without burns can be explained naturally or not, it is clear that our culture has prematurely rejected the possibility that many such happenings can actually take place.

d.   Laboratory Psychokinesis

Modern parapsychologists have described many important observations involving various psychokinetic activities and have conducted systematic laboratory research of this phenomenon with some remarkable results. Their methodology evolved from simple dice-throwing experiments to sophisticated designs using randomization based on the emission of electrons in radioactive decay, electronic devices, and modern computers. They have studied psychokinesis on targets in motion (PK-MT), such as dice thrown by special machines, electric clocks, the flow of liquids, and the emanation of electrons. Significant advances have been made in the area of studying psychokinesis on the more difficult static targets (PK-ST). Parapsychological experiments with living targets (PK-LT) involved controlled studies of healing in animals, growth in plants, and activity of enzymes.

Some other studies conducted in the United States, in the Soviet Union, and elsewhere focused on systematic observation of individuals capable of moving objects without touching them, projecting mental pictures onto photographic film, influencing others by hypnosis at a distance, and psychokinetic bending of metals. I am mentioning these here without making any conclusions; this has to be left to researchers and experts in this field. Interested readers will find more information in the writings of Charles Tart (Tart 1975a, 1977), Stanley Krippner (Krippner 1977, 1980), Jules Eisenbud (Eisenbud 1967), Russell Targ and Harold Puthoff (Targ and Puthoff 1978, Targ and Harary 1984), and Hans Bender (Bender 1984ab, 1985).

PHILOSOPHICAL CHALLENGES FROM
TRANSPERSONAL EXPERIENCES

Transpersonal experiences have many strange characteristics that shatter the most fundamental assumptions of materialistic science and of the mechanistic worldview. Researchers who have seriously studied and/or experienced these fascinating phenomena realize that the attempts of traditional psychiatry to dismiss them as irrelevant products of imagination or as erratic fantasmagoria generated by pathological processes in the brain are superficial and inadequate. Any unbiased study of the transpersonal domain of the psyche has to come to the conclusion that the observations involved represent a critical challenge for the Newtonian-Cartesian paradigm of Western science.

Although transpersonal experiences occur in the process of deep individual self-exploration, it is not possible to interpret them simply as intrapsychic phenomena in the conventional sense. On the one hand, they form an uninterrupted experiential continuum with biographical-recollective and perinatal experiences. On the other hand, they seem to be tapping directly, without the mediation of the sensory organs, into sources of information that are clearly outside of the conventionally defined range of the individual.

The reports of subjects who have experienced episodes of embryonal existence, the moment of conception, and elements of cellular, tissue and organ consciousness abound in medically accurate insights into the anatomical, physiological and biochemical aspects of the processes involved. Similarly, ancestral experiences, racial and collective memories in the Jungian sense, and past incarnation memories frequently bring specific details about architecture, costumes, weapons, art, social structure and religious practices of the cultures and periods involved, or even concrete historical events. Subjects who experienced phylogenetic sequences or identification with existing life forms not only found them unusually convincing and authentic, but also acquired, in the process, extraordinary insights concerning animal psychology, ethology, specific habits or unusual reproductive cycles. In some instances, this was accompanied by archaic muscular innervations not characteristic for humans, or even such complex performances as enactment of a courtship dance.

Those individuals who experience episodes of conscious identification with plants or parts of plants occasionally report remarkable insights into such botanical processes as germination of seeds, photosynthesis in the leaves, the role of auxins in plant growth, the exchange of water and minerals in the root system, or pollination. Equally common is a convinced sense of conscious identification with inanimate matter or inorganic processes — the water in the ocean, fire, lightning, volcanic activity, tornados, gold, diamond, granite, and even stars, galaxies, atoms, and molecules. Even these experiences sometimes can mediate accurate information about various aspects of nature.

There exists one interesting subcategory of transpersonal phenomena that can be frequently validated and even researched experimentally. Here belong telepathy, psychic diagnosis, clairvoyance, clairaudience, precognition, psychometry, out-of-body experiences, traveling clairvoyance, and other instances of extrasensory perception. This is the only group of transpersonal phenomena that has been occasionally discussed in academic circles, although unfortunately with a strong negative bias. Of particular theoretical interest are, of course, the problems associated with the transpersonal phenomena of psychoid nature.

From a broader perspective, there is no reason to sort out the so-called paranormal phenomena as a special category. Since many other types of transpersonal experiences quite typically involve access to new information about the universe through extrasensory channels, the clear boundary between psychology and parapsychology disappears, or becomes rather arbitrary, when the existence of the transpersonal domain is recognized and acknowledged.

The philosophical challenge associated with the observations described above — formidable as it may be in itself — is further augmented by the fact that in nonordinary states of consciousness, transpersonal experiences correctly reflecting the material world appear on the same continuum as — and are intimately interwoven with — others whose content, according to the Western worldview, is not part of objective reality. We can mention in this context the Jungian archetypes — the world of deities, demons, demigods, superheroes and complex mythological, legendary and fairy-tale sequences. Even these experiences can impart accurate new information about religious symbolism, folklore, and mythical structures of various cultures previously unknown to the subject.

The existence and nature of transpersonal experiences violate some of the most basic assumptions of mechanistic science. They imply such seemingly absurd notions as relativity and the arbitrary nature of all physical boundaries; nonlocal connections in the universe; communication through unknown means and channels; memory without a material substrate; nonlinearity of time; or consciousness associated with all living organisms (including lower animals, plants, unicellular organisms and viruses) and even inorganic matter.

Many transpersonal experiences involve events from the

microcosm and macrocosm — realms that cannot be directly reached by human senses — or from periods that historically precede the origin of the solar system, formation of planet Earth, appearance of living organisms, development of the central nervous system, and appearance of *homo sapiens*. This clearly implies that, in a yet unexplained way, each human being contains the information about the entire universe or all of existence, has potential experiential access to all its parts, and, in a sense, is the whole cosmic network, as much as he or she is just an infinitesimal part of it, a separate and insignificant biological entity.

Transpersonal experiences have a special position in the cartography of the human psyche. The recollective-analytical level and the individual unconscious are clearly biographical in nature. The perinatal dynamic seems to represent an intersection or frontier between the personal and transpersonal. This is reflected in its deep association with birth and death — the beginning and end of individual human existence. The transpersonal phenomena reveal connections between the individual and the cosmos which are at present beyond comprehension. All we can say is that somewhere in the process of perinatal unfolding, a strange qualitative Moebius-like leap seems to occur, in which deep self-exploration of the individual unconscious turns into a process of experiential adventures in the universe-at-large, which involves what can best be described as cosmic consciousness or the superconscious mind.

While the nature of transpersonal experiences is clearly fundamentally incompatible with mechanistic science, it can be integrated with the revolutionary developments in various scientific disciplines that have been referred to as the emerging paradigm. Among the disciplines and concepts that have significantly contributed to this drastic change in the scientific worldview are quantum-relativistic physics (Capra 1975, 1982), astrophysics (Davies 1983), cybernetics, information and systems theory (Bateson 1972 and 1979, Maturana and Varela 1980, Varela 1979), Sheldrake's theory of morphic resonance (Sheldrake 1981), Prigogine's study of dissipative structures and order by fluctuation (Prigogine and Stengers 1984), David Bohm's theory of holomovement (Bohm 1980), Karl Pribram's holographic model of the brain (Pribram 1971, 1977), and Arthur Young's theory of process (Young 1976).

The expanded cartography described above is of critical importance for any serious approach to such phenomena as psychedelic states, shamanism, religion, mysticism, rites of passage, mythology, parapsychology, thanatology, and psychosis. This is not just a matter of academic interest; it has deep and revolutionary implications for the understanding of psychopathology and offers new therapeutic possibilities undreamed of by traditional psychiatry (Grof 1985).

II

New Perspectives in Psychotherapy and Inner Exploration

THE HOLOTROPIC strategy of psychotherapy represents an important and effective alternative to the traditional approaches of depth psychology, which emphasizes verbal exchange between the therapist and the client. The name holotropic literally means aiming for totality or moving toward wholeness (from the Greek *holos* = whole and *trepein* = moving in the direction of). The basic philosophical assumption of this strategy is that an average person of our culture operates in a way that is far below his or her real potential and capacity. This impoverishment is due to the fact that the individual identifies with only one aspect of his or her being, the physical body and the ego. This false identification leads to an inauthentic, unhealthy, and unfulfilling way of life, and contributes to the development of emotional and psychosomatic disorders of psychological origin.

The development of distressing symptoms that do not have any organic basis can be seen as an indication that the individual operating on false premises has reached a point where it has become obvious that the old way of being in the world does not work any more and is untenable. Such a breakdown can occur in a certain limited area of life — such as marriage and sexual life, professional orientation, or pursuit of various personal ambitions — or can afflict simultaneously the totality of the individual's life. The extent and depth of this breakdown correlates approximately with the development of neurotic or psychotic phenomena. The resulting situation represents a crisis or even emergency, but also a great opportunity.

The emerging symptoms reflect the effort of the organism to free itself from old stresses and traumatic imprints and simplify its functioning. This development is, at the same time, a process of discovery of one's true identity and of the dimensions of one's being that connect the individual with the entire cosmos and are commensurate with all of existence. Under favorable conditions and with good support, this process can result in radical problem-solving, psychosomatic healing, and consciousness evolution. It should therefore be seen as a potentially beneficial, spontaneous healing activity of the organism that should be supported rather than suppressed. This understanding of the nature of psychopathology represents the basic credo of holotropic therapy.

The main objective of the techniques of experiential psychotherapy is to activate the unconscious, to unblock the energy bound in emotional and psychosomatic symptoms, and to convert the stationary balance of this energy into a stream of experience. Holotropic therapy favors activation of the unconscious, which is so powerful that it results in a nonordinary state of consciousness. This principle is relatively new in Western psychotherapy, but has been used for centuries or millenia in the context of shamanic procedures, aboriginal healing ceremonies, rites of passage, meetings of various ecstatic sects, and the ancient mysteries of death and rebirth.

For psychotherapies that utilize mind-altering techniques of such power, the personalistic and biographically oriented model of current academic psychiatry is clearly insufficient and inadequate. During such experiential work, it will become obvious, frequently in the first session, that the roots of psychopathology reach far beyond the events of early childhood and beyond the individual unconscious. Experiential therapeutic work will uncover — behind the traditional biographical roots of symptoms — deep connections with clearly transbiographical domains of the psyche, such as elements of profound encounter with death and with birth, characteristic of the perinatal level, and an entire spectrum of factors of transpersonal nature.

For this reason, the use of narrow biographical models in combination with experiential techniques functions necessarily as a conceptual straitjacket and is inhibiting and counterproductive. Truly effective treatment cannot be limited to work on biographical issues. The model of the psyche used in therapeutic approaches based on holotropic principles has to be, therefore, extended beyond the biographical level of the individual unconscious to include the perinatal and transpersonal domains.

Principles of Holotropic Therapy

WE can now summarize the basic principles of holotropic therapy. Its main contribution is the recognition of the healing, transformative, and evolutionary potential of nonordinary states of consciousness. Since in these states the human psyche seems to show spontaneous healing activity, holotropic therapy uses techniques to activate the psyche and induce nonordinary states of consciousness. This tends to change the dynamic equilibrium underlying symptoms, transform them into a stream of unusual experiences, and consume them in the process. The task of the facilitator or therapist (the term is used here in the original Greek sense of assisting to heal) is then to support the experiential process with full trust in its healing nature, without trying to change it.

It is important that the therapist supports the experiential unfolding, even if he or she does not understand it at the moment. Some powerful transforming experiences might not have any specific content at all. They consist of sequences of intense build-up of emotions or physical tensions and subsequent deep release and relaxation. Frequently, the insights and specific contents emerge later in the process, or even in the following sessions. In some instances the resolution occurs on the biographical level, in others in connection with perinatal material or with various transpersonal themes. Occasionally, dramatic emotional and psychosomatic healing and personality transformation with lasting effects are associated with experiences that elude rational comprehension altogether. I will describe one such situation that occurred in our experiential seminar at the Esalen Institute. Additional examples of unusual therapeutic mechanisms are described in a later section of this book (p. 244 ff.)

Gladys, who participated in one of our five-day workshops, had suffered, prior to attending this seminar, for many years from serious attacks of depression accompanied with intense anxiety. They had usually started every day after four o'clock in the morning and lasted several hours. It was very difficult for her to mobilize her resources to face the new day.

In the session of holotropic breathing, Gladys responded with an extraordinary activation of physical energy, but in spite of intense bodywork in the termination period, she did not reach a satisfactory resolution. This is a situation that is quite exceptional when systematic effort is used to facilitate the integration of the session. The next morning, her depression came as usual, but was considerably more pronounced. Seeing her condition, we decided to change our program for the morning session and do experiential work with her without delay.

We asked her to lie down in the middle of the group, do some deep breathing, surrender to the flow of the music we were playing, and accept any experience that might emerge under these circumstances. For about fifty minutes, Gladys experienced violent tremors, made loud noises, seemed to fight invisible enemies, and showed other signs of strong psychomotor excitement. Retrospectively, she reported that this part of her experience involved reliving of her birth.

Later in the session, her screams became more articulate and started resembling words in an unknown language. We encouraged her to let the sounds come out in whatever form they took, without censoring them or judging them, even if they made no sense to her. Gradually, her movements became extremely stylized and emphatic and she chanted a powerful repetitive sequence that sounded like some kind of prayer.

The impact of this event on the group was extremely strong. Without understanding the words or knowing what happened to Gladys internally, most participants felt deeply moved and started to cry. When Gladys completed her chant, she quieted down and moved into a state of bliss and ecstatic rapture, in which she stayed for more than an hour, entirely motionless. Later, when giving a retrospective account of her experience, she described that she had felt an irresistible urge to do what she did. She did not understand what had happened and indicated that she had absolutely no idea what language she was using in her chant.

An Argentinian psychoanalyst who participated in the group recognized that Gladys had chanted in perfect Sephardic language, which he happened to know. This language, also called the Ladino, is a Judeo-Spaniolic hybrid which consists of medieval Spanish and Hebrew. Gladys was not Jewish and did not even speak modern Spanish. She had never heard about the Ladino and did not know that it existed and what it was.

The literal translation of the chant that had such a powerful effect on the group was: "I am suffering and I will always suffer. I am crying and I will always cry. I am praying and I will always pray." This episode and the profound influence it had on Gladys have remained a mystery for her, as well as us.

The most powerful technique of inducing nonordinary states of consciousness and activating the psyche is, without any doubt, the use of psychedelic substances. However, this is a radical approach that involves potentially serious risks: it requires, therefore, special precautions, skills, and observance of a set of strict rules. In this context, I will not discuss the principles of psychedelic therapy and will refer the interested readers to my previous publications dedicated specifically to this subject (Grof 1977, 1980 and 1985). It seems more useful and appropriate to focus on nonpharmacological techniques that are readily available to all those who want to experiment with them and are not associated with complicated political, administrative, and legal concerns. Those for whom the parallels with psychedelic therapy are of special importance wil find a brief survey of the main psychedelic plants and substances and their ritual and therapeutic use in the appendix of this book.

During the last ten years, my wife Christina and I have developed a powerful nondrug approach that we call holonomic integration or holotropic therapy. As discussed above, the holotropic strategy in therapy in the broadest sense is characteristic for many different approaches, including various shamanic procedures, aboriginal healing ceremonies, the healing trance dance of the !Kung Bushmen and other groups, rites of passage, psychedelic therapy, certain forms of hypnosis and other experiential psychotherapies, and for different spiritual practices. However, I would like to reserve the term holotropic therapy for our treatment procedure, which combines controlled breathing, music and other forms of sound technology, and focused bodywork. In the following text, I will describe this process by discussing its various elements.

THERAPEUTIC EFFECTS OF INTENSE BREATHING (PNEUMOCATHARSIS)

It has been known for centuries that it is possible to induce profound changes of consciousness by techniques which involve breathing. The procedures that have been used for this purpose by various ancient and non-Western cultures cover a very wide range from drastic interferences with breathing to subtle and sophisticated exercises of the various spiritual traditions. Thus the original form of baptism as it was practiced by the Essenes involved forced submersion of the initiate under water, which typically brought the individual close to death by suffocation. This drastic procedure thus induced a convincing experience of death and rebirth, a far cry from its modern form involving sprinkling of water and a verbal formula. In some other groups,the neophytes were half-choked by smoke, by strangulation, or by compression of the carotid arteries. Profound changes in consciousness can be induced by both extremes in the breathing rate — hyperventilation and prolonged withholding of breath — or a combination of both. Sophisticated and advanced methods of this kind can be found in the ancient Indian science of breath, or *pranayama*.

Specific techniques involving intense breathing or withholding of breath are also part of various exercises in Kundalini Yoga, Siddha Yoga, the Tibetan Vajrayana, Sufi practice, Burmese Buddhist and Taoist meditation, and many others. More subtle techniques which emphasize special awareness in relation to breathing rather than changes of the respiratory dynamics have a prominent place in Soto Zen Buddhism, and in certain Taoist and Christian practices. Indirectly, the breathing rhythm will be profoundly influenced by such ritual performances as the Balinese monkey chant or *Ketjak*, the Inuit Eskimo throat music, and singing of *kirtans*, *bhajans*, or Sufi chants.

We have ourselves experimented, particularly in the context of our month-long seminars at the Esalen Institute in Big Sur, California, with various techniques involving breathing: some of these came from the spiritual traditions, others from the experiential psychotherapies of humanistic psychology. Of all these methods, we have opted for simple increase of the rate of breathing. We have concluded that a specific technique of breathing is less important than the fact that the client is breathing faster and more effectively than usual, and with full concentration on and awareness of the inner process. It is a general strategy in holotropic therapy to trust the intrinsic wisdom of the body. The clients should therefore be encouraged to listen to the inner clues from their organism, rather than to follow any specific conceptual scheme.

We have been able to confirm repeatedly Wilhelm Reich's observation that psychological resistances and defenses use the mechanism of restricting the breathing. Respiration has a special position among the physiological functions of the body. It is an autonomous function, but it can also be easily influenced by volition. Increase of the rate and of the depth of breathing typically loosens the psychological defenses and leads to release and emergence of the unconscious (and superconscious) material. Unless one has witnessed or experienced this process personally, it is difficult to believe on theoretical grounds alone the power and efficacy of this technique.

The nature and course of the experiential sessions using the method of hyperventilation vary considerably from one person to another and can be described only in general and statistical terms. In some instances, continued hyperventilation leads to increasing relaxation, sense of expansion and wellbeing, and visions of light. The individual can be flooded with feelings of love and mystical connection to other people, nature, the entire cosmos, and God. Experiences of this kind are extremely healing, and the individual should be encouraged to allow them to develop; this should be discussed during the preparation period.

It is surprising how many people in the Western cultures, because of strong Protestant ethics or other reasons, have great difficulty accepting ecstatic experiences unless they follow suffering and hard work, or even then. They might have a strong feeling that they do not deserve them and respond to them with guilt. If this has been clarified and the subject accepts the experience, the session can run from the beginning to the end without the slightest intervention of the therapist and be extremely beneficial and productive. The probability of such smooth a course tends to increase with the number of holotropic sessions.

In most instances, however, the hyperventilation brings a first more or less dramatic experiential sequences in the form of intense emotions and psychosomatic manifestations. Before discussing the use of breathing for therapeutic purposes, it seems appropriate and necessary, particularly for the readers with medical background, to discuss briefly certain misconceptions about hyperventilation that seem to be deeply ingrained in the Western medical model. The textbooks of physiology of breathing describe the so-called hyperventilation syndrome — an allegedly standard and mandatory physiological response to rapid breathing. Here belong particularly the famous carpopedal spasms — tetanic contractions of the hands and feet.

The symptoms of the hyperventilation syndrome are usually seen in a pathological context and are explained in terms of biochemical changes in the composition of blood, such as increased alkalinity and decreased ionization of calcium. It is well known that certain psychiatric patients tend to develop spontaneous episodes of hyperventilation with dramatic emotional and psychosomatic manifestations; this is particularly frequent in hysterical patients. The usual approach to these episodes is to combat them by the administration of tranquilizers, intravenous calcium, and a paper bag placed over the face to prevent depletion of pulmonary carbon dioxide.

We have now conducted the breathing sessions with many thousands of persons and have found this understanding of the effects of hyperventilation to be incorrect. There exist many individuals in whom even dramatic hyperventilation carried over a long period of time does not lead to a classical hyperventilation syndrome, but to progressive relaxation, intense sexual feelings, or even mystical experiences. Others develop tensions in various parts of their bodies, but in patterns that are quite different from the carpopedal spasms. Moreover, continued hyperventilation does not lead to progressive increase of these tensions, but to their climactic culmination followed by a profound relaxation. This sequence typically has a pattern resembling a sexual orgasm.

In addition, in repeated holotropic sessions, there is a general trend toward progressive decrease of the overall amount of muscular tensions and difficult emotions. What seems to happen in this process is that the organism tends to respond to the changed biochemical situation by bringing to the surface, in certain more or less stereotyped patterns, various old, deep-seated tensions and disposes of them by peripheral discharge. This elimination or reduction of pent-up energies during holotropic sessions can happen in two different ways.

The first of these is the form of catharsis and abreaction, which involves tremors, twitches, dramatic body movements, coughing, gagging, vomiting, screaming and other types of vocal expression, or increased activity of the autonomous nervous system. This is a mechanism well-known in traditional psychiatry since the time when Sigmund Freud and Joseph Breuer (Freud and Breuer 1936) published their studies on hysteria. It has been used in traditional psychiatry, particularly in the treatment of traumatic emotional neuroses, and is very common in the new experiential psychotherapies, such as the neo-Reichian work, Gestalt practice, and primal therapy. When it is not limited to the biographical level and is allowed to proceed to the perinatal and transpersonal realms, it is an effective therapeutic mechanism and means for reduction of emotional and psychosomatic tensions.

The second mechanism represents a principle which is new in psychiatry and psychotherapy and seems to be, in many ways, even more effective and interesting. Here the deep tensions surface in the form of lasting contractions and prolonged spasms. By maintaining such sustained muscular tension for long periods of time, the organism is consuming enormous amounts of pent-up energy and is simplifying its functioning by getting rid of them.

These two mechanisms have their parallels in sport physiology, where it is well known that it is possible to do work and train the muscles in two different ways — the isotonic and the isometric. As the names suggest, during isotonic exercises the tension of the muscles remains constant while their length oscillates; during isometric exercises the tension of the muscles changes, but their length remains the same all the time. A good example of isotonic activity is boxing, while weightlifting is distinctly isometric. In spite of their superficial differences, these two mechanisms have much in common, and in holotropic therapy they complement each other very effectively.

A typical result of a good holotropic session is profound emotional release and physical relaxation; many subjects report that they feel more relaxed than they have ever felt in their lives. Continued

a

b

Figure 17a–d Four paintings of the same subject from holotropic breathing sessions. They represent a powerful death-rebirth experience, experiential identification with the archetypal figures of Shiva Nataraja (Lord of Dance) and of the Great Mother Goddess, and a sense of unity with the sunset on the Pacific Coast at Big Sur.

c

d

hyperventilation thus represents ultimately an extremely powerful and effective method of stress-reduction and leads to emotional and psychosomatic healing. The spontaneous episodes of hyperventilation in psychiatric patients can thus be seen as attempts at self-healing. This is also the understanding that one finds in the spiritual literature. In Siddha Yoga and Kundalini Yoga, intentional hyperventilation (*bastrika*) is used as one of the meditation techniques, and episodes of rapid breathing often occur spontaneously as one of the manifestations of Shakti (or activated Kundalini energy) referred to as *kriyas*. These observations suggest that spontaneous episodes of rapid breathing occurring in psychiatric patients should be supported rather than suppressed by all means.

The nature and course of holotropic sessions varies considerably from person to person and, in the same person, also from session to session. As I mentioned earlier, for some individuals the experience can run from the beginning to the end without any emotional or psychosomatic turmoil. In most instances, however, hyperventilation brings, at first, more or less dramatic experiential sequences. After an interval that varies from person to person, the individual starts experiencing strong emotions and develops stereotyped patterns of muscular armoring.

The emotional qualities observed in this context can cover a wide spectrum; the most common of these are anger and aggression, anxiety, sadness and depression, feelings of failure and inferiority, guilt, and disgust. The physical manifestations include, beside the muscular tensions, headaches and pains in various other parts of the body, gagging, nausea and vomiting, choking, hypersalivation, sweating, sexual feelings, and a variety of motor movements.

Some individuals remain entirely quiet and almost motionless; they might have profound experiences, yet they give the impression to an external observer that nothing is happening, or that they are sleeping. Others are agitated and show rich motor activity. They experience violent shaking and complex twisting movements, they roll and flail around, assume fetal positions, behave like infants struggling in the birth canal, or look and act like newborns. Also crawling, swimming, digging, or climbing movements are quite common. The acoustic manifestations of the process can be very rich and include sighing, moaning, weeping, screaming, baby talk, gibberish, spontaneous chanting, talking in tongues, and a broad spectrum of animal sounds.

Sometimes the movements and gestures can be extremely refined, complex, differentiated, and very specific. Here belong, for example, strange animal movements emulating snakes, birds, or feline predators, associated with the corresponding sounds. Sometimes individuals assume spontaneously various yogic postures and gestures (*asanas* and *mudras*) that they are not intellectually familiar with. Occasionally, the automatic movements and/or sounds can take the form of ritual dances or other performances from different cultures — shamanic healing, Javanese dances, the Balinese monkey chant, symbolic movements of the Indian Kathakali or Manipuri school of ballet, The Inuit Eskimo throat music, Tibetan or Mongolian multivocal and overtone chanting, or the Japanese Kabuki.

Physical tensions tend to develop during the breathing in certain specific areas of the body. Far from being simple physiological reactions to hyperventilation, they have a complex psychosomatic structure. They vary greatly from one person to another and usually have specific psychological meaning for the individuals involved. Sometimes they represent an intensified version of tensions and pains that the person knows from everyday life, either as a chronic problem or as symptoms that appear at certain special times such as periods of intense emotional or physical stress, extreme fatigue, lack of sleep, weakening by an illness, and use of alcohol or marijuana. Other times, they can be recognized as reactivation of old difficulties that the individual had at the time of infancy, childhood, puberty, or during severe emotional stress.

In most instances, it is possible to identify the specific biographical, perinatal, or transpersonal sources of various forms of psychosomatic discomfort occurring during holotropic breathing, or at least to discover their general psychological meaning. In what follows, I will describe the typical predilection areas where physical tensions occur during breathing sessions and discuss their most common psychological connections. It is important to emphasize that the description is statistical in nature; it outlines all the major manifestations that are observed in a large group of people and during a large number of sessions. In a specific session, a person will have only a personalized selection of these manifestations, sometimes a rather limited one.

When the spasms develop in the hands and the feet (the carpopedal spasms of traditional medicine), they usually reflect a deep conflict between strong impulses toward some specific actions and the opposing and equally strong inhibiting tendencies. It is thus a dynamic equilibrium that involves simultaneous activation of the extensor and flexor muscles of comparable intensity. Individuals experiencing these spasms frequently report that they sense a history of an entire lifetime (or even more than a lifetime) of repressed aggression, withheld impulses to reach out to other people, or unexpressed sexual tendencies. Sometimes painful tensions of this kind can represent blocked creative expressions such as an impulse to paint, to write, to dance, to play a musical instrument, to do specific craftwork, or to heal with one's hands.

It is common to gain in this context deep insights into the nature of the conflict underlying the tensions and into their biographical, perinatal, or transpersonal roots. In the process, the tension typically reaches a culmination followed by a profound release. When it happens, the individual feels that the energetic block has been removed and that the energy can now flow freely through the hands. We have seen over the years repeatedly that a subjective sense of unblocking was followed by an extraordinary liberation of the repressed impulse underlying the spasms. The individuals involved would frequently find ways of creative expression and show remarkable achievements in painting, dancing, writing, handiwork, or in healing activities.

The release of the energetic block in the hands has important medical implications. As a rule, an energetically blocked area has an insufficient blood supply. People who develop intense tensions in their extremities during holotropic breathing are usually those who in everyday life suffer from poor circulation and complain about cold hands or feet. Opening of the energetic block can result in a dramatic and permanent improvement of circulation. We have seen instances of this on several occasions in individuals who had extreme circulation problems medically diagnosed as Raynaud's disease.

Another important source of muscular tensions are memories of old physical injuries incurred during operations or accidents. At the time of such painful afflictions, the individual had to suppress, often for a long time, any emotional and physical responses to the pain. During the process of healing, the traumas were corrected anatomically, but the emotional components have not been worked through and adequately integrated. Memories of such situations represent unfinished psychological gestalts of considerable importance. They can significantly contribute to future psychological problems, and, conversely, experiential work on them can result in emotional and psychosomatic healing.

Tensions in the legs and feet have a similar dynamic structure as those in the arms and hands, only far less complex. This reflects the fact that the legs and feet are much less specialized than the arms and hands and their role in human life is much simpler. Many of the problems are related to the use of legs and feet as instruments of aggression, particularly earlier in life. The tensions and spasms in the thighs and in the buttocks are often associated with sexual defenses, fears, and inhibitions, particularly in women. An archaic anatomical term for one of the adductor muscles of the thigh was actually "custodian of virginity" — *musculus custos virginitatis*. Much of the tension in the legs can also be associated with a history of physical trauma.

On a deeper level, the dynamic conflicts underlying tensions in the arms, legs, and many other parts of the body are related to the hydraulic circumstances of biological birth. Here the organism of the infant is trapped, often for many hours, in a situation that involves extreme vital anxiety, pain, and suffocation. This generates an enormous amount of neuronal stimuli, for which there is no peripheral outlet, since the child does not have access to breathing, and cannot scream, move, or escape. Blocked energy that is thus stored in the organism involves equally the flexor and the extensor muscles. When this dynamic conflict surfaces for belated discharge, it manifests as intense and often painful spasms. On occasion, deeper roots of the tensions in the arms and legs can be traced to the transpersonal experiential domain, particularly to various past life memories.

It is interesting that many of the tensions in the remaining parts of the body occur in the areas where the Tantric systems place the centers of psychic energy in the subtle body, the so-called *chakras* (for a more detailed description see p. 113). This is not particularly surprising, in view of the similarity between the technique of holotropic therapy and the exercises used in the Tantric tradition that put great emphasis on breathing.

Energetic blockage in the area of the head — the crown center, Thousand Petal Lotus, or *sahasrāra chakra* — will typically manifest as a painful experience of compression, often described as a tight steel band crushing the head. This is particularly common in people who have a history of tension-, pressure-, belt-, or migraine headaches. The most frequent and quite obvious connection links this problem to the memory of biological birth when the frail head of the fetus was wedged into the pelvic opening by the enormous pressure of uterine contractions. Occasionally, there can be associations to memories of head injuries suffered in this lifetime or experienced in the context of a past life memory.

Blockage in the area of the brow center, or *ajñā chakra*, manifests during the breathing in the form of intense tensions or even pains around the eyes, sometimes connected with a flutter of the eyelids. This occurs particularly frequently in the sessions of people who have in their everyday life vision problems. Some of these difficulties — such as certain forms of myopia — can be caused by chronic tension of the eye muscles. When the tensions are discharged in therapy, this can result in a far-reaching correction of the disorder. However, this can be expected only if the person involved is in the first few decades of life and the changes have not yet become organic and thus irreversible.

The biographical material underlying problems of this kind usually involves situations from early life in which the individual was forced to see things that he or she did not want to see, was not ready to see, or found extremely frightening. A classical situation of this kind would be childhood in a family with an alcoholic parent with daily upsetting and embarassing scenes, or the famous Freudian "primal scenes," where the child witnessed sexual intercourse of adults. As it is the case with other parts of the body, a significant source of pent-up energies in the area of the eyes is the trauma of birth. Less frequently, there can be a connection with memories of eye injuries, particularly those associated with past incarnation memories.

The area of the throat center, or *viṣuddha chakra*, is a site of significant blockages for many people, and the work on these blockages presents special problems that will be discussed later. During the breathing sessions, this will manifest itself in the form of tensions in the muscles around the mouth, particularly the chewing muscles, locking of the jaws, constriction of the throat, and subjective feelings of suffocation. The most frequent biographical material associated with this problem involves traumatic memories of situations that threatened oxygen supply. Here belong childhood pneumonia, whooping cough, diphtheria, near-drowning, aspiration of a foreign object, or assaults by parents or their surrogates, older siblings, peers, and other persons that are associated with strangling.

Conflicts around extreme oral aggression can also significantly contribute to problems in this area. They can be associated with emotional deprivation and oral frustration of unsatisfactory nursing, or with painful surgical interventions in the area of the mouth, pharynx, and larynx. The pain of teething, insensitive interventions of a dentist, application of strong solutions of disinfectant liquids, and the infamous tonsillectomy can be mentioned here as salient examples.

However, most frequently oral aggression, locking of the jaws, and suffocation can be traced back to biological birth and its various vicissitudes and complications, or to intubation and other interventions immediately following it. Another frequent source of problems in the area of the throat are various past life experiences involving choking, strangling, or hanging. On a more subtle level, one can also find significant conflicts around expressing verbal aggression. In the extremes, repressed oral anger can lead to stammering.

Next is the heart center, or *anāhata chakra*, which is traditionally related to feelings of love, compassion, and spiritual birth. The individual who has a significant blockage in this area, will experience during the breathing session a strong constriction around the chest, sometimes with cardiac discomfort. It feels as if a steel band is being tightened around the ribcage. This problem is most frequently connected with memories of situations that have caused obstructions in the free emotional flow between the individual and other people. For some persons, this can involve primarily difficulties in giving emotionally to others or expressing their emotions, for others an inability to receive, or even impediments of both giving and receiving.

When this blockage is released after temporary intensification, the individual feels suddenly flooded with love and light, and has a sense of grace and emotional liberation. He or she can be overwhelmed by warm feelings for and profound appreciation of other people, even strangers (see the account from a holotropic breathing session on p. 115). This is accompanied by a feeling of free flow of emotions and energy and by a sense of immediacy and belonging. The same deep connection can be experienced with animals, all of nature, and the entire cosmos. Some peope talk in this context about having lived up to this point as if in a glass cylinder or behind an intangible film that had separated them from the world. Such an experience of opening of the heart *chakra* can be extremely healing and have a profound influence on the individual's life. It usually has an important numinous dimension and is described as a spiritual or mystical experience.

The blockage of the navel center, or *maṇipūra chakra*, will manifest during the breathing session as tension, spasm, and pain around the umbilical area. This is typically related to ambition, self-assertion, competition, and specific problems related to self-image and self-esteem. These involve oscillations between a sense of inferiority, inadequacy, and childlike helplessness on the one hand, and compensatory grandiose fantasies, unrealistic ambitions, and autocratic or macho-type manifestations on the other. Such a combination of a sense of inferiority and will to power is the focus of Alfred Adler's individual psychology. There can be significant connections to biographical events in which security, satisfaction, and survival of the individual have been seriously threatened. However, the most common source of these problems can be found in the trauma of biological birth, particularly in situations involving insults to the umbilical cord, such as compression, excessive pull, or its severing at the time of the separation from the mother. Quite frequent are also connections of this area to traumatic past life memories.

The sexual center, or *svādiṣṭhāna chakra*, is located below the navel. The blockages in this area will lead during the breathing sessions to intense sexual arousal and various genital and pelvic spasms and pains. As can be expected from the name of this *chakra*, the main issues associated with blockages in this area are sexual in nature. They involve traumatic psychosexual memories from the life of the individual that underlie such problems as an inability to develop or maintain an erection, orgastic insufficiency or frigidity, satyriasis, nymphomania, sadomasochistic tendencies, and in women also painful menstrual cramps. There are, however, typical deeper links to biological birth (the sexual facet of BPM III) and often also to archetypal or past life themes.

And finally the root center, or *mulādhāra chakra*, has above all distinctly anal connections. Work on the blockages in this area is associated with anal spasms and pain or concerns about loss of control over the anal sphincter (flatulence or even defecation). The typical biographical material that tends to surface in this context involves a history of childhood colics, painful enemas, and harsh toilet training. It occurs particularly frequently in individuals who are obsessive-compulsive, have latent or manifest homosexual tendencies, or a rigid system of defenses and excessive fear of loss of control. Additional associations involve spastic diarrhea or constipation, irritable colon, ulcerous colitis and, on a more subtle level, serious difficulties in handling money.

Beside the tensions in the arms, hands, legs, feet, and in the above areas of the *chakras*, additional spasms and blockages can occur in the neck, in the stomach, in the long muscles along the spinal column, in the small of the back, and in the buttocks. These can either emerge independently or in combination with blockages in the individual *chakras*. They are associated with various issues and themes of a biographical, perinatal, and transpersonal nature.

In a typical breathing session, the tensions and blockages will be amplified and manifested. Continued breathing tends to bring them to a culmination point, resolution, and release. This is true no matter what the nature and location of the problem is, with one possible exception — the throat *chakra*. Here it can happen that the intensification of the problem leads to an actual constriction of the throat that interferes with further breathing. In this case, the client will be encouraged to shift to an abreactive technique that frees the throat and makes the continuation of the session possible. Basically, this means to do more of what is trying to happen already; it can be vocalization, coughing, gagging, shaking, or grimacing. The client is asked to amplify all such manifestations and continue with this process until the breathing is free. Then he or she returns to hyperventilation as the main tool. If the breathing itself does not result in complete resolution, the therapist uses an abreactive technique with similar principles as the one described for the work on respiratory blockage.

The interventions in the termination period of the sessions will be described later (p. 194).

The Healing Potential of Music

In holotropic therapy, the use of hyperventilation to induce nonordinary states of consciousness for healing purposes is combined with evocative music. Like breathing, music and other forms of sound technology have been used for millenia as powerful mind-altering tools. Since time immemorial, monotonous drumming and chanting have been the principle tools of shamans in many different parts of the world. Many non-Western cultures have developed quite independently drumming rhythms that have been demonstrated to have in the laboratory remarkable effects on the physiological activity of the brain, as reflected in the changes of the brain waves (Neher 1961, 1962). The archives of cultural anthropology contain countless examples of extraordinary trance-inducing instrumental music, chanting, and dancing.

In many cultures, sound technology has been used specifically for healing purposes in the context of intricate ceremonies. The Navajo healing rituals conducted by trained singers have astounding complexity that has been compared to that of the scripts of Wagnerian operas. The trance dance of the !Kung Bushmen in the African Kalahari Desert has enormous healing power, as has been documented in several anthropological studies and movies (Lee and DeVore 1976, Katz 1976). The therapeutic potential of the syncretistic religious rituals of the Caribbean and South America, such as the Cuban Santeria or the Brazilian Umbanda is recognized by many professionals of these countries with Western education. In our own tradition remarkable instances of emotional and psychosomatic healing occur in the meetings of ecstatic Christian sects that use trance dancing, singing, and music, such as the Black Southern Baptists, Revivalists, Pentecostals, and the Virginian Snake Handlers, or the Holy Ghost People.

Many great spiritual traditions have developed sound technology that does not induce just a general trance state, but has a more specific effect on consciousness. Here belong above all the Tibetan multi-vocal chanting, the sacred songs and chants of various Sufi orders, the Hindu *bhajans* and *kirtans* and, particularly, the ancient art of *nada* yoga, or the way to union by sound. The Indian teachings postulate a specific connection between sounds of certain frequencies and the individual *chakras*. With the systematic use of this knowledge, it is possible to influence the state of consciousness in a predictable and desirable way. Those are just a few examples of the extensive use of music for ritual, healing, and spiritual purposes. Those interested in more information on the effects of music on the human psyche can find it in special books on the subject (Hamel 1976, Berendt 1985).

We have used music systematically in the program of psychedelic therapy at the Maryland Psychiatric Research Center in Baltimore, Maryland, and have learned much about its extraordinary potential for psychotherapy. Good music seems to be of particular value in nonordinary states of consciousness, where it has several functions. It helps to mobilize old emotions and make them available for expression, intensifies and deepens the process, and provides a meaningful context for the experience. The continuous flow of music creates a carrying wave that helps the subject move through difficult experiences and impasses, overcome psychological defenses, surrender, and let go.

Skillful use of musical selections can also facilitate the emergence of specific contents, such as aggression, emotional or physical pain, sexual and sensual feelings, birth struggle, ecstatic rapture, or the oceanic atmosphere of the womb. In the work with a group, loud and dynamic music has an additional function, namely to mask sounds made by participants in various stages of the process and weave them into a unified artistic form. Helen Bonny, music therapist and member of our team at the Maryland Psychiatric Research Center, recognized early the enormous therapeutic potential of music and developed, as a result of her experiences in psychedelic research, an independent nondrug treatment technique, the Guided Imagery with Music (GIM) (Bonny and Savary 1973).

To use music as a catalyst for deep self-exploration and experiential work, it is necessary to learn a new way of listening to music and relating to it that is alien to our culture. In the West, we use music frequently as an acoustic background that has little relevance: for example, modern music at cocktail parties or piped music (Muzak) in shopping areas and work spaces. An approach quite characteristic for more sophisticated audiences is the disciplined and intellectualized style that dominates the atmosphere of traditional concert halls. The dynamic and elemental way of using music that one finds in rock concerts comes closer to the use of music in holotropic therapy, but it is extroverted and lacks an important element — sustained focused introspection.

In holotropic and psychedelic therapy, it is essential to surrender completely to the flow of music, let it resonate in one's entire body, and respond to it in a spontaneous and elemental fashion. This includes manifestations that would be unthinkable in a concert hall, where even silent tears or coughing might be a source of embarassment. Here one has to give full expression to whatever the music is triggering — crying ot laughing, grimacing, shaking, various contortions of the body, sensual pelvic movements, and any other emotional, vocal, and motor manifestations.

It is particularly important to suspend any intellectual activity in relation to the music that is being played, such as trying to guess who its composer might be or from which culture it comes, exploring its resemblance to another piece that one knows, judging the performance of the orchestra, attempting to identify the key, or criticizing the technical quality of the recording or the music equipment in the room. The music has to be allowed to act on the psyche and the body in a completely spontaneous and elemental fashion. Used in this way, it becomes a powerful means for inducing and supporting unusual states of consciousness. The music used for this purpose should be of superior technical quality and have sufficient volume to drive the experience. When such mind-altering sound technology is used together with the technique of intense breathing described earlier, the two elements seem to potentiate each other. The combination of the two is a therapeutic and exploratory tool of remarkable power.

When music is used in psychedelic therapy, where the experiential momentum is provided by the drug, the basic rule is to choose music in such a way that it supports the experience and is as fully congruent with it as possible. Thus, for example, in working with LSD, the therapist should use initially some music that has a flowing and opening quality and slowly builds as the drug effects are increasing. In the middle part of the session, the music should be powerful, driving, and of relatively little oscillation in terms of intensity. Between the third and fourth hour, the therapist would shift to a "breakthrough" type of music, since at this time, most individuals experience a culmination and sudden resolution. As the experience is quieting down, the music should become more and more flowing, peaceful, and meditative.

In addition, when the therapist is aware of the specific content of the experience, he or she can support it by an appropriate choice of music. When the subject's comments and body movements indicate that the experience has a strong sexual emphasis, the music should be sensual and erotic. Rimsky-Korsakov's *Scheherazade*, Wagner's Venusberg music from *Tannhaeuser* and Isolde's Death from *Tristan and Isolde*, or Prokofiev's love scene from *Romeo and Juliet* could be used here as prime examples. Similarly, aggressive experiential episodes indicate choice of dynamic music, such as sequences of powerful drumming and primitive human voices from aboriginal rituals or shamanic procedures, "Mars" from Holst's *Planets*, or dramatic orchestral selections from Wagner's operas.

Episodes of oceanic ecstasy, unitive cosmic feelings, or a sense of overwhelming love will require a choice of music that conveys corresponding emotions and states of consciousness. Sometimes it is possible to be even more specific. If the subject reports experiential sequences from specific cultures, such as a past life memory from Russia, India, or Japan, the therapist should choose music characterizing that culture, or at least music that sounds similar.

Occasionally, recordings of natural sounds might be very effective. Here belong, for example, the intra-abdominal sounds of a pregnant woman ("Lullaby from the Womb"), songs of the humpback whales, voices of the wolves, noises of insects, such as chirping of crickets or humming of the bees, singing of passerine birds, rushing of creeks and rivers, the rhythms of the splashing waves aproaching the ocean shore, or the astronomical sound tracks portraying the emissions from the pulsars.

When using psychedelics other than LSD, the choice and timing of the music has to be, naturally, adjusted to the specific quality of the drug effect, the onset and duration of its action, and the dynamic curve of the experience. Thus the onset of the effects of tryptamine derivatives that have to be inhaled or injected, such as DMT or DPT, is almost instant and their duration shorter. The amphetamine-related empathogens (MDA, MMDA, 2CB, or Ecstasy) require music that is much gentler and more flowing. The dissociative anesthetic ketamine, in addition to producing an experience of very short duration (about one hour), requires a particularly slow and expansive ("spacy") type of music.

The principles of the use of music in holotropic breathing are very similar to those that I have just described for psychedelic treatment. The major difference here is that the nonordinary state of consciousness is the result of deliberate effort of the subject, rather than the chemical effect of a drug. Also its continuation depends on sustained hyperventilation and the impact of music, and is not automatic. We have found it useful to start from the beginning with music that is evocative and driving to help initiate the unusual state of consciousness. For much of the holotropic session, the music should also be, in general, more powerful and emphatic than in psychedelic therapy.

As far as the specific choice of music is concerned, I will outline only the general principles and give a few suggestions based on our experience. Each therapist or therapeutic team develops, after a certain time, their own list of favorite pieces for various stages of the sessions and for certain specific situations. The basic rule is to respond sensitively to the phase, intensity, and content of the experience, rather than try to impose a specific pattern on it. This is in congruence with the general philosophy of holotropic therapy, particularly with the deep respect for the wisdom of the collective unconscious and the autonomy and spontaneity of the healing process.

In general, preference should be given to music of high artistic quality that is not well known, and has little concrete content. One should avoid playing songs and other vocal pieces in which the verbal content conveys a specific message or suggests a definite theme. When vocal compositions are used, they should be in a language that is not known to the experient, so that the human voice is perceived as an unspecific stimulus. For the same reason, it is preferable to avoid pieces with which clents have specific intellectual associations.

Thus the wedding marches from Wagner's *Lohengrin* or from Mendelssohn-Bartholdy's *Midsummer Night's Dream* immediately suggest a nuptial atmosphere to most Westerners. The overture to Bizet's *Carmen* will evoke the image of the arena, the toreador, and the bullfights. Similarly, famous masses or oratoria will activate one's memories related to the Christian church and religious upbringing. Although programming of the experience should generally be avoided, specific connotations of certain pieces can be very useful when the therapist deliberately wants to support a spontaneously emerging theme of a particular kind.

The associations to various pieces of music will naturally vary, not only from individual to individual, but also from culture to culture and from nation to nation. For example, in many middle-aged and older Europeans, Liszt's *Les Préludes* tends to activate memories of World War II, because it was used by the Nazi propagandists as an introduction to the daily news broadcast by street loudspeakers of all the major cities occupied by the Germans. In our experiential workshop in Bombay, we noticed a remarkable emotional response of a large number of participants to the Indian chant *Ragupati Raja Ram*. In the discussion following the session, we found out that we had unknowingly chosen the piece of music that was broadcast all over India nonstop for several days after Gandhi's assassination.

The major objection against the use of music in holotropic and psychedelic sessions is that the choice of music has a strong structuring influence on the experience, even if we avoid gross programming and try to adjust the music to the nature of the experience. This is particularly true if holotropic therapy is used in the context of a large group. Here the best a therapist can do is to observe the situation in the room and use statistical principles — adjust the choice according to what seems to be the prevailing atmosphere in the room. In this way, it is inevitable that the choice of music will be less than optimal for some of the members of the group.

However, the danger of programming associated with specific music is not as serious as it might seem. The potential for manipulating and controlling the experience of a person in a nonordinary state of consciousness has its definite limits. If the subject is in an extremely difficult emotional place, any music, no matter how inspired and uplifting, will be distorted and sound like a dirge. Conversely, during a deep ecstatic experience, the subject will accept enthusiastically just about any piece of music, will find it fitting, and will perceive it as interesting from some point of view. Only in the middle range between these two extremes will the choice of music really effectively shape the experience.

Even then, although the music will suggest a certain general atmosphere or emotional tone, the subject will elaborate it in a very personal way. The situation here is similar to what I will later describe in relation to the possibility of programming the session by the preparation and verbal instructions preceding it. What the subject does with the incoming information will still be a reflection of his or her own memory banks and unconscious dynamics. This becomes clear when one compares the wide variety of reactions to the same music within a large group of people. Whatever the role of the music is in structuring the individual experiences, they can be healing and transformative for the individuals involved, and can have a deep personal meaning for each of them.

Over the years, we have developed our own library of audiotapes that seem to work well with most of the subjects. The pieces we have found very useful in the initial stages of the holotropic sessions are *Time-Wind* and selections from the *X* album by the German composer Klaus Schultze, John McLaughlin's *Shakti*, and Sergei Rachmaninov's *Isle of the Dead*. We have also experimented with specialized audiotapes, where all the music of one holotropic session was drawn from one thematic area (e.g. a shamanic breathing tape or a Sufi breathing tape). Here we used in the initial phase Michael Harner's shamanic drumming, a recording of Pakistani Sufis, or a Sufi tape called the *Islamic Mystical Brotherhood*.

Particularly effective selections for the middle parts of holotropic sessions are certain compositions by the American composer of Scotch-Armenian extraction, Alan Hovhanness (*All Men Are Brothers, The Mysterious Mountain, And God Created the Great Whales*), "Mars" from Holst's *Planets*, Alexander Scriabin's *Poem of Ecstasy*, selected pieces from Sergei Prokofiev's ballet *Romeo and Juliet* ("Monteques and Capulets," "Tomb of Romeo and Juliet"), the first symphony by Samuel Barber and his famous *Adagio for Strings*, and compositions by the contemporary artists Vangelis Papathanassiou and Georg Deuter. Among the unique ethnic pieces that can be used at this time are the *Balinese Monkey Chant* or *Ketjak*, parts of the *Dhikr of the Halveti-Jerrahi* dervishes, and authentic recordings of the African tam-tams (Drums of Passion).

In the later stages of holotropic sessions, as the clients are quieting down, the choice of music gradually shifts to less dramatic, slower, and finally timeless and meditative pieces. Our own favorite selections for the termination periods of sessions include Hector Berlioz's *Harold in Italy*, Pachelbel's *Canon in D*, Alan Stivell's *Renaissance of the Celtic Harp*, Paul Horn's albums *Inside the Taj Mahal* and *Inside the Great Pyramid*, Charles Lloyd's *Big Sur Tapestry*, the American Sufi music *Habibbiyya*, flute music from the Andes (*Urubamba*), the Japanese *shakuhachi*, Tony Scott's *Music for Zen Meditation* and *Music for Yogic Meditation*, Tibetan multivocal chanting, various Indian *ragas*, *bhajans* and *kirtans* (particularly the *Om Namah Shivaya* chant and other recordings of the Ganeshpuri group), and the music by Steven Halpern, Georgia Kelly, Paul Winter, and Brian Eno.

In systematic work with holotropic therapy, it is good to start with more conservative selections and later move to powerful mind-altering sound technology, particularly pieces of music that were specifically developed in various cultures and spiritual traditions to change consciousness and for healing purposes. The therapeutic potential of music is quite remarkable and this field is open for future explorations. Marilyn Ferguson dedicated an entire issue of her *Brain/Mind Bulletin* to what she called "music medicine" — systematic scientific research of aesthetic, emotional, psychological, physiological, and biochemical effects of music (Ferguson 1985).

Among the possibilities that should be systematically explored in holotropic therapy is the use of "white noise," random acoustic stimulation produced by a sound generator. Years ago, I conducted some preliminary work with it in psychedelic sessions and found it most interesting. The use of "white noise" eliminates the possibility of programming of the experience by music, since it consists of rapid sequences of acoustic stimuli that do not have any specific patterning. In psychedelic sessions, most subjects will illusively transform such monotonous sounds into music. This music is then perceived as perfectly fitting, since it comes from the same source as the rest of the experience — the subject's psyche. It remains to be seen if the same is true for holotropic sessions.

Another interesting avenue of future research is the study of the effects of specific sound frequencies on the psyche and body. This work is a modern version of the system known in India as *nada* yoga, or yoga of sound. Its basic assumption is the existence of a deep connection between vibrations of different frequencies and the activity in the centers of psychic energy, the *chakras*. It is conceivable that it will be possible in the future to incorporate some of the findings in this area into holotropic therapy. However, by far the most promising perspectives for further developments of holotropic therapy can be found in the rapidly developing field of holophonic sound. The possibilities in this area are so exciting and far-reaching that they deserve some elaboration.

The inventor of the holophonic sound technology is the Argentinian-Italian researcher Hugo Zucarelli. Because of patent considerations, he has not yet disclosed all the information necessary for full understanding of his important discovery. In the following discussion, I will use the data from the lectures of his I attended, from our personal discussions, and from my experience with holophonic sound during a three-day seminar in Millbrae, California, that my wife Christina and I participated in.

Early in his life, Zucarelli had a profound personal experience during which he was almost killed by a car. What saved his life was his ability to locate precisely the sound of the approaching vehicle without actually seeing it. Subsequently, he became fascinated by the problems associated with the capacity of various animals to localize sounds in auditory perception. By careful study and analysis of the mechanisms by which different species in the evolutionary pedigree arrive at precise identification of the sources of sound, he came to the conclusion that the existing models of hearing cannot account for important characteristics of human acoustic perception.

The traditional explanation of the ability to localize sounds is based on comparing the intensity of sound entering the ears on the right and left sides. Studying the evolution of this mechanism, Zucarelli found that organisms whose head is connected firmly with the body, such as a crocodile, tend to move the entire body when localizing sounds. In those species where the movements of the head can be isolated from those of the body, such as in birds, the organism will use them in the process of localizing the sound. In most mammals, the head can remain steady and its movements are replaced by positioning of the earlobes.

The fact that humans can locate the source of sounds without movements of the head or positioning of the earlobes clearly suggests that the comparing of the intensity of acoustic input between the right and left ear is not the only mechanism responsible for human abilities in this area. In addition, even individuals whose hearing has been destroyed on one side can still localize sounds. On the basis of the above data, Zucarelli concluded that to explain adequately all the characteristics of spatial hearing in humans, one has to assume that human acoustic perception is using holographic principles. This required the acceptance of the fact that, contrary to the model of traditional medicine, the human ear has to function not only as a receiver, but also as a transmitter.

By replicating this mechanism electronically, Zucarelli developed the holophonic technology. Holophonic recordings have an uncanny capacity to reproduce acoustic reality with all its spatial characteristics to such an extent that, without constant visual control, it is virtually impossible to distinguish the perception of recorded phenomena from actual events in the three-dimensional world. In addition, listening to holophonic recordings of events that stimulated other senses tends to induce synesthesias — corresponding perceptions in other sensory areas.

Remarkable examples of such synesthesias can be experienced while listening to Zucarelli's experimental tape. Here the sound of scissors opening and closing near one's scalp will convey a realistic sense of one's hair actually being cut. The hum of an electric hairdryer can produce sensations of the stream of hot air blowing through the hair. Listening to a person striking a match might be accompanied by the vision of light and/or distinct smell of burning sulphur. While hearing the sound of a paper bag near one's ears, one has a convinced sense that somebody is pulling a shopping bag over one's head. And the voice of a woman whispering into one's ear will make one feel her breath.

The discovery of the holophonic principles and the holophonic technology has great relevance for many fields of science and areas of human life. It can revolutionize the understanding of physiology and pathology of hearing and have undreamed of implications for psychiatry, psychology, and psychotherapy. One can at this point only fantasize about all the broader possibilities of theoretical implications for religion and philosophy and practical applications in mass media, entertainment, art, and many other realms. The possibilities for the use of holophonic sound in the context of holotropic therapy are extremely intriguing and promising. Of particular interest would be holophonic recordings of musical performances aimed specifically at inducing or communicating a nonordinary state of consciousness — Balinese trance-dancing music, shamanic rituals, Sufi music and chants, music and drumming for a Huichol or Native American peyote ceremony, songs of the Peruvian *ayahuasqueros*, and others.

FOCUSED BODY WORK

The last component of holotropic therapy, the focused body work, is used only when it is indicated. There are many sessions with a smooth course where no interventions are required. In some of these sessions, the hyperventilation does not trigger any difficult emotions or unpleasant physical manifestations and leads to progressive relaxation and to feelings of an ecstatic nature. In others, emotional and psychosomatic distress develops, but continued breathing brings about quite automatically a good resolution and good integration of the session.

There are only a few situations when focused body work is necessary in the early phases of holotropic sessions. The most important of these was mentioned earlier; it is a situation where the major blockage is in the area of the throat and it reaches such a degree that it interferes with further breathing. Occasionally, abreactive body work has to be used when the intensity of the reaction — spasms, physical pain, or anxiety — reaches such a degree that the subject would not be able or willing to continue unless the discomfort was reduced. In rare instances, it is useful to employ this approach when the subject presents serious problems for the sitters or other participants in the group by becoming too agitated or too deeply involved in the experience.

However, the main indication for the use of focused body work is a situation during the termination period of the session (usually after about an hour and a half to two hours) in those individuals where the breathing and music did not bring a complete resolution. At this time, the facilitator should check with the subject and find out if there is any residual discomfort and what its nature is. The work on such prob-

Figure 18a–b   Pictorial representations of an alternating experiential identification with a poisonous spider (**a.**) and an aboriginal mask (**b.**) that occurred during abreactive work in the final stage of a holotropic session. These experiences resulted in a dramatic relief in general and particularly facial tension.

lems is desirable, since it brings the session to a cleaner resolution and better integration, but it is in no way mandatory. We always ask the clients if they want to do the work, or if they want to leave the situation as it is. In any case, the residual symptoms tend to disappear with time.

The basic principle of focused body work in the termination period of holotropic sessions is to exteriorize the various forms of physical discomfort associated with the emotional distress, while taking the clues from the client's body. Whatever the nature and localization of the problem, the individual is asked to accentuate the symptom. For example, if the issue is a headache or pain in the neck, it can be often intensified by assuming a certain focused posture of the head, making a grimace, or tensing up the neck muscles. Pelvic discomfort can be exaggerated by lifting the pelvis and tensing the abdominal muscles (the bridge pose of hatha yoga) or by trying to hold the legs together while the knees are being pulled apart. Similarly, when there is too much energy or cramping in the hands, this can be voluntarily accentuated and the tension further increased by external intervention, such as steady pull of "Mexican hand-wrestling". The same general principle can be applied to any other area of the body.

While the presenting problem is being accentuated and the tension in the area maintained, the rest of the body is allowed to express anything that it spontaneously tends to do. It is important that the client (or therapist) does not attempt to judge what is happening or to change it. However, it can be helpful to use certain interventions that cooperate with the process, deepen it, and intensify it. Here belong, for example, massage or pressure in the areas that are tense or painful, or offers of specific resistances that increase existing tensions, such as those that I mentioned earlier in connection with the maneuvers for releasing the tensions in the pelvis or in the hands.

Among the reactions that might spontaneously occur under these circumstances are violent shaking, grimacing, coughing, gagging, vomiting, a variety of movements, and a wide range of sounds that include screaming, baby talk, animal voices, talking in tongues or a language foreign to the client, shamanic chanting, and many others. This activity should be encouraged and continued until the emotional and psychosomatic discomfort disappears and the person feels relaxed and comfortable.

Another important aspect of body work in holotropic therapy is the use of supportive physical contact. This is naturally a controversial issue from the point of view of academic psychiatry, psychology, and psychoanalysis, where there is a strong taboo against it. However, this form of therapeutic approach has become natural and routine in many groups practicing various forms of experiential psychotherapy. Although the use of physical support might seem objectionable and unacceptable to a traditional therapist with psychoanalytic training, it is a powerful and effective tool, particularly in individuals with a history of severe emotional deprivation in infancy and childhood.

To understand the importance of physical contact as a therapeutic tool, one has to examine the nature of traumatic experiences and the measures that can remedy them. The traumas that play an important role in the developmental history of the individual and in the dynamics of psychopathology fall into two large categories. Paraphrasing the terminology of the law, we can say that some of them happen by commission, others by omission. These two groups are very different from each other in their basic nature and require different therapeutic measures.

Figure 19 Painting expressing an authentic identification with a large cat that was experienced during focused body work in the terminal phase of a holotropic session. The hand in the upper part of the picture belongs to the facilitator who was at the time applying pressure on the subject's forehead.

In the first category are memories of situations that inflicted severe physical pain on the individual, or evoked strong negative emotions, such as fear, confusion, shame, despair, disgust, and others. Here belong memories of physical abuse, painful injuries or medical interventions, discomfort associated with childhood diseases, sexual abuse, or threatening events. Traumatic memories of this kind can be likened to foreign bodies in the psyche; they can be expelled through expressive emotional work and abreaction.

The second category of traumas involves situations in which the infant or child had at different periods of his or her life legitimate needs for security and satisfaction that were not met by parents or their surrogates. Of special importance here are the so called anaclitic needs (from the Greek *anaklinein* = to lean onto). Here belong the need for nourishing symbiotic contact with the mother, satisfactory nursing, cuddling, rocking, and caressing. When these needs have not been satisfied, they leave a vacuum in the psyche. The individual can express anger and frustration about having been deprived, but that does not fill the empty space. The only possibility here is to offer satisfaction of these needs when the client is regressed to the level of the original trauma.

The use of physical contact in therapy requires an impeccable approach and observation of basic ethical rules. It has to be clear that offering physical contact — or asking for it — should be a response to the demands of the therapeutic situation and should not involve any other motives. This does not necessarily mean only adult sexual needs which, of course, are the first to consider. We have had in our workshops over the years several women with strong unfulfilled maternal needs, who were insensitively and inappropriately imposing their mothering on the persons they worked with. They tried to rock and cuddle them at times when it was absolutely contrary to the nature of their experience, which was, for example, reliving of a past life memory as a great African chieftain, a Viking warrior during a maritime conquest, or a Roman soldier on a military expedition.

The issue of physical contact should be discussed and clarified with the client before the session. It is important to realize that the attitudes toward physical contact cover an extremely wide range. For some people, it is an absolutely natural thing; for others, it is associated with serious conflicts and problems. In our workshops, we always encourage experiencers and sitters to discuss this issue before they start working with each other, to reach a clear understanding, and to make a "contract" as to how they will proceed in this matter.

The choice of the form of physical contact and its timing involves a strong element of intuition and it is difficult to set strict objective rules for it. However, it is possible to give some general guidelines. The facilitator should consider the use of physical contact when the client is clearly deeply regressed and seems helpless and vulnerable. Typical situations of this kind would be the reliving of episodes involving emotional deprivation in childhood, or the period following the reliving of biological birth. The best approach seems to be to offer first tentatively some limited physical contact, such as touching the hand or forehead of the client. If this is eagerly accepted, one can offer more; eventually, this can reach the point of full body contact.

In our own work, the problem of physical contact is significantly simplified by the fact that we almost always work in a group context. The reasons and rules for the use of intimate support are clearly explained and they are accepted by the group as part of the procedure. The areas of the body that are being touched are determined by the inner process of the experient, not by the choice of the sitters. In addition, all that happens along these lines happens publicly and under collective supervision of the group. This is a situation that differs considerably from the context of individual work in private practice. The feasibility of this approach for individual therapy would have to be assessed from case to case.

We have found that using holotropic therapy in a group context adds entirely new dimensions to the therapeutic process. The most obvious advantage is, of course, the economic factor. Up to twenty persons can have, with the assistance of two skilled facilitators, significant healing and transformative experiences in the time span of only three sessions of classical psychoanalysis.

In addition, the sessions in a group context generally are much more powerful than individual holotropic work. They tend to create what can best be described as a strong catalytic energy field that has a facilitating influence on the therapeutic process. An interesting aspect of collective holotropic work is the occurrence of many synchronistic events in the sense of Carl Gustav Jung (Jung 1960) between the experients and facilitators, among the experients, as well as between all the participants and various aspects of the external world.

However, there exists yet another advantage of group work, which is the profound effect it has on many of the sitters. The usual arrangement we use is such that every participant in the group chooses a partner with whom he or she wants to work. In the sessions, participants function alternately as experients and sitters or facilitators. It is not unusual that the experience of being a sitter has a deep and significant impact on the person involved. The privilege of assisting another human being in an experience which is profoundly personal and intimate is an event the power of which should not be underestimated.

The way partners choose each other turns out often to be psychologically significant and can also involve synchronistic factors. It is not uncommon that the process of the two partners has elements of unusual complementarity or antagonism; these can be of special significance and present an opportunity for emotional learning of an extraordinary kind. If the holotropic sessions continue on a systematic basis, the partners have the option to switch, if they do not find it rewarding to work together, or if they have developed a special affinity to somebody else in the group.

THE PROCEDURE OF HOLOTROPIC THERAPY

After having described the basic elements of holotropic therapy — the use of hyperventilation, music, and body work — I will now discuss the therapeutic procedure as we have been practicing it. The principles of holotropic therapy are very simple. During the preparation that precedes the experiential sessions, the clients are acquainted with the extended cartography of the psyche that includes the biographical-recollective level, the elements of the death-rebirth process, and the spectrum of transpersonal experiences. It is made quite clear that any of these experiences are absolutely natural and that they occur under these circumstances in any group of randomly selected individuals.

In verbal approaches to psychotherapy, the resistance takes the form of emotional and even psychosomatic defenses, as has been clearly demonstrated by Wilhelm Reich (Reich 1949) with his concept of the character armor. The new experiential techniques can effectively overcome the emotional and psychosomatic blockages so that they cease to be a problem. Surprisingly, the most important barrier of defense in the work with these modern therapies, according to our experience, is of an intellectual or philosophical nature. These techniques can open access to areas of experience for which our culture does not have an adequate conceptual framework. In spite of the fact that such experiences as perinatal sequences and transpersonal phenomena can be healing and transformative, an uninformed Westerner tends to fight against them and block them because they appear strange, bizarre, or even indicative of severe psychopathology.

For this reason, cognitive preparation that includes a discussion of the new comprehensive cartography of the psyche is a very important part of the holotropic procedure. In some of our past workshops, participants with traditional scientific training occasionally raised the objection that the preparation might have included "indoctrination" and might have actually induced by suggestion the experiences in the sessions. In my experience, the danger of such indoctrination is minimal. I saw repeatedly in the early years of my psychedelic research that my patients moved spontaneously and without any programming into the perinatal and transpersonal realms — long before I developed the cartography of the unconscious that we now discuss before psychedelic or holotropic sessions.

We have also seen many instances where perinatal and transpersonal experiences occurred in unsupervised psychedelic sessions or in psychedelic and holotropic sessions that were conducted by others with inadequate preparation or without any preparation at all. There is, therefore, no doubt that they represent genuine manifestations of the psyche that do not require any programming. It is also important to realize that, during the preparation, the clients hear about practically the entire spectrum of possible human experiences. Since their actual experience in the holotropic session represents only a small and very selective fragment of what was discussed, this choice has to have significant personal determinants. While the danger of "indoctrination" seems to be minimal, entering the session without the necessary information and warning can represent a serious disadvantage and obstacle, in view of our strong cultural programming against such experiences.

Another important part of the preparation focuses on the technical aspects of the process. The client is asked to spend the entire session in a reclining position with the eyes closed, focused on the emotional and psychosomatic processes induced by breathing and music, and surrendering to them with full trust and without judgment. In this context, it is recommended to abstain from intentional use of abreactive techniques or any other attempts to change and influence the experience. The general attitude should be similar to certain techniques of Buddhist meditation — simply watching the emerging experiences, registering them, and letting them go.

The preparation includes also discussion of certain important rules of the procedure and the principles of the bodywork, which I have described at some length earlier. When the preparation has covered adequately all the above points, the therapist can schedule the experiential session.

An important requirement and necessary prerequisite for holotropic therapy is the right setting. The room has to be large enough for half of the participants to lie down with enough space around them. It has to be in a location that is sufficiently isolated from disturbing external influences of any kind and, in turn, allows loud noises without limitations. This involves the possibility of using a high volume of music and giving participants the freedom of full vocal expression, if necessary.

The floor has to be padded or covered with mattresses, and a sufficient supply of pillows, cushions, and other soft material should be readily available. It seems to be best to conduct sessions in a semidarkened room or to use eyeshades for experients. Many people find that bright light in the room disturbs them and interferes with their experience. An adequate supply of tissues and buckets or plastic bags for those who might develop nausea and vomit are indispensable items in a room for holotropic therapy.

The clients should come to the session dressed in casual and comfortable clothes. It is important to remove everything that could interfere with breathing, and with the inner process. This includes glasses and contact lenses, artificial dentition, heavy earrings, bracelets, and necklaces, bras, belts, and watches. Holotropic therapy has also important contraindications that should be considered before the individual starts experiential sessions. There exist other conditions that do not constitute contraindications, but require special precautions. These also have to be discussed before this form of self-exploration can begin.

Holotropic therapy can involve dramatic experiences accompanied by strong emotional and physical stress. It is mandatory to screen out all individuals with serious cardiovascular problems, for whom this situation could be dangerous. These include persons with a history of heart attacks, cardiosurgery, cerebral hemorrhage, malignant hypertension, advanced atherosclerosis, or arterial aneurysma. For the same reason, it could be precarious to conduct sessions with individuals a short time after operations or injuries, whose surgical wounds have not yet adequately healed.

Another important contraindication is pregnancy, particularly if it is in more advanced stages. The placenta is one of the areas of the body where hyperventilation causes vasoconstriction; this results in reduced blood supply to the fetus. In addition, women reliving their birth in psychedelic sessions or in holotropic therapy frequently experience simultaneous powerful contractions of the uterus and a convincing sense of delivering. As a result of this, they can oscillate between determined pushing with their heads first, like a fetus, and using the abdominal press with their legs in a gynecological position, like a delivering mother. We have seen repeatedly in our workshops women who started their menstrual periods in the middle of the cycle as a result of powerful holotropic sessions of this kind. The limited blood supply in combination with intense uterine contractions could endanger the pregnancy and lead to a miscarriage.

A condition that belongs to relative contraindications is epilepsy. In medicine, hyperventilation is used to augment the epileptic brain waves for diagnostic purposes. Theoretically, fast breathing could thus trigger a seizure in a person with epileptic history. We have had in our workshops over the years six persons suffering from epilepsy and all of them decided to do the breathing, since the danger is minimal for a person in a reclining position, if the sitter protects the tongue in the case of seizure.

The most important danger associated with epilepsy is the risk of accidents that happen when the seizure occurs in a person who is swimming, driving, or is in an unprotected high place. In most instances, the consequences of the seizure are more dangerous than the seizure itself. In a person lying on a soft mattress the risks would be minimal, if the tongue were safeguarded by a towel. However, none of the six epileptic persons in our seminars experienced a seizure during the breathing sessions. Several of them reported that the experience led to a substantial reduction of their organismic tension. They talked about the possibility that this process could actually function as a preventive measure by keeping the tension below the level that is necessary for an explosive epileptic discharge. However, the history of epilepsy requires caution, mainly because of another possible — if unlikely — complication, called *status epilepticus*. This is an uninterrupted sequence of seizures that is serious and might be difficult to stop without expert medical intervention and a well-equipped pharmacy.

The remaining conditions that represent contraindications or require special precautions are obvious even without deep medical knowledge; they can be easily understood by common sense. Participation in the sessions poses emotional and physical demands on the organism. Persons weakened and exhausted by serious diseases of any kind should be, therefore, excluded from participation. Infectious diseases deserve a special notice in this context, since coughing, spitting, and vomiting, which are common in experiential work, are among the most common means of transfer of bacteria and could represent a real risk for the sitters.

Many individuals get involved during the breathing sessions in intense body movements, sometimes with extreme excursions. Thus, special caution is required with persons who suffer from such conditions as habitual dislocation of knees or shoulders or pathological fragility of bones, where this situation could lead to injuries or complications. If the problem is not sufficiently serious to exclude the person from participation, the sitter should know the problem and protect the client from movements or positions that are risky.

As far as emotional contraindications are concerned, a history of serious psychopathology and psychiatric hospitalization requires special considerations. Holotropic therapy can be very effective in persons with deep emotional problems, including certain psychotic states. From a practical point of view, there are two important elements to consider — the intensity of the symptoms and the ego strength. Dramatic emotional and psychosomatic symptoms indicate that important unconscious material with strong emotional charge is close to the surface. That in itself does not mean a difficult prognosis for holotropic therapy. On the contrary, we have seen many instances where in such cases remarkable results could be achieved in a few holotropic sessions. This happened in individuals with severe isolated psychotraumas and relatively stable personalities.

A more important factor in regard to prognosis is the ego strength. Experiential work is generally more difficult and lasts longer in clients who do not have sufficient grounding in consensus reality, show an unstable and precarious personality structure, and find it difficult to maintain clear boundaries between their inner process and the external world. This situation reflects lack of nourishing symbiotic contact ("good breast" and "good womb") in the early history. Here the expressive and uncovering work on emotional traumas has to be supplemented with systematic use of nourishing body contact in a regressed state. This seems to be the only way to fill the emotional vacuum created by early deprivation. Gradually, the nourishing experiences of this kind become internalized and constitute the client's source of inner strength and stability.

Such experiential work with severely disturbed individuals requires a special residential facility with trained staff where continuous support is available for twenty-four hours a day; it should not be conducted on an outpatient basis. Individuals with less extreme emotional difficulties, such as psychoneuroses and psychosomatic disorders, can participate in regular individual or group sessions of holotropic therapy supervised by experienced facilitators. Here it is of special importance to reach the best possible completion and integration of each session by doing systematic body work in the termination period. Supportive physical contact might also be strongly indicated in some instances.

Holotropic work is an expressive form of therapy and is incompatible with tranquilizing medication that suppresses emotions. It would not make sense to conduct holotropic sessions with individuals who are on major tranquilizers. Sudden discontinuation of tranquilizing medication can lead to a dramatic upsurge of the suppressed unconscious material; it should not be attempted outside of a residential treatment center.

It seems useful to start the session of holotropic therapy with a brief period of meditation and relaxation. We usually ask the clients to assume a position with the legs and arms somewhat apart and palms facing the ceiling. This is a physical expression of the basic attitude with which one should approach the experience — that of openness, receptivity, and acceptance. Crossing of legs and arms usually expresses resistance or reservation. If the client has a technique of relaxation that has proved effective in the past, it is possible just to allow him or her a short period of time to use it.

Another possibility is for the facilitator to guide the relaxation by mentioning successively different parts of the body, beginning with the feet and moving gradually upward through the calves, thighs, buttocks, the abdominal muscles, small of the back, the long muscles of the back, chest, shoulders, arms and hands, the throat and neck, jaws and facial muscles, to the forehead and finally to the scalp. During this procedure, the client attempts to relax the individual parts of the body as they are being mentioned. The areas that are reasonably relaxed usually do not present any problem and can be influenced directly. In the areas where the individual experiences intense muscular tension, this might not be possible. In that case it can be useful to first exaggerate the tension, hold it for a while, and then let go.

For some individuals it can be very effective to use guided imagery involving the elements of the ocean, waves, aquatic life forms, such as jellyfish or kelp, or beautiful scenery associated with pleasant memories of leisure and satisfaction. According to our experience, each facilitator using holotropic therapy develops his or her own favorite sequence of instructions to introduce the client into the experience and might even use specific modifications and variations adjusted to the personalities of the clients. When the sessions are repeated, this introductory period can be shortened as the client is becoming more experienced.

When the body is as relaxed as it can be under the circumstances, the next task is to quiet the mind and generate an attitude that is optimal for the experience. At this stage, we suggest that the clients bring their awareness and attention as much as possible to the present moment and present location — to the "here and now". They should try to leave behind all the memories of the past — what happened in their previous self-exploration with other techniques or in preceding sessions of holotropic therapy, what they heard about the procedure from other people, what happened to them earlier that day or in the more remote past, and even what they were told during the preparation, with the exception of the specific instructions for the session.

In a similar way, they should give up thinking about the future and, particularly, let go of any programs involving the session itself. We specifically discourage people from coming into the session with concrete ideas as to what issues they would like to work on, what the experience should be like, what they would like to experience, or what they would like to avoid. The nature of holotropic therapy, and also of psychedelic therapy, is such that the process itself automatically selects in each session the material that is most emotionally relevant at the time. From a broader perspective, it also determines in a series of consecutive sessions the sequence of themes and issues that is optimal for healing. By far the best strategy is to suspend the analytical process ("turn off the head") and to surrender with full trust to the wisdom of the body and of the unconscious and superconscious processes.

A parallel procedure should occur at this time in the sitter (or sitters, if this is a group session). Like the client, the sitter should clear his or her mind from involvement with the past and from fantasies about the future. It is important to have absolutely no expectations or plans for the session. The best attitude seems to be deep human concern for the client, interest in the process, and trust in the wisdom and spontaneous healing potential of the psyche, combined with a certain degree of detachment. This is a safeguard that the facilitator does not get excessively personally drawn into the process by too much emotional investment in the outcome or through idiosyncratic resonance with the content of the session.

To work systematically as a facilitator in holotropic therapy requires not only sufficient personal experience during training, but continuous awareness of one's own process and additional personal work whenever necessary. The nature of the emotional response to different aspects of the process of the clients is the best barometer indicating which areas of one's own psyche require more attention and experiential work.

It is important to realize that holotropic work is completely open-ended. It is best to think about it as an ongoing research project and psychological experiment. The model of the psyche used in academic psychotherapy is based on the assumption that one can acquire comprehensive knowledge of the psychological processes applicable to all individual patients one works with. The theory of holotropic therapy is very explicitly open to and prepared for surprises. During daily therapeutic work, phenomena and problems can emerge that the facilitator has not seen, experienced, or read about before, and possibly some that are absolutely new and that nobody has seen and described before. The training of the facilitator never should be considered a fait accompli. Holotropic therapy is a process of continuous learning, rather than mechanical application of a closed system of concepts and rules.

The final part of the introduction, after the physical relaxation and mental preparation, involves specific suggestions for the experiential process. The clients are now asked to focus on the breathing and get in touch with its natural rhythm, first without trying to change it. It can be useful at this point to actually visualize the breath as a cloud of light and follow it in the mind's eye all the way down to the pelvis, legs, and feet, and back again. One can imagine that as it travels down and up the body, it is creating a sense of open space and is filling every cell of the body with light.

Then the suggestion is given to increase the frequency of the breathing rhythm and to make the breath fuller and more effective than usual. The specifics of the process, such as the rate and depth of breathing, the use of the nostrils or the mouth as respiratory pathways, as well as the engagement of the upper parts of the lungs or the diaphragmatic area and the abdomen, are left up to the client's organismic intuition. When the breathing rhythm has been sufficiently increased, the facilitator prepares the client for the beginning of the music, encouraging him or her to surrender to the flow of the music, to the breathing rhythm, and to any experiences that might emerge, without analyzing them or attempting to change them, and with full trust in the process.

Ideally, a holotropic session requires only minimal intervention from the sitters. Their main role is to observe the process and make sure that the experiencers maintain a breathing rhythm that is faster and more effective than usual. The rate of breathing, its depth and style, vary from individual to individual and from session to session. The facilitator and client (or the partners in group sessions) should have a "contract" as to the degree and nature of the intervention. This is particularly important in initial sessions, before the subject becomes familiar with the experience and develops his or her own style. Some newcomers want to explore as deeply as possible what this technique has to offer. They ask the sitters to watch their breathing closely, make sure it is adequate, and not to let them get away with anything. Others just want to get a "warm-up," explore the possibilities of the technique at their own pace, and ease their way into the process. Some persons do not want to be touched, or ask the sitter not to interfere at all. Requests of this kind should be respected.

Occasionally, it happens that an experiencer forgets to hyperventilate, or gets drawn into the experience and withholds the breath. If the facilitator wants to remind the client that the breathing should be more effective, this should be done nonverbally, by gentle touch on the shoulder, chest, or belly. Talking is generally discouraged during the sessions, with the exception of occasional words or simple sentences. The emphasis in holotropic therapy is on deep emotional and psychosomatic experience. Cognition, conceptualization, and verbal exchange seriously interfere with the depth and the flow of the process. Thus, all the talking is done during the preparation period before the first breathing session and in the sharing sessions following each of the holotropic experiences.

In most instances, the breathing experience follows an orgastic curve, with a build-up of emotions and physical manifestations, culmination, and more or less sudden resolution. When the clients reach this turning point, the facilitators should not intervene at all and should let them choose their own rhythm. At this time, the breathing can actually be extremely slow — two to three breaths a minute. Occasionally, the client can enter even earlier in the session an experiential realm that is incompatible with forced or fast breathing, such as identification with an embryo or a fish. In such situations, the sitter should not insist on hyperventilation. In any case, the interventions should be gentle reminders and not urgent demands. Once the sitter is clear that the message has been received, it should be up to the experient to decide what to do with it.

The other situations where interventions might be necessary during the breathing (pneumocathartic) part of the session have been already discussed (p. 194). They include abreactive work on respiratory blockages, reduction of excessive intensity of emotions or physical manifestations, and situations where the client poses management problems. Otherwise, the work of the sitters during much of the session is support, protection, and caring. This includes supplying pillows to buffer kicking or pounding, preventing people from moving into each other's space and separating them if they get dangerously close, providing plastic bags or buckets in case of nausea and vomiting, and bringing tissues or a glass of water if necessary. In the termination period of the sessions, the role of the sitter becomes more active, if there are any residual problems. The technique of focused bodywork used at this time has already been described earlier. Providing emotional and physical support for the experiencer and offering an opportunity for verbal sharing are also important functions of the sitter.

The therapeutic outcome of the sessions is frequently indirectly proportionate to the amount of external intervention. Some of the most productive experiences are those where the client did everything himself or herself. Many traditional psychotherapeutic methods see the therapist as the active agent who uses specific techniques to change the psyche of the client in a certain direction, predicated by the theory of a particular school. Individuals who have been trained in such traditions might find it difficult to function as facilitators in holotropic therapy, where much emphasis is put on the spontaneous healing potential of the psyche.

We like to combine the holotropic work with *mandala drawing* as it was developed by Joan Kellogg, a psychologist and art therapist who participated in the project of psychedelic therapy at the Maryland Psychiatric Research Center (Kellogg 1977). Although perhaps of limited value as an independent therapeutic tool, it is extremely useful when combined with various experiential approaches. The procedure is very simple: the subject is given a set of crayons or magic markers and a large piece of paper with the outlines of a circle, and is asked to fill the circle in any way that seems appropriate. It can be just a combination of colors, an abstract composition of geometrical patterns, or a more-or-less complex figurative drawing.

The resulting mandala can be subjected to formal analysis according to the criteria developed by Joan Kellogg on the basis of her work with large groups of psychiatric patients and LSD subjects. However, it can also be used as a unique device documenting unusual experiences and helping in their integration. When used in groups, it contributes an important graphic dimension to the understanding of unusual experiences of others and facilitates sharing. In addition, certain mandalas render themselves to further experiential work with the use of Gestalt practice, expressive dancing, or other techniques. In our four-week workshops at the Esalen Institute, it has become very popular among participants to keep a "mandala log", in which the process of self-exploration is documented on a continuous basis in daily mandala drawings.

After the general discussion of the principles and techniques of holotropic therapy, I would like to illustrate this procedure by an account of a 45-year-old woman who participated in one of our five-day workshops at Esalen. In addition to the two sessions of holotropic breathing that we usually offer in the context of our five-day seminars, she also participated in a third one (number two) that was being conducted for the Esalen community by people who have trained with us. The entire process that she describes thus happened in less than a week.

> I arrived at the Grof workshop with little preconception about what it would be like. I had read nothing about the method other than the brief paragraph in the Esalen catalogue. I have never taken any psychedelic drugs, nor have I even been drunk. One of the main

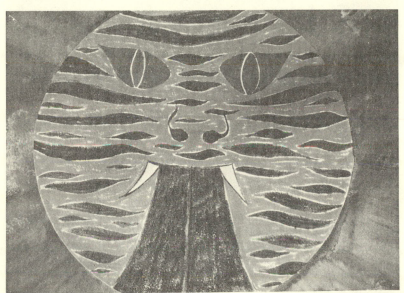

Figure 20 Examples of mandalas illustrating experiences during holotropic breathing. The content of the session and the symbolism of the mandalas reflected Tantric motifs related to Kali and Shiva.

a

b

Figure 21   Paintings by the artist Ann Williams inspired by holotropic breathing.

c   d

e

issues in my life has been an intense need to be in control — of myself, others, situations, everything! The idea of letting go of this control was very frightening. I came to the workshop feeling angry, tense, and confused about how to live my life; I merely thought that this "technique" might be a way to release some of that tension in a safe place.

My first experience of the Grof Breathing was as a sitter for Peter. He had a fairly quiet session, so I spent much time observing what was going on in the rest of the room. Ruth, in particular, impressed me. She did much writhing, moaning, and struggling. Several people held her to protect her from hitting the wall. It was very scary and yet exhilarating to watch. It looked as if she would never be able to return to sanity, yet she sat up at the end looking ten years younger — just glowing from somewhere inside. Seeing her gave me lots of permission to let go on the following day.

First Breathing Session

When it was my turn, we first went through a process of relaxing our bodies and then began breathing more deeply and rapidly. The music poured around us. Within perhaps ten minutes, my hands and feet were cramping up. For the next ten or fifteen minutes, my mind fought for control. Feelings of panic, loss, loneliness, "going under" engulfed me. An image came. The day before, I had seen a small black water bird searching for food along the shore below the Esalen hot baths. As each big wave came, the bird would calmly dive deeper under the turbulence. When the wave had passed, he popped to the surface again.

I held to the image that I was like that water bird; that the only safety for me lay in diving deeper. I kept going, releasing hold on ordinary identity, letting go of thinking, fears, ideas, members of my family, other supports. Near the end of this entry phase, I called out silently: "Here I come, Mother!", meaning not my human mother, but the great ocean crashing below. After some twenty to twenty-five minutes (as I judged it later), I was fully into the process. Whatever my body seemed to want to do, I let it do it.

My head began to turn rhythmically from side to side on the mattress. My legs pulled up until the heels touched my buttocks. One arm began to rise and fall, with my fist pounding the mattress. I had no pictures, emotions, or psychedelic colors, just a deeply felt need for this rhythmic movement. Soon both my feet were lifting and beating down, one after the other, in a marching or tribal dancing manner. An image came of being a dancer in a ceremony in an African village.

My arms and fists joined in the movement of my legs. An impulse came to let out a sound. I threw my head back and almost howled.

The sound went up and up, higher than I remember my voice ever sounding before. I felt like an opera singer "stuck" on a long high note. Then my voice, at fullest volume, began to come into rhythm with my body. I felt I was a native American Indian, chanting a tribal song. Repeated images of the Esalen/Big Sur headlands looking south along the ocean came to me. (The name Esalen is the name of a group of American Indians who inhabited the area around the Esalen Institute. The present premises of the institute were their sacred burial grounds and the hot springs were a healing place.)

This chanting/dancing kept up for about an hour at full steam, with a few rest periods and renewed breathing in between. At the end, I had rested for about twenty minutes when Stan came over and asked if I had any residual tensions in my body. I replied that my neck was still tense. He pressed on my neck and asked me to express whatever I felt. Although I had not hyperventilated for some time and felt "back to normal," I was instantly able to begin chanting and dancing again for several minutes. Later, I felt drained of excess energy and really relaxed for the first time in years.

Second Breathing Session

In my second breathing session, I was fully in the experience within about ten minutes. I began tossing my head from side to side and went into the same rhythmic movements as the day before. These quickly escalated into a full-on "tantrum". I thrashed around on the mattress, pounding it in great anger and yelling loudly. James, Paul, and Tara held my arms, legs, and shoulders tightly. I was totally panic-stricken. Images of being a child trapped in a too-tight place came to me. I felt I would have to tell them to stop — the terror was too much to bear.

Suddenly, I remembered Pia's courage during the session when I had been a sitter. Four people had held her down as she thrashed, off and on, for nearly two hours. I stayed with my fear and my tantrum until the need to struggle left me, and I relaxed into calmness. After a bit, I resumed the deep breathing. This time I lay on my stomach and pushed as hard as I could against the pillow and the wall. Tara held my feet, so that I could push against her hands. I pushed and strained and yelled. Images of struggling to get out of the womb, out of the crib, out of a cage, out of my confining life situation came to me. After maybe twenty minutes, I was quiet again.

I resumed deep breathing and my legs drew up into a "missionary intercourse" position. I felt that I was being raped simultaneously by my father, my husband, and the steeple of the Christian Science Church in Boston! I yelled and protested several minutes while this continued. Then the image came of having my mouth crammed with pages of Christian Science literature. I was being forced to swallow a whole worldview that denied my body, my sexuality, myself. An alien universe filled me, teaching me that I was no good. I began a ritualistic "throwing up," using my hands to motion bringing up the bile from my whole body, up through my throat and then out — with all the guttural sounds of vomiting.

I became more and more frantic, efforting, panting, willing myself to throw up. This lasted for nearly an hour. I felt that if I did not throw up, I would carry that bile, that foreign universe, out of the room and would have it with me for the rest of my life! I thought of my daughter. If I do not get rid of that stuff, she would be trapped too, stuck with the same universe that poisoned my grandmother, my father, my husband, and me. The "sins of the fathers" would be vested upon her. I kept telling her I was doing it for her and that I would stay with it forever, if necessary. And then the strong need to control the experience by vomiting left me. I rested quietly, releasing my daughter to the care of the universe.

As I lay there, an image filled me. I was dancing and running joyfully around the empty Mother Church in Boston with Mary Baker Eddy. I caught up with her in the Mother's Room. We had playful sex together, then ran up to the second balcony on the left side of the church. One by one, all the important people in my life joined us there. I recognized my Christian Science teacher, my parents, my husband, my daughter, my closest friend, my sister, my therapist, Ram Dass, Muktananda, Jesus . . . They all looked at me beatifically and said: "It is all O.K.; we were just kidding, we were just playing roles. It is all O.K." As I came up, I was holding Paul's hand on my right and Tara's hand on my left. James was gently stroking my face. I told them what a joke it all was, and thanked them for helping me find God again. I said, I had never felt so connected, after feeling so alone in my life.

Third Breathing Session

At the beginning of my third breathing session, I was still anxious as I waited for the process to begin, although I had done it twice before. I joked about feeling like an astronaut waiting for blast-off, wondering if the rockets will fire and where the destination will be. Within minutes, I was "under." A very clear image came. It was my daughter's face, minutes after her birth. She looked at me from the glass bassinet they put next to me as I lay on the delivery table. I was totally overwhelmed with love for her. All the locked-in emotion flooded out of me and I began to weep heavily. I realized for the first time in my life how much I love my child.

And then the image changed. I saw her skeleton lying there in the bassinet and then immediately afterward her body again, but this time with my mother's face looking at me. I wept harder. All the love

I have never allowed myself to feel for my mother poured through me. I hugged my arms around myself, curled into a tight fetal position, and wailed. Deep sadness filled me. I cried for all the love I had been unable to feel for her. Her face faded out and I saw her mother's face. I wept for my grandmother, for the sorrows of her life. Then I saw us deep in an underground cave. My grandmother's skeleton was on the bottom, cradling my mother's skeleton, which in turn cradled my skeleton, while I held my daughter's skeleton. I wailed some more.

For the next hour or so, I continued to mourn and rock all the important women in my life, crying for the losses, the missed chances to love, the partings, the confusion, the separations. Finally, I took my husband (at the age of three) in my arms and wept for him — for the loss of his mother, the loss of his childhood, the lack of tenderness in his life. And then, the scene shifted, and I was watching children being torn from their mothers in a concentration camp. I wept and wailed and rocked them. Then I was holding the skeletal, bloated body of a starving Ethiopian child and wailing at the mother's grief. Following this, I was in the South, holding a black mother whose son was shot by the police and lay dying in the gutter, while the police restrained her from cradling him. I felt as if I were weeping for the entire world.

After some calm, I went back down and found myself comforting and stroking all the anguished ones — the man in Atlanta accused of eleven sexual murders of young boys, other rapists and murderers, everyone I could remember hurting me or others. I was singing and crooning softly a childhood hymn: "Shepherd, Show Me How To Go." The others in my group were yelling and thrashing around in the room, while I crooned my lullaby over and over again. More deep breathing and I had an experience of being out in the universe looking back at the world. I heard the sounds of the Balinese Monkey Chant; it seemed loud and violent, like anticraft fire! Pow, pow! I saw the Civil War going on, the Spanish Armada, people of South America and Africa fighting, First World War, Second World War, Vietnam . . . all at once. Fighting was going on over the whole globe as time was eclipsed. And through all this, a small and quiet strand of comforting music — my lullaby for the world.

As I lay there afterwards, I became aware of the others in the room who were still writhing and moaning. I felt such compassion for them, as though the fullest floods of the energies of the universal Mother were flowing through me. My femininity was unblocked and loosened for the first time; I had touched the power of the female nature! The tears were pouring down my face. I stayed in a meditative state and had some more strong visual images, including a very powerful one of brilliant clouds parting in the sky and revealing an incandescent giant eagle. Her feathers were dazzling white, soft, and strong. I was caught up to this eagle and held lovingly against her breast.

Two hours after this session, our group gathered again to share our experiences. As I looked around, the tenderness and compassion flooded me again and I felt deeply connected to everyone present. I had this powerful feeling that I had flown thousands of miles to be with me! That all the "me's" I was ready to be with had gathered together to be with me. I felt strongly that I could never be lonely again; I was surrounded by me.

I would like to conclude this report by a passage from a letter which we received a year after the Esalen seminar as a response to our request for a follow-up evaluation of the effects of the above experiences:

You asked about any lasting effects I have had from the breathing workshop. It has been just about a year since that time, so I feel that what is with me now is indeed lasting. Perhaps the most satisfying and amazing result is that I have truly and totally accepted the place where I live as my home — after some sixteen years of struggling with a strong desire to leave here! I mentioned in my earlier comments about the workshop that I had suddenly realized that I had flown thousands of miles to be with myself. At that moment, high on the cliffs of Esalen, I began living at home. That realization of home has been with me without a moment of wavering for this whole year since then. All who know me have been amazed.

In addition, there have been some other very substantial changes in my life, which I feel are directly the result of the workshop. After many years of talking, thinking, and reading about spirituality, I actually experienced during the workshop what seemed to me a very spiritual state. This spiritual experiencing has continued to pervade my life. The "issues" continue to come up — work, family, marriage, purpose, and so forth — but there is an increasing tendency to go deeply within myself, and to let these issues heal up from within, rather than trying to control or manipulate external circumstances.

I have been meditating each day for a couple of months now. This just seems like a good path for me. I am not using a particular teacher or spiritual discipline. This is just a time of focusing, of coming into the present moment. The result has been an increasing sense of calmness and quiet joy. I am noticing more love flowing out of me, something that has definitely been blocked throughout my life. I have always longed to share, yet the sharing has too often degenerated into domination and control, with ego getting in the way of Self! I am feeling freer now, and the love is flowing more freely. A number of people have come to me for help and support of various kinds — a spontaneous recognition from "outside" of the progress within.

Effective Mechanisms of Healing and Personality Transformation

THE extraordinary and often dramatic effect of psychedelic and holotropic therapy on various emotional and psychosomatic disorders naturally raises the question about the mechanisms involved in these changes. In the context of the traditional systems of psychotherapy based on psychoanalysis, lasting changes of the deeper psychodynamic structures underlying psychopathological symptoms require years of systematic work. Psychiatrists and psychotherapists, therefore, tend to disbelieve that profound and lasting changes of personality can occur within a matter of days or even hours, since the current theories do not have explanatory frameworks for such a possibility.

Descriptions of dramatic healing in the context of shamanic procedures, aboriginal healing ceremonies, meetings of ecstatic sects, or trance dancing have not been taken seriously by most Western scholars, or have been attributed to the influence of suggestion in superstitious natives. Occasional dramatic changes in the personality structure known as conversions are usually seen as too capricious and unpredictable to be of interest from a therapeutic point of view. However, it is an undeniable fact that religious, ethical, sexual, political, and other types of conversions can have profound and often lasting influence on the individual involved. Their impact is not limited to beliefs, attitudes, systems of value, and life strategies, but often includes emotional and psychosomatic healing, changes in interpersonal adjustment, and disappearance of such deeply ingrained behavior patterns as alcoholism or drug abuse.

I would like to mention in this context the most dramatic and extreme example of the healing and transformative potential of non-ordinary states of consciousness — the changes observed in many individuals who have come close to death. David Rosen, a psychiatrist from the Bay Area, has interviewed eleven survivors of suicidal jumps off the Golden Gate Bridge and the San Francisco-Oakland Bay Bridge (Rosen 1973). He reconstructed their life situation and psychosomatic condition before the attempt, explored their motivation for suicide, discussed the experience during the fall and the rescue operations, and studied thoroughly the resulting changes of personality and life style.

Rosen found profound changes in all the survivors. These involved striking emotional and psychosomatic improvement, active enjoyment of life, and discovery of the spiritual dimension of existence, or validation of previous religious beliefs. The experiences that had led to these changes involved the fall and a stay of up to ten minutes in cold water, which is the time period during which the survivors had to be rescued. If help is not available within that time, the currents will carry the person to the open ocean, which means certain death. Since the few minutes in cold water do not have such profound transformative effect (this was more than sufficiently tested and proved in the pre-tranquilizer era of institutional psychiatry), the findings have to be clearly related to the experience during the fall.

Using simple mathematical formulas of elementary physics, one can compute that the fall from the railing of the bridge to the surface of the bay lasts only about three seconds of clocktime. The results cannot be easily attributed to a physical shock effect; in spite of the fact that the general mortality of these jumps is about 99%, most of Rosen's survivors emerged from the situation virtually unscathed. A compelling inner experience lasting only three seconds thus produced results that years of Freudian analysis could not possibly match. However, it is important to realize that the subjective experience of time is radically changed in nonordinary states of consciousness. Within seconds of clocktime, one can experience a rich and complex sequence of events that lasts subjectively a very long time, or even seems to involve eternity.

In his recent book, *Heading Toward Omega*, thanatologist Kenneth Ring came to a similar conclusion. He dedicated a special section of this volume to the study of the long-term effects of near-death experiences (Ring 1984). These included an increase in self-esteem and self-confidence, appreciation of life and nature, concern and love for fellow humans, a distinct decrease of emphasis on personal status and material possessions, and development of universal spirituality transcending the divisive interests of religious sectarianism. These changes were remarkably similar to those, described by Abraham Maslow following spontaneous "peak experiences" (Maslow 1962, 1964).

The ancient history of psychiatry offers many examples of attempts to utilize powerful experiences for healing. One of the techniques used in ancient India was the simulated charge by a trained elephant who stopped just before hitting the patient. In some instances, the disturbed individual was placed in a pit full of cobras with extracted fangs. Other times, a surprise fall into water was arranged when the patient was crossing a bridge with a special falltrap mechanism. For important individuals, an entire fake trial was conducted that included death sentence and execution procedures with a last minute pardon from the king (Hanzlíček 1961). Discussing these observations, I am naturally not advocating exposure to real or simulated life-threatening situations as a therapeutic strategy for modern psychiatry. However, I am trying to illustrate that there exist mechanisms in the psyche, the therapeutic and transformative power of which transcends anything the current theories of psychotherapy can conceive of.

Psychedelic and holotropic therapy make it possible to utilize the healing and transforming potential of powerful experiences without the risk involved in actual biological crises, or the complex deceptive ploys associated with the situations described above. The unconscious dynamics stimulated by appropriate unspecific techniques will produce spontaneously powerful sequences of confrontation with death. These have comparable healing power as the above externally determined situations. However, before approaches of this kind can be accepted by academic psychiatry, it is important to clarify the mechanisms involved in such dramatic changes and present them in the context of a comprehensive theory of personality. Only the more superficial experiences and the changes following them can be interpreted in the context of traditional psychiatric thinking. Most of them require not only substantial revisions of the conceptual frameworks of psychiatry and psychology, but also a new scientific worldview, or paradigm.

Intensification of Conventional
Therapeutic Mechanisms

Some of the therapeutic changes occurring in psychedelic and holotropic sessions can be explained in terms of the mechanisms described in traditional psychotherapy. However, even in relatively superficial nonordinary states of consciousness, these mechanisms are greatly intensified in comparison with the verbal procedures. In more profound holotropic states, one typically encounters many mechanisms of therapeutic change that are entirely new and have not yet been discovered and acknowledged by traditional psychiatry.

Nonordinary states of consciousness certainly change dramatically the relationship between the conscious and unconscious dynamics of the psyche. They tend to lower the defenses and decrease psychological resistances. Under these circumstances, one observes typically not only enhanced recall of repressed memories, but also complex reliving of emotionally important events from the past occurring in total age regression. Unconscious material can also appear in the form of various symbolic experiences that have a structure similar to dreams and can be deciphered by the techniques of Freudian dream interpretation. The emergence of these otherwise unavailable contents from the individual unconscious is often associated with rich emotional and intellectual insights into the nature of the client's psychopathological symptoms and distortions of interpersonal relations.

The therapeutic potential of the reliving of emotionally relevant episodes from childhood involves several important elements. Psychopathology seems to draw its dynamic power from deep repositories of pent-up emotional and physical energies. This fact was first described by Freud and Breuer in their studies of hysteria (Freud and Breuer 1936). Freud himself later played down the significance of this factor, and it was up to the famous psychoanalytic renegade Wilhelm Reich to discover the theoretical and practical significance of the bioenergetic dynamics of the organism (Reich 1949, 1961). In psychedelic and holotropic therapy, the release of these energies and their peripheral discharge play a very significant role. Traditionally, such a release is known as abreaction, if it is associated with specific biographical content. Discharge of more generalized emotional and physical tension is usually referred to as catharsis.

Abreaction and catharsis deserve a brief discussion in this context, since their role in psychotherapy has to be significantly reevaluated in view of the observations from both psychedelic and holotropic therapy. The recognition of the healing power of emotional catharsis can be traced back to ancient Greece. Plato gave a vivid description of emotional catharsis in his dialogue *Phaedrus,* while discussing the telestic or ritual madness in the Korybantic mysteries. He saw a remarkable therapeutic potential in wild dancing to flutes and drums that culminated in an explosive paroxysm and resulted in a state of profound relaxation and tranquility (Plato 1961). Being himself allegedly an initiate of the Eleusinian mysteries, he seems to have drawn on personal experience.

Another great Greek philosopher, Plato's disciple, Aristotle, is the author of the first explicit statement that full experience and release of repressed emotions are an effective treatment of mental illness. In agreement with the basic thesis of the members of the Orphic cult, Aristotle believed that the chaos and frenzy of the mysteries were eventually conducive to order. According to him, initiates experienced through the use of wine, aphrodisiacs, and music extraordinary arousal of passions followed by a healing catharsis (Croissant 1932).

The mechanism of abreaction was described by Freud and Breuer and played an extremely important role in Freud's early speculations about the origin and therapy of psychoneurosis, particularly hysteria. In his original model, the future neurotic had experienced in childhood traumatic situations under circumstances that did not allow adequate peripheral discharge of the emotional energy generated by this trauma. This resulted in repositories of pent-up emotions or "jammed affects." The goal of therapy then was to bring the repressed memory into consciousness in a safe situation, facilitating belated discharge of this affect.

Freud later abandoned this concept in favor of other mechanisms, particularly analysis of transference. Under his influence, traditional psychotherapy does not see abreaction as a mechanism capable of inducing permanent therapeutic changes. However, there has been general agreement that abreactive techniques are a method of choice in dealing with emotional difficulties due to a single massive psychotrauma, such as war neuroses or other types of emotional traumatic disorders.

In view of the observations from psychedelic and holotropic

therapy, Freud made a mistake when he eliminated abreaction from psychoanalysis and focused his attention on more subtle and superficial mechanisms and techniques. Exclusively verbal approaches are clearly inadequate to deal with the bioenergetic situation underlying psychopathology. The reason why abreaction did not bring lasting therapeutic changes was that in most cases it was not deep and radical enough.

For abreaction to be fully effective, the therapist has to encourage its full development. This frequently leads far beyond biographical traumas of a psychological nature to memories of life-threatening physical events (childhood pneumonia, diphtheria, operations, injuries, or near drowning), various aspects of biological birth, and even into past life experiences and other phenomena from the transpersonal domain.

It can take very dramatic forms and lead to temporary loss of control, projectile vomiting, high level of choking, momentary lapse of consciousness (blacking-out), and other dramatic manifestations. This seems to explain why abreaction has been effective in treating traumatic emotional neuroses where the therapist was prepared to deal with reliving of a life-threatening situation. A therapist who is not ready, emotionally or conceptually, to face the full spectrum of the abreactive phenomena described above will allow only abortive and truncated forms and levels of abreaction that do not bring permanent results.

Although abreaction has a significant role in holotropic therapy, it is just one of many effective mechanisms that contribute to the therapeutic changes. Even on the level of biographical traumas, important additional factors exist. An individual who is experiencing full regression to the time in childhood when a certain trauma took place literally becomes again an infant or a child. This includes a corresponding body image, primitive emotions, and a naive perception and understanding of the world. At the same time, he or she also has access to the mature conceptual world of the adult. This situation makes it possible to integrate traumatic events by releasing their energetic charge, becoming fully aware of them, and evaluating them from an adult point of view. This is particularly important in those situations where conceptual immaturity or confusion was an important element in the trauma. Factors of this kind were described most clearly in Gregory Bateson's "double-bind" theory (Bateson 1972) and more recently in the work of Alice Miller (Miller 1985).

An interesting question in relation to reliving of childhood traumas is why reliving of a painful situation from the past should be therapeutic, or even why it should not be traumatic rather than healing. The usual answer is that the adult person is capable of facing and integrating experiences that he or she could not deal with as a child. In addition, the supportive and trusting context of the therapeutic situation is quite different from the original traumatic circumstances. This might be an adequate explanation for some relatively subtle psychological traumas. However, in the case of major traumas, particularly situations threatening survival and body integrity of the individual, an additional important mechanism seems to be involved.

It is very likely that in situations of this kind, the original traumatic event was not really fully experienced at the time when it was happening. A massive psychological shock can lead in certain persons to loss of consciousness and swooning. It is conceivable that somewhat less dramatic circumstances can lead to a situation where the experience is shut out partially rather than completely. As a result of it, the event cannot be psychologically "digested" and integrated, and remains in the psyche as a dissociated foreign element. When it then emerges from the unconscious during psychedelic or holotropic therapy, it is not as much reliving of what happened as it is the first full experiencing of this event which makes it possible to complete it and integrate it. The problem of reliving as compared to the first full conscious experience of a traumatic event was discussed in a special paper by the Irish psychiatrist Ivor Browne and his team (McGee et al. 1984).

The last traditional therapeutic mechanism that should be discussed in this context is transference. In psychoanalytically oriented psychotherapy, it is considered essential that the patient develops in the course of analysis a transference neurosis. This consists in projecting on the therapist an entire spectrum of emotional reactions and attitudes originally developed in childhood or even infancy in relation to parental figures or their surrogates. The critical therapeutic mechanism is then analysis of this transference. In psychedelic and holotropic therapy, the potential for developing transference is, in principle, tremendously enhanced. However, it is seen as a complication of the therapeutic process rather than a necessary prerequisite for successful treatment.

Unlike the verbal approaches, deep experiential therapy has the potential to take the client in a very short time to the original traumatic situations and thus to the roots of the problem. It is not unusual that individuals reach, within the first psychedelic or holotropic session, the early oral level of development, relive sequences of their biological birth, or connect with the transpersonal domain. Under these circumstances, the development of transference has to be seen as a manifestation of resistance to facing the original trauma.

In many instances, it is less painful for the client to create an artificial problem in the therapeutic relationship by projecting on it elements of the original trauma than to face the real issue, which is much more devastating. The task of the therapist then is to redirect the attention of the client to the introspective process, which alone carries promise for an effective solution. When the therapeutic work is conducted in this spirit, it becomes more than obvious that transference represents a defensive attempt to avoid an overwhelming problem from the past by creating a less threatening and more manageable pseudoproblem in the present.

Another possible source of transference seems to be a history of severe emotional deprivation in childhood. In this situation, the client tends to seek in the therapeutic process the anaclitic satisfaction which he or she did not experience in childhood. The best solution for this problem is the therapeutic use of physical contact. Although this approach clearly violates the Freudian taboo of touch, it tends to diminish rather than increase the transference problems, and its therapeutic effects are truly remarkable. The issue of physical contact in holotropic sessions was discussed at some length in another context (p. 196).

The potential of psychedelic and holotropic therapy is not limited to intensification of conventional therapeutic mechanisms. The most exciting aspect of these approaches is that they offer access to many additional, powerful, and radical mechanisms of healing and transformation which have not yet been discovered and acknowledged by Western academic psychiatry. In the following text, I will describe and discuss the most important of these new therapeutic possibilities and perspectives.

DYNAMIC SHIFTS IN THE PSYCHE'S GOVERNING SYSTEMS

Many dramatic changes resulting from deep experiential sessions can be explained in terms of dynamic interplay of unconscious constellations that have the function of governing systems. The most important systems of this kind have been described earlier in the context of the new cartography of the psyche. The systems of condensed experience, or the COEX systems, organize important emotional material on the biographical level. The basic perinatal matrices, or BPMs, have a similar function in relation to experiential repositories on the perinatal level. There exists also a rich spectrum of dynamic matrices associated with different types of transpersonal experiences.

During episodes of nonordinary states of consciousness, the dynamic governing systems determine the content of the individual's experience. The system that controls the experience during the termination period of the sessions tends to influence, in a more subtle way, the subject's future experience of him/herself, the perception of the environment, emotional reactions, values and attitudes, and even various psychosomatic functions. According to the nature of the emotional charge, we can distinguish negative governing systems (negative COEX systems, BPM II, BPM III, negative aspects of BPM I, and negative transpersonal matrices) and positive governing systems (positive COEX systems, positive aspects of BPM I, BPM IV, and positive transpersonal matrices).

The general strategy in psychedelic and holotropic sessions is the reduction of the emotional charge of the negative systems, conscious integration of the painful material that emerges, and facilitation of experiential access to positive dynamic constellations. A more specific tactical rule is to structure the termination of each individual session in such a way that the psychological gestalt that was manifested that day is successfully completed and integrated. The manifest clinical condition of the individual is not a global reflection of the overall amount and nature of the unconscious material. It depends much more on specific tuning into a particular dynamic system that accentuates a certain aspect of the psyche and makes it selectively experientially available.

Figure 22 A synoptic painting representing a cluster of birth- and death-related childhood memories that emerged in a holotropic breathing session as the process was approaching the perinatal level.

Figure 23 A painting representing a powerful death-rebirth experience from a holotropic breathing session.

Figure 24 A painting representing a combined experience of being born and giving birth; it involved a simultaneous identification with the mother, the child, and the Great Mother Goddess.

Individuals who are tuned into various levels of negative matrices perceive themselves and the world in a pessimistic way and experience various forms and degrees of emotional and psychosomatic distress. Those persons who are under the influence of positive dynamic systems are in a state of emotional well-being and optimal psychosomatic functioning. The specific qualities of the resulting states depend in both instances on the level of the psyche that is activated, on the type of the dynamic matrix, and on the nature of the unconscious material involved.

An individual who is under the influence of a particular COEX system and, more specifically, under the influence of its specific layer will experience himself and the world in terms of its leading theme and behave in a way that tends to reproduce the original traumatic elements in the present situation. Depending on the material, this can involve parents and other authority figures, peers, sexual partners, various specific situations, and many other elements. The dynamic influence of a COEX system introduces into the life of the individual archaic and anachronistic elements. The role of COEX systems in

Figure 25 A painting from a psychedelic session representing the discovery of a horrifying Shadow aspect of one's own personality in the sense of Dr. Jekyll and Mr. Hyde or The Picture of Dorian Grey (from the collection of Dr. M. Hausner, Prague).

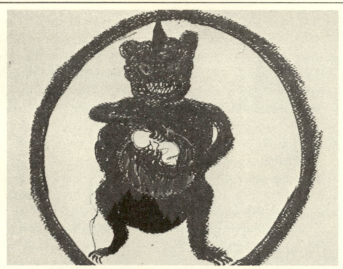

Figure 26 A painting representing the experience of being born and simultaneously tortured by a vicious demonic figure. Mandala from a holotropic session.

Figure 27 A synoptic painting representing the experiences of torture, mutilation and demonic assault alternating with a sense of identification with a demonic entity; they emerged in a holotropic session focusing on the perinatal level of the unconscious.

human life and the mechanisms associated with them have been discussed and illustrated by typical clinical examples in my book *Realms of the Human Unconscious* (Grof 1975).

Under the influence of the positive aspects of BPM I (the amniotic universe), the individual sees the world as incredibly beautiful, radiant, safe, and nourishing. This is associated with a deep awareness of the spiritual and mystical dimension in the universal scheme of things and with a sense of oneness and belonging. The general image of life is that of a divine play to the flow of which one can surrender with full trust. The negative aspects of BPM I introduce the element of psychotic distortion of the world. The dissolution of boundaries is not ecstatic and mystical, but confusing and threatening. The individual feels endangered, under attack by demonic forces, frightened, and often poisoned. In this state, the entire world seems to be full of uncertainty and triggers feelings of panic and paranoia.

The beginning phase of BPM II (cosmic engulfment) is quite similar to the negative aspects of BPM I. This is logical, since the beginning of birth represents a fundamental and irreversible disturbance of the intrauterine state. The only major difference is a sense of mechanical entrapment and claustrophobia that characterizes BPM II, but is missing in BPM I. Under the influence of a fully developed BPM II (no exit or hell), the world is seen as a hopeless place, full of absurd and meaningless suffering, or as a cardboard play of inanimate robots. The individual feels deeply ridden with guilt and identifies with the role of a helpless victim.

The person who is under the influence of BPM III (the death-rebirth struggle) feels under great emotional and physical tension and has, typically, problems with the control of self-destructive and destructive impulses. This can be associated with strong sadistic and/or masochistic fantasies and inclinations, sexual disturbances, and preoccupation with demonic, perverted, and scatological themes. Under the perceptual stencil of BPM III, the world is seen as a dangerous place — an existential battlefield governed by the law of the jungle, where one has to be strong to survive and satisfy one's needs.

The dynamic hegemony of BPM IV (the death-rebirth experience) is characterized — if the biological birth was not confounded by heavy anesthesia or some other severe adverse circumstances — by feelings of physical and spiritual rebirth, rejuvenation, and emotional renewal. The individual feels full of excitement and energy, yet centered and peaceful, and perceives the world as if through cleansed senses. He or she experiences the joy of life and a significant increase in zest in relation to various ordinary aspects of existence — nature, music, food, sex, work, and human relationships.

It is difficult to describe in a synoptic way the influence of the transpersonal matrices, because of the great richness and variety of possibilities involved. The theme dominating an individual's life can be a powerful past incarnation experience, a positive or demonic archetype, an ancestral, racial, or phylogenetic memory, a sense of shamanic connection with nature, loose boundaries toward the domain of extrasensory perception, and many others.

Changes in the governing influence of dynamic matrices can occur as a result of various biochemical and physiological processes inside the organism, or as a reaction to a number of external influences of a psychological or physical nature. Many instances of sudden clinical improvement can be explained as a shift from psychological dominance of a negative dynamic system to a selective influence of a positive constellation. Such a change does not necessarily mean that all the unconscious material underlying the psychopathological state involved has been worked through. It simply indicates an inner dynamic shift from one governing system to another.

This situation can be referred to as transmodulation and can occur on many different levels. A shift from one biographical constellation to another can be called COEX transmodulation. A comparable shift from the dominance of one basic perinatal matrix to another would then be referred to as BPM transmodulation. And, finally, transpersonal transmodulation involves shifts among dynamic systems of transindividual nature. Depending on the emotional quality of the governing systems involved and of the resulting clinical change, we can talk about positive, negative, and substitutive transmodulation.

A typical positive transmodulation has a biphasic course; it involves intensification of the dominant negative system followed by a sudden dynamic shift to the positive one. However, if a strong positive system is easily available, it can dominate the psychedelic or holotropic session from the very beginning; in this case, the negative system recedes into the background. A shift from one dynamic constellation to another does not have to result in clinical improvement. A negative transmodulation involves a shift from a neutral situation, or even from a positive system, to a negative one. This results in the appearance of new clinical symptoms that the individual did not have before.

A particularly interesting dynamic change is substitutive transmodulation, which involves a shift from one negative system to another. The external manifestation of this intrapsychic event is a remarkable qualitative change in psychopathology from one clinical syndrome to another. Occasionally, this transformation can be so dramatic that the client moves to a completely different diagnostic category. Although the resulting condition might appear to be entirely new, careful analysis reveals that all its dynamic elements pre-existed in the psyche before the dynamic shift occurred. A dramatic example of a shift from deep depression to a hysterical paralysis is described in my book *LSD Psychotherapy* (Grof 1980, p. 219). Substitutive shifts from one positive system to another can also occur; however, the differentiation is more difficult. This is due to the fact that the spectrum of negative experiences is much richer and much more variegated than that of the positive ones.

A therapist using psychedelic or holotropic therapy should be familiar with the above mechanisms and be aware of the fact that, in addition to lasting changes resulting from the thorough working-through of unconscious material, these forms of treatment can also involve dramatic dynamic shifts that change its experiential relevance.

THERAPEUTIC POTENTIAL OF THE DEATH-REBIRTH PROCESS

Powerful experiential sequences of dying and being born can result in dramatic alleviation of a variety of emotional, psychosomatic, and interpersonal problems that have previously resisted all psychotherapeutic work focusing on postnatal biographical issues. Negative perinatal matrices are an important repository of emotions and physical sensations of extraordinary intensity. As I have described in another context (Grof 1985), they function as a potential experiential source of many psychopathological syndromes. It is, therefore, not surprising that significant work on the perinatal level of the psyche can influence a broad spectrum of psychiatric problems. In this context, deep experiences of undisturbed intrauterine existence and cosmic unity (BPM I) have a universal healing potential of extraordinary power.

Such crucial symptoms as anxiety, aggression, depression, fear of death, feelings of guilt, sadomasochistic tendencies, general emotional and physical tension, or an inferiority complex seem to have their deep roots in the perinatal domain of the unconscious. Similarly, pathological preoccupation with various physiological functions or biological material, a variety of psychosomatic symptoms, and strange hypochondriacal complaints can often be traced to various aspects of the death-rebirth process. Here belong, for example, ordinary or migraine headaches, muscular spasms and pains in different parts of the body, and various tremors and diskinesias. Among other physical symptoms with clearly perinatal roots are cardiac distress, nausea and vomiting, neurotic feelings of lack of oxygen and suffocation, psychogenic asthma, and menstrual cramps.

Experiential work involving the perinatal matrices is typically necessary to influence significantly inhibited or agitated depression, self-hatred, and self-destructive tendencies. A powerful experience of ego death and rebirth seems to eliminate or greatly reduce suicidal ideation and inclinations. Clients who experience psychological death-rebirth and/or feelings of cosmic unity tend to develop a negative attitude toward the states of mind induced by alcohol and narcotics. This has proved extremely useful in the treatment of alcoholism and drug addiction. William James was well aware that a deep religious conversion is the best therapy for alcoholism, that the "best remedy for dipsomania is religiomania" (James 1961). The importance of deep spiritual experiences for overcoming alcoholism was also well known to Carl Gustav Jung. His famous recipe *"spiritus contra spiritum"* became the philosophical basis for Alcoholics Anonymous (AA), the most successful program for combating this disorder (Jung 1963).

Malignant aggression, impulsive behavior, self-mutilation, and sadomasochistic tendencies also have important roots on the perinatal level. Activation of BPM III typically results in experiences involving scenes of violence, mass destruction, war, and sadomasochistic orgies. Exteriorization of deep destructive and self-destructive potential in the individual is one of the most important aspects of the death-rebirth struggle. In this context, enormous amounts of destructive energy are mobilized and discharged. The result is a dramatic reduction of aggressive feelings and tendencies. The experience of psychological and spiritual rebirth (BPM IV) is typically associated with a sense of love, compassion, and reverence for life.

Perinatal elements also play an important role in the dynamics of various anxiety states and phobias, particularly claustrophobia, thanatophobia, and nosophobia. The same is true for hysterical conversion symptoms and certain aspects of obsessive-compulsive neuroses. Many sexual disorders and deviations are anchored in the perinatal domain of the psyche and can be logically explained from the strong sexual component of BPM III. This is most evident for impotence, inability to reach sexual orgasm, menstrual cramps, and painful vaginal spasms during sexual intercourse (dyspareunia). Indulgence in biological material in a sexual context, such as coprophagia (eating feces), urolagnia (drinking urine), and sadomasochistic inclinations also have significant perinatal determinants. Deep and effective experiential work on these problems always reaches back at least to biological birth.

It should also be mentioned that many nonordinary states of consciousness that traditional psychiatry sees as psychoses, and thus as manifestations of mental diseases of unknown etiology, seem to result from activation of perinatal matrices. Successful completion of the psychological death-rebirth process can lead to dramatic therapeutic results that by far surpass what can be achieved by the present indiscriminate use of suppressive therapy (Grof and Grof, 1986).

THERAPEUTIC MECHANISMS ON THE TRANSPERSONAL LEVEL

Probably the most interesting and challenging observations from experiential therapy are those related to the healing potential of transpersonal experiences. In many instances, specific emotional and psychosomatic symptoms or distortions of interpersonal relations are anchored in dynamic matrices of a transpersonal nature and cannot be resolved on the level of biographical or even perinatal experiences. If that is the case, the individual has to confront dramatic transpersonal experiences in order to solve the problems involved.

In some instances, the roots of difficult emotions or psychosomatic symptoms can be found in various embryonal and fetal experiences. They disappear or are considerably mitigated when the subjects relive various intrauterine traumas related to an imminent miscarriage or attempted abortion, maternal disease or emotional crisis during pregnancy, toxic conditions in the womb, or feelings of being unwanted ("bad" or "rejecting womb"). In this case, therapeutic use of physical contact ("fusion therapy") can be of particular value (McCririck n.d.).

Occasionally, various problems can be traced to specific experiences from the lives of one's ancestors and be resolved by reliving and integrating the ancestral memories. Some individuals identify certain problems as internalized conflicts between the families of their ancestors and resolve them on that level. It is not uncommon to find significant connections to racial or collective memories in the sense of Carl Gustav Jung, or to discover even evolutionary or phylogenetic roots of a difficult issue.

Particularly dramatic instances of therapeutic change that involve the subject's emotional and psychosomatic well-being and many other dimensions of his or her life can be observed in connection with past life experiences. Sometimes these occur simultaneously with various aspects of perinatal experiences, other times as independent experiential gestalts. Problems that are identified as related to a karmic pattern disappear when the traumatic memories involved are fully relived and the subject reaches a sense of forgiving and being forgiven (for example, see the patient of Dennys Kelsey and Joan Grant on p. 244). This is frequently associated with remarkable independent and synchronistic changes in the lives and attitudes of the people the subject denoted as protagonists in the karmic episode.

Other emotional or psychosomatic symptoms have underlying holotropic gestalts that involve various life forms, such as animals on different levels of the Darwinian evolutionary pedigree, or even plants. To resolve a problem of this kind, the individual has to allow full experiential identification with the organism involved (see the cases of Marion and Martha on p. 245). Very frequently, symptoms, attitudes, and behaviors are manifestations of an underlying archetypal pattern. Sometimes, the energy involved has an uncanny quality and is identified as "evil" by the subject and often also by the people witnessing the experience. The condition then resembles strikingly what has been described as "spirit possession" and the therapeutic session can have many characteristics of exorcism, as it has been practiced by the Catholic Church, or of the expulsion of evil spirits in aboriginal cultures (for examples, see the story of Flora on p. 246).

Two transpersonal experiences of an abstract and highly generalized nature deserve special notice in this context. The first one can be described as identification with the Universal Mind, with Cosmic Consciousness, or with the Absolute. The second one is the experience of identification with the Supracosmic and Metacosmic Void. These have an extraordinary therapeutic potential; they involve mechanisms that stand in a metaposition to all the others and cannot be adequately described in words. They can bring spiritual and philosophical understanding of such high level that everything is redefined and appears in a new perspective.

The importance and value of transpersonal experiences is extraordinary. It is a great irony and one of the paradoxes of modern science that phenomena with a therapeutic potential transcending most of what Western psychiatry has to offer are, by and large, seen as pathological, and are indiscriminately treated by suppressive therapy. A therapist who is unwilling to recognize them because of his or her philosophical bias is giving up a therapeutic tool of remarkable power.

HEALING AS A MOVEMENT TOWARD WHOLENESS

As I have described earlier, the therapeutic mechanisms operating in psychedelic and holotropic therapy cover an extremely wide range. As the psyche gets activated and symptoms become converted into a flow of experience, significant therapeutic changes can occur in connection with the reliving of childhood memories, with various aspects and facets of perinatal dynamics, and with many different types of transpersonal phenomena. This raises an interesting question, as to whether all these most variegated experiential events can be reduced to a common denominator. It is clear that the effective mechanism that would account for phenomena of such diversity and happening on so many different levels would have to be extraordinarily general and universal.

The recognition of such a general healing mechanism requires an entirely new understanding of human nature and a radical revision of the Western scientific worldview. The fundamental aspect of this new paradigm for psychology and for science in general is the realization that consciousness is a primary attribute of existence rather than an epiphenomenon of matter. I have discussed, in another context, at some length this new vision of reality emerging independently in a variety of scientific disciplines, such as quantum-relativistic physics, astrophysics, information and systems theory, cybernetics, thermodynamics, biology, anthropology, thanatology, and modern consciousness research (Grof 1985). In this context, I will only briefly summarize its implications for the understanding of psychotherapy and refer the interested reader to the original source.

Modern research clearly indicates that human beings have a strange paradoxical nature. In the contexts traditionally explored by mechanistic science, it seems appropriate to think about people as separate Newtonian objects — complex biological machines made of cells, tissues, and organs. However, recent discoveries confirm the claims of perennial philosophy and the great mystical traditions that humans can also function as infinite fields of consciousness, transcending the limitations of time, space, and linear causality. This image has its subatomic parallel in the famous particle-wave paradox in relation to matter and light described by Niels Bohr's principle of complementarity.

These two complementary aspects of human nature are connected experientially with two different modes of consciousness that were briefly mentioned earlier (p. 38, 39). The first of these can be referred to as *hylotropic consciousness*, which translates as matter-oriented consciousness. The name is derived from the Greek *hylé* = matter and *trepein* = to move toward. It is the state of mind that we experience in everyday life and that Western psychiatry considers as the only one that is normal and legitimate — one that correctly reflects the objective reality of the world.

In the hylotropic mode of consciousness, an individual experiences himself or herself as a solid physical entity with definite boundaries and with a limited sensory range. The world appears to be made of separate material objects and has distinctly Newtonian characteristics: time is linear, space is three-dimensional, and all events seem to be governed by chains of cause and effect. Experiences in this mode support systematically a number of basic assumptions about the world, such as: matter is solid; two objects cannot occupy the same space; past events are irretrievably lost; future events are not experientially available; one cannot be in more than one place at a time; one can exist only in one temporal framework at a time; a whole is larger than a part; or something cannot be true and untrue at the same time.

In contrast to the narrow and restricted hylotropic mode, the *holotropic variety* involves the experience of oneself as a potentially unlimited field of consciousness that has access to all aspects of reality without the mediation of senses. Holotropic literally translates as aiming for totality or moving toward wholeness (from the Greek *holos* = whole and *trepein* = moving in the direction of). Experiences in this state of mind offer many interesting alternatives to the Newtonian world of matter with linear time and three-dimensional space.

They support systematically a set of assumptions which are diametrically different from those characterizing the hylotropic mode: the solidity and discontinuity of matter is an illusion generated by a particular orchestration of events in consciousness; time and space are ultimately arbitrary; the same space can be simultaneously occupied by many objects; the past and the future are always available and can be brought experientially into the present moment; one can experience oneself in several places at the same time; it is possible to experience simultaneously more than one temporal framework; being a part is not incompatible with being the whole; something can be true and untrue at the same time; form and emptiness or existence and nonexistence are interchangeable; and others.

In the human psyche, these two modes seem to be in a dynamic interplay. The hylotropic consciousness seems to be attracted by elements of the holotropic mode and, vice versa, the holotropic forms show a tendency to manifest in everyday consciousness. An average, "healthy" individual has a sufficiently developed system of psychological defenses to protect him or her from holotropic intrusions. Psychopathological symptoms of psychogenic origin can be seen as an interface amalgam or hybrid between the elements of the two modes, interpreted as distortion of the consensual Newtonian image of reality. They thus reflect a situation in which holotropic and hylotropic elements compete for the experiential field. This occurs when the defense system has been weakened or the holotropic gestalt is particularly strong.

It is important to realize that in the hylotropic mode it is possible to experience only the present moment and the present location ("here and now") in the phenomenal world of consensual reality, as it changes from one second to another. This is all we can ever experience while in the hylotropic mode of consciousness. In addition, the nature and scope of the segment of the material world that we can perceive depends critically on the physical characteristics of the Newtonian world and on the properties of the sensory organs. In contrast, an individual in the holotropic mode has, potentially, experiential access to all the remaining aspects of the phenomenal world in the present, past, and future, as well as the subtle and causal realms and the Absolute.

Some of these holotropic experiences — when they emerge into full consciousness — are interpreted by the subject in possessive terms from the position of the body-ego: my childhood memory, my birth, my embryonal development, my conception, the memory from the life of my human or animal ancestors, my past life, or an episode from my future. Others take the form of an encounter with something that is clearly other than the body-ego or its extension. This could be exemplified by an experience of telepathic connection with another person or an animal, animistic communication with plants or even elements of inanimate nature, and encounter with extraterrestrial entities or intelligence. The third possibility is full experiential identification with various aspects of the world without possessive interpretation. Here belong, for example, mediumistic experiences, identification with animals and plants, experiences of inorganic objects or processes, collective and racial memories in the sense of Carl Gustav Jung, and others.

The reach of holotropic consciousness is not limited to the material world and to spacetime. It can extend beyond the boundaries of the Newtonian reality altogether and access nonordinary dimensions of existence. Here belong, for example the astral realms of discarnate entities, the domains of suprahuman beings, the hells and heavens inhabited by blissful deities and demons, the world of Jungian archetypes, or various mythological and legendary regions. It is surprising enough to discover that the dynamic forces behind psychopathological symptoms are holotropic gestalts representing various domains of the phenomenal world. However, in many instances the symptoms clearly draw their power from elements of nonordinary realities. It is not uncommon that factors of both kinds participate in the dynamic structure of a particular problem.

A psychogenic symptom represents a hybrid between the hylotropic experience of the world and a holotropic theme that is trying to emerge into consciousness. The individual is incapable of suppressing the unconscious material, nor does he or she allow its full surfacing and conscious integration. The hylotropic experience of the world in its pure form does not present any problems. Similarly, a pure holotropic experience is quite acceptable and even desirable, provided that it happens in a safe context, where the subject does not have to deal with external reality. It is the confusing and incomprehensible mixture of both that constitutes psychopathology.

When I discussed with Karl Pribram this concept and its relation to the holographic model of the universe and the brain, he offered an interesting parallel. A person swimming in the ocean far from the shore deals exclusively with the world of waves and does not get into trouble no matter how big they are. If the same individual climbs up high on the shore and is facing only the world of solid forms, there is again no problem. It is the waterline, where the two worlds mix and neither of them can be experienced in its own right that presents the difficulties.

However, this interesting simile has to be further specified and refined. As the research in subatomic physics has clearly demonstrated, even the material world reflected in the hylotropic mode is not a realm of solid forms. The universe is in essence a vibratory dynamic system. Similarly, a gnoseological analysis of the process of perception in the hylotropic mode breaks down the solid world of Newtonian objects into a system of subjective experiences related to different senses. A better metaphor thus would be competition of two television channels, which broadcast programs with different characteristics for the same television set.

The understanding of the nature of psychopathology as interference of the holotropic and hylotropic modes of consciousness then suggests new therapeutic strategy. The client is offered a technique that induces a nonordinary state of consciousness and mediates access to the holotropic mode. Under these circumstances, the holotropic theme underlying the symptoms automatically emerges into consciousness. Various aspects of the symptoms that appeared bizarre and incomprehensible suddenly make perfect sense as derivatives of the underlying holotropic gestalt. As I mentioned above, it can be a biographical memory, a sequence from biological birth, or a transpersonal experience. Full conscious experience and integration of the previously unconscious material consumes the symptom and the client returns to the hylotropic mode of everyday consciousness. An important characteristic of holotropic therapy is that each therapeutic episode of this kind moves the individual's life philosophy in the direction of the mystical worldview.

The techniques that make the holotropic mode of consciousness available for therapeutic purposes cover a wide range from meditation, exploratory hypnosis, use of biofeedback, various methods of experiential psychotherapy, and trance dancing to psychedelic drugs. However, it should be emphasized that not all altered states of consciousness mediate access to the holotropic mode. As far as the psychoactive substances are concerned, this is limited to genuine psychedelics, such as LSD, psilocybine, mescaline, ibogain, harmaline, tryptamine derivatives (dimethyl-, diethyl-, dipropyl-, and methoxy-dimethyltryptamine), and the amphetamine-related empathogens (MDA, MMDA, 2-CB, and MDMA — known as Adam or Ecstasy). Many other substances that alter consciousness induce trivial deliria characterized by confusion, disorientation and amnesia, rather than a holotropic change in consciousness. Similar deliriant conditions are also associated with a great variety of physical diseases and disorders.

Since the above abstract description of the therapeutic mechanisms involving the holotropic mode of consciousness might not be easy to follow, I would like to use as illustrations several clinical examples. The first of these comes from regressive hypnotherapy, as conducted by Joan Grant and Dennys Kelsey. However, it is reminiscent of many situations that we have witnessed during psychedelic or holotropic therapy. Joan Grant is a French woman who has the unusual ability to reconstruct in autohypnotic states what appears to be her past lives. She has published many books based on the results of this karmic self-exploration, such as *The Winged Pharaoh*, *Life As Carola*, *The Eyes of Horus*, *So Moses Was Born*, and many others. Although she has stayed deliberately away from any historical studies, she has been able to describe the periods involved with uncanny accuracy.

Joan's husband, Dennys, is an English psychiatrist using regressive hypnosis in the treatment of various emotional and psychosomatic problems. After hypnotic induction, he asks the client to go back in time as far as necessary to find where the problem started. The Kelseys work together as a therapeutic team; they have described their treatment technique and their results in the book *Many Lifetimes* (Kelsey and Grant, 1967). Joan seems to have as easy an access to other persons' past life material as she has to her own. Using this gift, she is able to facilitate this process for her clients. In the late 1960s, Joan and Dennys spent three weeks as consultants at the Maryland Psychiatric Research Center. During this time, they conducted experiential sessions with all the members of the therapeutic team. Having worked with them myself, I speak from personal experience.

> After many years of unsuccessful treatment for a severe phobia of birds and feathers, a patient consulted Joan Grant and Dennys Kelsey with the intention to find the roots of her problem through regressive hypnosis. Dennys hypnotized her and asked her to go as far as she had to go to find what this problem meant and where it started. After some time, the patient reported that her body was strong and muscular and very definitely masculine; she felt that she was a soldier in an ancient army. As the session progressed, a dramatic story started to unfold.
>
> The patient was getting deeply involved in the process and described that she was involved in a vicious battle in ancient Persia. Suddenly, she experienced sharp pain in her chest which was penetrated by an arrow. She was lying on the ground dying in the dust on a hot day. In the blue sky above her, she noticed vultures, approaching her in large circles. They all landed and surrounded her, waiting for her to die. While she was still alive, some of them approached her and started tearing pieces of her flesh.
>
> Screaming and beating around herself, she fought a desperate, but losing battle with the scavenger birds. Finally, she surrendered and died. When she emerged from the experience, she was free from the phobia that had tormented her life for a long time.

Here we have a situation where an adult and intelligent woman had in her everyday life (hylotropic consciousness) a strange and incomprehensible experiential enclave: she was afraid of birds and even isolated feathers. In the hypnotic state (holotropic consciousness), she connected with the underlying transpersonal gestalt involving a battle in medieval Persia. In the context of the theme that emerged during this process — a seriously wounded soldier dying on the battlefield and surrounded by hungry vultures — the fear of birds is certainly more than justifiable. To get rid of the phobia, it was necessary to bring the underlying holotropic theme from the unconscious into consciousness, experience it fully, and integrate it.

The second example is a story of a young woman who attended our five-day workshop at the Esalen Institute, where we used the technique of holotropic therapy. Prior to this workshop, she had suffered for many months from intense muscular spasms and pains in her neck, upper back, and shoulders. All she had done up to that point to get rid of this problem, including repeated massage and hot baths, had brought only partial and transient relief.

> After about half an hour of intense breathing, the tensions in Marion's neck and shoulders intensified considerably; her trapezius muscles became hard and tender. Suddenly, she opened her eyes and sat up. When we asked her what was happening, she refused to continue breathing. "I do not want to do this any more; it is absolutely crazy. I have the feeling I am turning into a crab." After reassurance and encouragement that she might find the roots of her problem, she decided to continue after all.
>
> With the muscles of much of her upper trunk completely stiff for a very long time, Marion experienced total identification with a crab associated with some interesting zoological insights. When she discontinued the hyperventilation, she still felt intense tension in her neck and shoulders. Using the technique of focused body work, described earlier (p. 194), we asked her to exaggerate the tensions and proceeded to massage the muscles involved.
>
> Marion tuned again into a convincing experience of being a crab and dragged the two of us four times from wall to wall in a room about thirty feet long, moving sideways in a most determined fashion, very much like a crab. This session completely released the tensions and pains that had up to that time resisted all other types of experiential work and body work.

Many years ago, I witnessed a similar, yet even more unusual, therapeutic mechanism during psychedelic therapy. The underlying holotropic gestalt involved in this case a combination of plant consciousness and some archetypal elements.

> Martha, a 32-year-old woman, was undergoing psychedelic therapy for a variety of psychopathological symptoms. The most striking of these were complaints about strange sensations in the legs that she had great difficulties describing. Her psychiatric diagnosis included terms like bizarre hypochondriacal complaints and borderline psychosis with distortions of the body image.
>
> In one of her psychedelic sessions, the sensations in the legs reached such proportions that Martha found them unbearable and demanded termination of the session by Thorazine. However, after a

brief discussion she decided to continue and try to find out what was involved. As she fully focused on her legs, she suddenly started experiencing herself as a beautiful large tree. The identification was quite authentic and convincing and was associated with many interesting insights into various botanical processes.

She stood up for a long time with her arms stretched up, experiencing them as branches with rich foliage. This was associated with cellular awareness of the process of photosynthesis in the leaves, the mysterious process that is the basis of all life on our planet. She felt the sap circulating up and down her body through the pathways in the cambium and sensed the exchange of minerals and water in the root system. What appeared to be bizarre distortions of the human body image turned out to be perfectly normal, fascinating experiences involving a tree.

However, the experience was not limited to the botanical level. What at first appeared to be the physical sun, became also the Cosmic Sun — the source of creative power in the universe. Similarly, the earth became Mother Earth, a fantastic mythological figure of the Great Mother Goddess. The tree itself assumed a deep archetypal meaning and became the Tree of Life. The experience that was at first so frightening became ecstatic and mystical. Martha emerged from the session without the disturbing distortions of the body image and with deep reverence for plant life on earth.

The final example is probably the single most unusual and dramatic episode I have experienced during three decades of my research in nonordinary states of consciousness. The situation described here happened in the context of the program of psychedelic therapy with LSD during my stay in Baltimore. Unlike in the preceding cases, the underlying holotropic gestalt did not involve elements from the phenomenal world, but was purely archetypal.

While working at the Maryland Psychiatric Research Center, I was invited to a staff conference at the Spring Grove State Hospital. One of the psychiatrists was presenting the case of Flora, a 28-year-old single patient, who had been hospitalized for more than eight months in a locked ward. All available therapy, including tranquilizers, antipressants, psychotherapy, and occupational therapy, had been tried, but failed, and she was facing transfer to the chronic ward.

Flora had one of the most difficult and complicated combinations of symptoms and problems I have ever encountered in my psychiatric practice. When she was sixteen years old, she was a member of a gang that conducted an armed robbery and killed the night watchman. As the driver of the getaway car, she spent four years in prison and was then placed on parole for the rest of her sentence.

During the stormy years that followed, Flora became a multiple drug addict. She was an alcoholic and heroin addict, and used frequently high doses of psychostimulants and barbiturates. Her severe depressions were associated with violent suicidal tendencies. She often had impulses to drive her car over a cliff or to collide with another automobile. She suffered from hysterical vomiting in situations where she became emotionally excited.

Probably the most agonizing of her complaints was a painful facial cramp, *tic douloureux*, for which a Johns Hopkins neurosurgeon recommended a brain operation consisting in severing the nerve involved. Flora was also a lesbian and had severe conflicts and much guilt about it; never in her life had she had a heterosexual relationship. To further complicate the situation, she was court-commissioned, because she had severely wounded her girlfriend and roommate while trying to clean a gun under the influence of heroin.

At the end of the Spring Grove case conference, I was asked by Flora's attending psychiatrist if I would consider giving her LSD treatment as the last resort. This was an extremely difficult decision, particularly in view of the national hysteria concerning LSD at that time. Flora had a criminal record already, she had access to weapons, and had severe suicidal tendencies.

It was clear that, under these circumstances, if she were given LSD, anything that would happen in the future would be automatically blamed on the drug, without regard to her past history. On the other hand, everything else had been tried without success and Flora was facing a lifetime in a chronic ward. After long discussions, the therapeutic team of the Maryland Psychiatric Research Center decided to accept her into the LSD program, feeling that her desperate situation justified the risk.

Flora's first two high-dose LSD sessions were not much different from many others I had run in the past. She had to face a number of traumatic memories from her stormy childhood and repeatedly relived sequences of the struggle in the birth canal. She was able to connect her violent suicidal tendencies and painful facial spasms to certain aspects of her birth trauma and discharged enormous amounts of physical and emotional tension. Despite this, the therapeutic gain seemed minimal.

In her third LSD session, nothing extraordinary happened during the first two hours; her experiences were similar to those of the previous two sessions. Suddenly, she started complaining that the pain of the facial cramps was becoming unbearable. In front of my eyes, the spasms were grotesquely accentuated and her face froze into what can best be described as a mask of evil. She started to talk in a

deep, male voice and everything about her was so different that I
could not see much connection between her present appearance and
her former self. Her eyes had an expression of indescribable evil and
her hands were spastic and claw-like.

The alien energy that had taken over her body and voice introduced
itself as the devil. "He" turned directly to me, ordering me to stay
away from Flora and to give up any attempts to help her. She
belonged to him and he would punish anybody who would try to
invade his territory. What followed was quite explicit blackmail, a
series of dismal intimations of what would happen to me, my
colleagues, and the research program, if I decided not to obey.

It is difficult to describe the uncanny atmosphere that this scene
evoked; one could almost feel the tangible presence of something
alien in the room. The power of the blackmail and the sense of the
supernatural was further augmented by the fact that the patient could
not have had in her everyday life access to some of the information
that her voice was using in this situation.

I found myself under enormous emotional stress, which had
metaphysical dimensions. Although I had seen similar manifestations
in some earlier LSD sessions, they had never been so realistic and
convincing. It was difficult for me to control my fear and my strong
tendency to perceive the presence as real and to enter an active
psychological and spiritual combat with it. I found myself thinking
fast, trying to devise the best strategy for this situation. At one point,
I caught myself seriously entertaining the idea that we should have a
crucifix in the treatment room as a therapeutic tool. My rationalization
was that what I was witnessing was manifestation of a Jungian archetype
for which a cross would be the appropriate archetypal remedy.

It soon became clear to me that my emotions, whether it was fear or
aggression, were making the situation and the entity more real. I
could not help thinking of one of the programs of the television
science fiction series *Star Trek*, which featured an alien entity feeding
on human emotions. I realized that it was essential for me to remain
calm and centered. I decided to put myself in a meditative mood
while I held Flora's cramped hand, trying to imagine her the way I
had known her before. At the same time, I tried to visualize a capsule
of light enveloping us both; this was based on the archetypal polarity
of evil and light. The situation lasted for over two hours of clock-time.
In terms of the subjective time sense, these were the two longest
hours I have ever experienced outside of my own psychedelic
sessions.

After this time, Flora's hand relaxed and her face returned to its
usual form; these changes were as abrupt as the onset of this peculiar
condition. I soon discovered that she did not remember anything that
happened during the two preceding hours. Later, in her write-up of

the session, she described the first two hours and continued with the period following the "possession state". I seriously questioned whether I should discuss with her the time covered by amnesia and decided against it. There did not seem to be any reason to introduce such a macabre theme into her conscious mind.

To my great surprise, this session resulted in an astounding therapeutic breakthrough. Flora lost her suicidal tendencies and developed a new appreciation of life. She gave up alcohol, heroin and barbiturates and started to attend zealously the meetings of a small religious group in Catonsville, Maryland. For most of the time, she did not have any facial spasms; the energy underlying them seemed to have exhausted itself in the "mask of evil" that she maintained for two hours. The occasional recurrence of pain was of negligible intensity and did not require any medication.

She started even to experiment with heterosexual relations for the first time in her life and eventually got married. However, her sexual adjustment was not good; she was capable of intercourse, but found it unpleasant and painful. The marriage ended three months later and Flora returned to her lesbian relationship, this time, however, with much less guilt. Her condition was so improved that she was accepted as a taxi driver. Although the following years had their ups and downs, she did not have to return to the psychiatric hospital that could have become her permanent home. Flora probably would have made further progress had we been able to continue LSD therapy. Unfortunately, the NIMH protocol limited the psychedelic treatment to three high-dose sessions.

Potential and Goals of Experiential Self-Exploration

You never enjoy the world alright, till the sea itself flows in your veins, till you are clothed with the heavens and crowned with the stars; and perceive yourself to be the sole heir of the whole world, and more so, because others are in it, everyone sole heirs as well as you. — *Thomas Traherne*

IT must be clear from the preceding discussion that self-exploration with psychedelic drugs and powerful nondrug experiential techniques is a process that is not easy and should not be taken lightly. It can involve certain extreme states of mind, with considerable emotional suffering and difficult psychosomatic experiences. In addition, in emotionally unstable individuals, it is not without potential risks. It is only natural under these circumstances that one would ask the questions: What are the benefits of such an undertaking and why should anybody subject himself or herself to this procedure?

Both psychedelic and holotropic self-exploration grew out of clinical work with psychiatric patients and efforts to find more effective ways of helping them. The first and most obvious reason for experiential self-exploration is thus to offer a more effective alternative to conventional verbal psychotherapy, which is extremely time-consuming and expensive, and to treat various forms of psychopathology that do not respond to traditional approaches.

However, experiential work has shown that even individuals who would be considered normal by the ordinary standards of Western psychiatry are often using life strategies that are unfulfilling, self-defeating, or even self-destructive, and they do not live up to their full human potential. The second major reason for experiential self-exploration is thus to search for a more satisfying approach to life and a new way of being in the world.

Finally, modern consciousness research has confirmed the basic thesis of perennial philosophy that the consensus reality reveals only one aspect or fragment of existence. There are important realms of reality that are transcendental and transphenomenal. The impulse in human beings to connect with the spiritual domain is an extremely powerful and important force. It resembles, in its nature, sexuality, but is much more fundamental and compelling. Denial and repression of this transcendental impulse introduces a serious distortion into human life on both an individual and collective scale. Experiential self-exploration is an important tool for a spiritual and philosophical quest. It can mediate the connection with the transpersonal domain of one's own being and of existence.

In the following text, I will briefly explore the possibilities of experiential self-exploration for all these three areas and discuss the specific problems involved.

EMOTIONAL AND PSYCHOSOMATIC HEALING

Experiential forms of psychotherapy have the capacity to dissolve psychological resistances and loosen defense mechanisms in a much more effective way than approaches limited to verbal exchange. It is not uncommon to reach, in the first session with psychedelics or with holotropic breathing, early childhood material, birth memories, or even the level of transpersonal experiences. On occasion, dramatic and lasting psychological breakthroughs can occur within a matter of hours or days. Although this is in no way a norm, one psychedelic or holotropic experience can result in a major personal transformation or can resolve a chronic emotional or psychosomatic problem. Other times, one such session can be an important turning point in one's life. On a more modest and common scale, after a really good experiential session, the subject should have a clear feeling that something significant has been achieved and feel distinctly better than before it.

This compares favorably with historically oriented verbal therapies, where it often takes months or even years to reach early childhood material through memory recall and indirect reconstruction from free associations, dreams, "psychopathology of everyday life," neurotic symptoms, and transference distortions. The therapeutic changes — if they occur at all — develop slowly and gradually over a very long period of time.

It is not surprising that the power and efficacy of experiential therapies using the healing potential of nonordinary states of consciousness have their shadow side and that these procedures are not without certain risks. In general, there is very little problem if the sessions are conducted with individuals who show reasonable emotional balance, in a good set and setting, and under the supervision of an experienced guide. Under such circumstances, considerable benefits can be achieved with no or minimal risks. The more one moves into the realm of severe clinical psychopathology, the more caution and support is required.

Experiential work with individuals who have a history of psychiatric hospitalization should be conducted only if ongoing support is available when necessary. In the context of holotropic strategy, major activation of the unconscious dynamics is not considered a complication or obstacle, as it is in the case in traditional psychiatry, but a normal and lawful concomitant of the therapeutic procedure. However, if the process gets to be too active and extends beyond the framework of the sessions, it can require special measures.

A question that is asked very frequently is whether one can do deep experiential self-exploration without a guide or sitter. In general, this is something that is not recommended. Even if there are individuals who, after a certain initial experience under guidance, find that they can handle such sessions reasonably well, the solo approach changes considerably the ratio between potential risks and potential benefits.

There are several important reasons why one should not undertake the journey into the deep recesses of one's psyche without having the reality aspects of the situation covered. It is, in principle, impossible to know when a particular session will bring confrontation with unconscious material that is difficult and disorganizing. This can occasionally happen even in a well-adjusted person, after a series of sessions that did not pose any serious problems. When high dosages of psychedelic substances are used as a tool in self-exploration and when the subject works on serious emotional or psychosomatic problems, difficult and taxing episodes in the sessions seem to be a norm rather than an exception. Here the presence of a trusted person can be a critical factor in determining the safety of the procedure and the degree of success of a particular session.

But the possibility that certain aspects of the experience will be dangerous and the subject will not be able to handle them alone is not the only reason for having a sitter. There are other situations where the presence of a trusted person is a critical factor for therapeutic success and full benefit of the session. There exist certain important stages of the process of experiential self-exploration that require total loss of control and letting go. In principle, this is an extremely healing and transforming experience. However, it might be very difficult, or even impossible, for the subject to face it without the support of a trusted person. Unsupervised total loss of control could lead to serious dangers for the individual involved or for others. Under such circumstances, it is vitally important that a significant part of the personality remains dissociated from the experiential process and provides the necessary connection with reality. Only the presence of a facilitator who is entrusted with the task of keeping the situation safe makes it possible to surrender control totally and unconditionally.

Another important reason for having a facilitator or sitter in experiential sessions is work on critical problems that involve human relationships. I have already discussed earlier the importance of nourishing physical contact and anaclitic satisfaction during emergence of traumas that were caused by "omission" rather than "commission" (p. 196). Here the presence of a warm and understanding human being is essential. Reactivating the old memory and finding that one is again alone, as in the original traumatic situation, can be reinforcing rather than therapeutic. Similarly, the damaging impact of situations that involved breach of basic trust cannot be successfully resolved unless one can have a corrective human experience. Also, being able to share the innermost psychological events with another human being and being unconditionally accepted, irrespective of the nature of one's experience, is a factor that should not be underestimated.

The last reason for having an experienced sitter is the fact that focused body work is a very important component of holotropic therapy, particularly in the termination period of some sessions. When there are residual emotional and psychosomatic issues that remained unresolved, it is possible to facilitate good integration by using the principles that were described earlier (p. 194). For obvious reasons, this requires another person; this part of the procedure would have to be omitted or would be severely compromised in solitary sessions.

In discussing the therapeutic potential of nonordinary states of consciousness, I will not include those induced by psychedelic substances. That is a very extensive and complex topic that would require much time and space. There exist several major groups of psychedelics with somewhat different effects and specific problems associated with each of them. Researchers in this field have developed several treatment modalities that differ considerably in their basic philosophy, characteristic dosage range, elements of the set and setting, and the specific techniques used before, during, and after the drug sessions.

In addition, the issue of psychedelic substances is further complicated by many factors of an emotional, political, legal, and administrative nature. In this context, I will offer only a very brief and sketchy overview of this problem area and refer the interested readers to the appendix of this book and particularly to my earlier book, *LSD Psychotherapy* (Grof 1980). It focuses specifically on clinical use of psychedelics, its techniques, indications and contraindications, complications, therapeutic potential, and results.

Review of psychedelic literature shows that favorable results have been reported in a wide variety of clinical problems, including depressions, phobias and other types of psychoneuroses, psychosomatic diseases, character disorders, sexual deviations, criminal behavior, alcoholism, narcotic drug addiction, and even psychoses. Two areas where successful results have been achieved deserve special attention. The first of these is the use of psychedelic therapy to relieve the physical and emotional suffering of terminal cancer patients (Grof and Halifax 1977). The second one involves psychedelic sessions for former inmates of concentration camps to help them to overcome the so-called "concentration camp syndrome," a delayed traumatic reaction to incarceration (Bastians n.d.).

Although many of the claims of psychedelic therapists have been based on clinical impressions, some of them were confirmed in controlled studies. The team of psychiatrists and psychologists at the Maryland Psychiatric Research Center in Baltimore, Maryland, which I participated in for seven years, conducted such large-scale controlled clinical trials of LSD, DPT (dipropyl-tryptamine), and MDA (methylene-dioxy-amphetamine) in alcoholics, narcotic drug addicts, and cancer patients, with significant results (Grof 1980).

Therapeutic work with psychedelics has a long and rich history extending for more than a quarter of a century. It has been conducted by many individual researchers and therapeutic teams in different countries of the world. By contrast, systematic clinical research and controlled studies of holotropic therapy have yet to be performed. However, we have seen over the years many therapeutic changes that certainly justify systematic investigation of this promising mode of treatment. As a matter of fact, some of these changes were so dramatic and convincing that they hardly require confirmation by controlled studies.

When evaluating the results of holotropic therapy, one has to realize that the situation is different in some important aspects from the one encountered in regard to verbal psychotherapy. Dramatic changes can occur here within hours or days, even, on occasion, in emotional and psychosomatic conditions that have lasted for years. Since they are so clearly related to the therapeutic session and its specific content, the causal connection between the holotropic procedure and the results is beyond reasonable doubt.

In comparison, the dynamics of the symptoms in most of the typical verbal approaches in psychotherapy extends over many months or years. With such a broad temporal scale, the changes are so slow that they are difficult to assess. In addition, it is questionable if there is a causal link between these changes and the events in psychotherapeutic sessions. It is quite plausible that they reflect the spontaneous dynamics of the symptoms and would have happened without any treatment. They might also be caused by some of the many intercurrent events that occur in the life of the individual during such a long period of time. This has been the position of some of the major critics of psychoanalysis (Eysenck and Rachman 1965).

Among the changes we have observed in the context of our workshops have been the clearing of chronic depressions, dramatic relief from anxiety states and phobias, and the disappearance of headaches, migraine headaches, menstrual cramps, and a wide variety of psychosomatic pains. Very common is also release of generalized muscular tension, and opening of bioenergetic blockages in the sinuses, throat, chest, stomach, intestines, pelvis, uterus, and the rectum.

In some instances, such energetic unblocking has been followed by clearing of chronic infections in these areas, such as sinusitis, pharyngitis, bronchitis, and cystitis. It seems that energetic blocks are typically associated with vasoconstriction. Reduced supply of blood and its constituents that play an important role in protecting the organism against infection, such as white blood cells and various antibodies, then leads to a situation where the tissue or organ cannot defend itself against the common bacteria. When the blockage is removed, the subjects typically report feelings of warmth and flow of energy in the area involved. As this occurs, chronic infections often clear within days.

This suggests that holotropic therapy could, in the future, play an important role as an adjunct in the treatment of many conditions currently considered purely medical problems. I have already mentioned earlier that we have seen in our workshops several instances of dramatic improvement in individuals suffering from Raynaud's disease. The problems with peripheral circulation in the hands disappeared after a release of energetic blockage in the afflicted areas.

Our observations related to psychogenic asthma deserve special notice in this context. One might easily presume that a technique which puts primary emphasis on intense breathing would not be a feasible tool for asthmatic patients; however, this is not necessarily true. Although asthmatic patients tend to approach the sessions with many fears and apprehensions, we have now seen, in six individuals, profound improvements after only a few holotropic sessions. In several instances, persons previously suffering from daily attacks have been practically seizure-free for months or years. One important consideration in experiential work with asthmatic patients is a good cardiovascular situation, since the sessions can involve considerable emotional and physical stress.

Holotropic sessions with a person who suffers from asthma tend to trigger, sooner or later, asthmatic symptoms. When further breathing becomes impossible, the facilitator has to shift to focused body work and encourage full abreaction through vocal expression, various motor movements, coughing, and any other channels that become available. As soon as the respiratory pathways open up again, the subject is asked to return to fast breathing. This is repeated until continued hyperventilation does not lead to respiratory spasms. When sufficient work of this kind has been done, the respiratory pathways can remain permanently open and a lasting improvement occurs.

The fact that in psychedelic and holotropic therapy dramatic results can be sometimes achieved within a few days or even hours will sound unbelievable to those therapists who use exclusively verbal approaches and whose conceptual framework does not include the perinatal and transpersonal levels. To take such claims seriously, one has to have some awareness of the depth and intensity of the experiences occurring in experiential forms of therapy. This often includes an encounter with death so convincing that it cannot be distinguished from actual biological emergency and vital threat, episodes of mental disorganization that feel like insanity, total loss of control lasting several minutes, episodes of extreme choking, or long periods of violent tremors, shaking, and flailing around. The intensity these experiences can reach cannot be conveyed in words; it has to be experienced or at least observed.

Although the results of experiential therapy can be, on occasion, extremely dramatic, one should not consider it a panacea that guarantees fast and impressive results in every single case. While some individuals will have profound healing and life-transforming experiences, others will proceed only slowly or show little improvement. This is particularly true for those persons whose history was one of chronic lack of satisfaction and of deficiency. An example would be someone who as a fetus experienced a predominantly "bad womb," had a long and complicated delivery, and an emotionally deprived childhood. Here psychedelic or holotropic work will confront the individual with a long sequence of traumas and very few positive nourishing experiences. In a situation like this, it is important to use systematically nourishing physical contact for a gradual building of the ego and not to expect instant therapeutic success.

Another problem in experiential psychotherapy can be a specific impasse. It occurs in situations where a good resolution is in principle possible, but would require an extreme experience of some kind that the client is unable or unwilling to face. Such psychological stumbling blocks vary considerably from individual to individual. It could be fear of facing psychological death ("ego death"), fear of losing control, or fear of insanity. Other times, the obstacle can be a reluctance to experience extreme physical pain, suffocation, or some other form of intense physical distress. It is common for the subject to recognize the problems involved as something that he or she knows from everyday life in the form of specific fears or uncomfortable symptoms. ("The last thing in the world I would do is to throw up"; "The idea of having to face pain drives me crazy"; "The most important thing for me is to be in control under all circumstances," etc.) In situations of this kind, the therapist has the important task to identify the nature of the impasse and to help the client to overcome the psychological resistance that prevents him or her from facing it.

I have already discussed earlier that special precautions have to be taken when experiential work is conducted with individuals who show severe psychopathology and a history of psychiatric hospitalization. This requires an experienced guide and continuous support system, if necessary. However, if these conditions are met, the results can be very rewarding. The techniques and therapeutic principles described in this book can be used successfully in many individuals in severe transpersonal crisis ("spiritual emergency") who would be seen by traditional psychiatry as suffering from psychosis — mental illness of unknown etiology (Grof and Grof 1986).

The therapeutic potentials and promises of psychedelic and holotropic therapy are not easy to compare with those of traditional verbal approaches. These two therapies differ considerably from the mainstream approaches in their basic scientific and philosophical premises and have to be judged in the context of their own conceptual frameworks. Traditional psychotherapy uses techniques of self-exploration, such as free associations or face-to-face interviews, that are relatively weak and ineffective means of penetrating into the unconscious. However, since their conceptual framework is limited to biography, their focus is very narrow — to work on the postnatal traumatic material from the life of the individual. Similarly, their goal is very modest — to alleviate symptoms and to improve adjustment of the individual to the existing conditions of life.

Psychedelic and holotropic therapy are incomparably more effective ways of gaining access into the unconscious psyche. However, the work with these techniques has shown that the roots of most emotional and psychosomatic problems are not only biographical, but also perinatal and transpersonal. In addition, their goal is not just to return the symptom-free individual to the old worldview, lifestyle, and value system. The process here involves a profound personal transformation during which most aspects of the individual's life are drastically redefined. At a certain point this form of therapy automatically changes into a serious philosophical and spiritual quest addressing itself to the most fundamental questions of existence. When this occurs, the process is completely open-ended; the spiritual search and philosophical quest then become important new dimensions of life.

PURSUIT OF A MORE REWARDING LIFE STRATEGY

The possibility of improving the quality of one's experience of life goes beyond alleviation or elimination of clinical psychopathology. The lives of many people who do not suffer from manifest emotional and psychosomatic symptoms and have all the external conditions necessary for good existence are not rewarding and fulfilling. A good example of this situation is the condition tha' the Austrian psychiatrist and founder of existential analysis Viktor Frankl called noogenic depression (Frankl 1956). It refers to individuals who do not have an obvious emotional disorder and often show superior functioning in their personal and professional lives. Admired and envied by their friends and neighbors, they themselves do not experience their existence as meaningful and are not able to enjoy their successes. There are others who also would be considered "normal" by the traditional psychiatric standards, even though certain areas of their lives show various forms and degrees of distortion of perception, emotions, thoughts, and behavior.

In these situations, experiential self-exploration and psychotherapy reveal the factors underlying such distortions and offer an opportunity to correct them. On the biographical level, this can be specific traumatic events in childhood that interfere with the individual's proper functioning in a certain area of life and a certain segment of interpersonal relations. These are facts that are well-known in traditional dynamic psychotherapy. Thus a traumatic experience with parental authority can contaminate all future relationships with superiors and other people in positions of authority. Complications in the intimate emotional interaction with one's mother or father can cause recurrent problems with sexual partners. Absence of a sibling, sibling rivalry, or certain specific problems with brothers and sisters can lead to difficulties with one's peers, whether they are schoolmates, friends, fellow soldiers, or co-workers. Reliving and integrating the underlying traumas can have a beneficial effect on the afflicted segment of one's life.

Individuals whose experiential self-exploration transcends biography and reaches the perinatal level of the unconscious typically make a surprising and shattering discovery. They recognize that the inauthenticity of their lives is not limited to certain partial segments that are contaminated by specific childhood traumas, but that their entire approach to existence and their life strategy have been inauthentic and misdirected in a very basic way. This total distortion of existential emphasis is based on the fact that one's actions are dominated from a deep unconscious level by the unresolved trauma of birth and by fear of death that is associated with it. This leads to various behaviors that are useless or damaging and make it impossible to discover a strategy of life that would be more fruitful and fulfilling.

Numerous observations suggest that an individual who is dominated by one of the negative perinatal matrices approaches life in a way that not only fails to bring satisfaction, but also can be, in the long run, destructive and self-destructive. If the psyche is under the influence of BPM II, but not strong enough to result in manifest psychopathology, the individual will show a generally passive, resigned, and submissive attitude toward life. Under similar circumstances, BPM III will generate what can be referred to as a "workaholic", "tread-mill", or "rat-race" type of existence.

The dynamics of BPM III imposes on life a compelling linear trajectory and creates an unrelenting drive toward pursuit of future goals. Since the psyche of a person in this situation is dominated by the memory of the painful confinement in the birth canal, he or she never experiences the present moment and the present circumstances as fully satisfying. The world and one's life is always seen from the perspective of deficiency. That involves a selective focus on what is missing, what is unsatisfactory, or what is wrong, and, at the same time, engenders an inability or limited ability to appreciate and enjoy what is available and make the best of it. It is important to emphasize that this is a pattern that operates independently of the external circumstances and cannot be eliminated or corrected by achievements of any form and scope. This individual feels dissatisfied with his or her looks, talents and abilities, accomplishments, possessions, fame, or power, no matter what the actual situation is — often in sharp contrast with the opinions of other people. Like the fetus who is experiencing the painful constriction in the grip of the birth canal and is trying to escape into more comfortable circumstances, the person who is under the psychological spell of BPM III will always strive for something different from what the present situation offers. He or she will expect the solution and satisfaction from some attainment in the future.

In this situation, the specific goals that one's fantasy offers as unmistakable sources of future happiness can be easily identified as surrogates for the psychological completion of biological birth, and for postnatal or prenatal satisfaction and security. Since these goals are not really authentic, but are mere psychological substitutes, achieving them will not and cannot bring true satisfaction. The strategy based on the dynamics of BPM III is thus always a losing strategy, whether or not the goals are reached, since it is based on the wrong premises and does not bring the anticipated results.

A failure to achieve a specific goal from which satisfaction was expected perpetuates the self-deceptive belief that happiness depends on external factors. In this case, the individual typically presumes that success would have made a difference. When the goal is achieved, it typically does not bring the psychological result that was expected. However, this is not usually interpreted as an indication that the strategy linking happiness to success has failed. It is attributed to the fact that the goal was not sufficiently ambitious or that a wrong choice of the goal was made. The resulting frustration will then generate new plans or more ambitious ones of the same nature. The most important characteristic of this self-defeating strategy is that it disregards the actual present and focuses on imaginary projections into the future.

In this frame of mind, other people are seen as competitors and nature as something that is hostile and has to be conquered and controlled. Historically, the first explicit formulation of this attitude can be traced to Francis Bacon, who defined the basic strategies for the new empirical method in Western science. Referring to nature, he used such terms as: nature has to be hounded in her wanderings, raped, placed on a rack, tortured, and forced to give her secrets to the scientists, put in constraint, made a slave, and controlled (Bacon 1870). It has taken several centuries to realize that Bacon's suggestion was dangerous and ultimately destructive and self-destructive. With the development of modern technology, it proved to be a reliable recipe for planetary suicide.

On a collective and global scale, this frame of mind generates a philosophy and strategy of life that emphasizes strength, competition, and unilateral control; it glorifies linear progress and unlimited growth. In this context, material profit and increase of the gross national product are considered to be the main criteria of well-being and measures of the living standard. This ideology and the economic and political strategies resulting from it bring humans into a serious conflict with their nature as living systems and with basic universal laws.

Since all biological organisms and systems depend critically on optimal values, maximizing the pursuits is an unnatural and dangerous trajectory. In a universe, the very nature of which is cyclical, this strategy advocates an irreversible linear trend and unlimited growth. Seen from a broader perspective, this means in the long run depletion of nonrenewable natural resources, particularly the fossil fuels, and accumulation of toxic waste, which pollutes the air, water, and soil — all vitally important for the continuation of life. In addition, this approach to existence glorifies competition and the Darwinian "survival of the fittest" as natural and healthy principles of existence, and is unable to recognize the urgent need for synergy and cooperation.

When the individual is able to move away from the dominance of the negative perinatal matrices and to connect experientially with the memories of the positive symbiotic exchange with the maternal organism in the womb or during nursing, this situation changes radically. The experience with the mother during fetal or early post-natal existence is equivalent on the adult level to the individual's relationship with all of humanity and with the entire world. The former represents a prototypical model and experiential template for the latter. The type and quality of the perinatal matrix that influences the individual's psyche has, therefore, a profound influence, not only on his or her inner subjective experience, but also on his or her attitude and approach to other people, to nature, and to existence in general.

When the individual experiences during in-depth self-exploration a major shift from negative to positive perinatal matrices, the ability to enjoy life and the degree of zest increase considerably. The original experience of undisturbed prenatal existence and nursing associated with these matrices involves a sense of satisfaction and timelessness of the present moment. When these elements underlie the experience of everyday life, it becomes possible to draw intense satisfaction from each present moment and from many ordinary situations and functions, such as eating, simple human contact, work activities, sex, art, music, play, or walks in nature. This reduces considerably the irrational drive to pursue complicated schemes in the false hope of achieving satisfaction. In this state of mind, it becomes clear that the ultimate measure of one's living standard is the quality of one's life experience and not the quantity of achievements or material possessions.

The above changes are accompanied by the spontaneous emergence of deep ecological consciousness and awareness. The Baconian attitude toward nature ("Mother Nature") described earlier is modeled after the precarious and antagonistic experience of the fetus with the maternal organism in the process of biological delivery. The new values and attitudes reflect the symbiotic experience of the fetus with the mother during prenatal existence and during nursing. Synergistic, mutually nourishing, and complementary aspects of this situation tend to replace automatically the competitive and exploitative emphasis of the old value system. The concept of human existence as a life-and-death struggle for survival in a world governed by the law of the jungle gives way to a new image of life as a manifestation of a cosmic dance or a divine play.

The level of aggression decreases considerably and the sense of connection and fundamental unity with the world leads to sexual, political, national, cultural, and racial tolerance. In the new context, differences are not threatening any more. They are seen as interesting and desirable variations of the one undivided cosmic web. This new vision of the world often leads to "voluntary simplicity" in Duane Elgin's sense (Elgin 1981) that is now seen as an expression of profound wisdom. It also becomes obvious that the only hope for a political, social, and economic solution of the current global crisis can come from a transpersonal perspective that transcends the hopeless us-versus-them psychology, which produces at best occasional pendulum-like shifts in which the protagonists exchange the roles of oppressors and oppressed.

It is important to emphasize that the development of the changes described above does not necessarily mean loss of interest in creative activities. In most instances, the opposite is true. As more energy becomes available, work can be very productive, effortless, and flowing, if the individual finds it compatible with his or her new life philosophy. Occasionally, there is a tendency to give up some activities that seem inappropriate or that were in the past pursued for what is now seen as the wrong motivations.

The key to all these changes is a radical shift from the emotional and psychosomatic tuning into the dynamics of the negative perinatal matrices to an experiential connection with the positive elements of

BPM IV and BPM I. The same changes do not occur or are very compromised in those individuals whose early history does not include a sufficient amount of nourishing emotional and biological experiences and is predominantly traumatic ("bad womb" and "bad breast"). For these people, the movement in the described direction is slow and takes a long time. It requires, among other elements, direct anaclitic satisfaction during regressive therapeutic work that provides a corrective experience for the emotional deprivation and rejection in early childhood.

Up to this point, I have been discussing the potential of psychedelic and holotropic therapy to correct the negative psychological consequences of the trauma of birth. However, the observations from experiential work offer also important clues for their prevention. They provide strong support for the recent attempts to move obstetrics from its emphasis on dehumanized technological wizardry to a discipline that recognizes the paramount importance of the biological, psychological, and spiritual dimensions of pregnancy and birth as critical factors shaping the future of the individual and society.

Psychological and physical hygiene of pregnancy, good emotional and somatic preparation for birth, Frederic Leboyer's birth without violence (Leboyer 1975), Igor Tjarkovsky's underwater birth (Sidenbladh 1983), adequate time for symbiotic contact between mother and child, the opportunity for bonding, and the practice of breast-feeding seem to be factors of critical importance, not only for the future of the individual, but also possibly for the future of the planet. On the negative side, the fact that babies can be conceived and grown in test tubes, frozen fetuses can be implanted into the uterus, and miscarriages can be kept alive by artificial means does not necessarily mean that the conditions involved meet the minimum criteria required for healthy psychological development. Much more research should be conducted before these techniques are used on a mass scale.

In the above discussion, I have focused on the changes in the basic hierarchy of values and in existential strategy that occur in connection with perinatal sequences. These changes become more pronounced, lasting, and refined when a person connects experientially with the transpersonal domain. While the death-rebirth sequences initiate the process of spiritual opening, transpersonal experiences reveal and confirm in many different ways that the deeper dynamics of the human psyche are in their essence numinous, and that spirituality represents a critical dimension in the universal scheme of things. The importance of the spiritual and philosophical quest in human life will be the focus of the following section.

PHILOSOPHICAL AND SPIRITUAL QUEST

When self-exploration reaches the level of perinatal and transpersonal experiences, it changes automatically into a search for answers to basic spiritual and philosophical questions of existence. The individual connects with important aspects of reality that are transphenomenal — that is, inaccessible to perception under ordinary circumstances. When consciousness changes in a certain way, as in spontaneous mystical states or in psychedelic and holotropic sessions, some of these hidden aspects of reality will manifest as immanent divine dimension of the phenomenal world; others as transcendental realms radically different from the universe we live in. Using a modern technical analogy, the former situation could be compared to an opportunity to observe in colors a channel that up to that point was available only in black-and-white. The latter situation then could be likened to the possibility to tune into other channels and programs that were previously present but unavailable.

The spiritual dimension and the determination of those who pursue it will probably make sense only to those people who can relate it to some previous experience of their own. Without it, it might make as little sense as the concept of colors does to a person who is color-blind. When an individual whose only concern in the past has been to get rid of emotional and physical distress and to achieve success in this world is suddenly confronted with the realms of perinatal and transpersonal phenomena, he or she will discover the critical importance of the basic ontological and cosmological questions.

Who or what created this universe? How was it created and how am I related to the Creator or the creative principle? Who am I, where did I come from, and where am I going? What is the purpose of my life or life in general? Are there other levels and realms of existence as real as our own universe? Is it possible that the archetypal beings and mythological domains have an existence of their own and that they interact with our reality in a significant way? Do we go through an entire chain of existences and are these existences lawfully connected? If continuous rebirth is a source of suffering, is there knowledge and a chain of actions that lead to liberation? Questions of this kind, which have previously been seen as pseudophilosophizing reserved for primitive cultures, pre-adolescents, and psychiatric patients, suddenly appear in an entirely new light.

The process of experiential self-exploration not only shows these questions as being extremely real and important, but also provides access to critical information that can lead to a solution of these fundamental riddles of existence. Traditional Western scientists like to assume an all-knowing position and discard any notion of spirituality as primitive superstition, regressive magical thinking, lack of education, or clinical psychopathology. Psychiatry and psychology governed by the mechanistic worldview are incapable of making a distinction between the narrow-minded and dogmatic religious beliefs of mainstream religions and the profound wisdom of the great spiritual philosophies and mystical traditions, such as the different systems of yoga, Kashmir Shaivism, Tibetan Vajrayana, Zen, Christian mysticism, Kabbalah, Sufism, or certain forms of Gnosticism.

Western science is blind to the fact that the above traditions are the result of centuries of research into the human mind that has combined systematic observation, experimentation, and construction of theories in a way that resembles the scientific method. Many traditional scientists confuse the current Newtonian-Cartesian model of the universe with a definitive description of reality, the accuracy and truth of which has been proven beyond any reasonable doubt. In a universe where matter is primary and life, consciousness, and intelligence are its accidental products, there is no place for spirituality of any form as a relevant and meaningful aspect of existence.

If the mechanistic paradigm were actually a true and complete description of reality, an enlightened understanding of the universe based on science would involve acceptance of one's own insignificance as one of four billion inhabitants of one of the countless celestial bodies in a universe that has millions of galaxies. It would also require the recognition that humans are nothing but highly developed animals and biological machines composed of cells, tissues, and organs. In this context, our consciousness is a physiological product of the brain, and our psyche is governed by unconscious forces of a biological and instinctual nature.

When deep spiritual convictions are found in non-Western cultures with inadequate educational systems this is usually attributed to ignorance, childlike gullibility, and superstition. In our own culture, such an interpretation obviously will not do, particularly if it occurs in well-educated persons with superior intelligence. Here mainstream psychiatry resorts to the findings of psychoanalysis suggesting that the roots of religious beliefs can be found in unresolved conflicts from infancy and early childhood. It interprets the concept of deities as infantile images of parental figures, the religious attitudes of the believers as signs of emotional immaturity and childlike dependency, and ritual activities as results of a struggle against early psychosexual impulses, comparable to the mechanisms found in obsessive-compulsive neuroses.

Direct spiritual experiences, such as feelings of cosmic unity, death-rebirth sequences, encounters with archetypal entities, visions of light of supernatural beauty, or past incarnation memories are then seen as gross distortions of objective reality, indicative of a serious mental disease. Anthropologists have discussed shamanism usually in the context of schizophrenia, hysteria, or epilepsy, and psychopathological labels have been put on all the great prophets and sages. Even meditation has been discussed in a psychopathological context. The following passage from an article by the famous psychoanalyst Franz Alexander equating Buddhist meditation with artificial catatonia can be used here as an example: "From our present psychoanalytic knowledge it is clear that Buddhist self-absorption is a libidinal, narcissistic turning of the urge for knowing inward, a sort of artificial schizophrenia with complete withdrawal of libidinal interest from the outside world" (Alexander 1931). With a few exceptions, such as the work of Carl Gustav Jung, Roberto Assagioli, and Abraham Maslow, there has been no recognition of spirituality in Western psychiatry and no notion that there might be some difference between mysticism and psychosis.

I have tried to demonstrate in another context (Grof 1985) the errors involved in this approach to spirituality. To confuse the Newtonian-Cartesian model of reality with reality itself means to ignore the modern philosophy of science with its understanding of the nature of scientific theories and the dynamics of paradigms. In addition, it constitutes a serious logical error; by confusing the map with the territory in Korzybski's sense (Korzybski 1933), it violates the principle of logical typing, which used to be a favorite topic of the late Gregory Bateson (Bateson 1979). However, above all, this approach extrapolates the findings from basic sciences into psychology and ignores a vast body of observations from modern consciousness research, particularly those related to transpersonal experiences. Any serious scientific theory has to be an attempt to organize the existing facts, rather than a product of speculative extrapolation. It has to be based on observations of the universe and not on the beliefs of scientists as to what the universe is like or their wishes about what it should be like to fit their theories.

Modern consciousness research and experiential psychotherapy have thrown entirely new light on the problem of spirituality and religion and have returned to the human psyche its cosmic status. In full agreement with the Jungian perspective, spirituality or numinosity appears to be an intrinsic property of the deeper dynamics of the psyche. Whenever the process of experiential self-exploration reaches the perinatal and the transpersonal levels, it leads to spiritual awakening, and the individual becomes interested in the mystical quest. I have seen many highly educated persons undergo this process in our psychedelic training program and in holotropic workshops, and have yet to see a single individual, including atheists, Marxists, and positivistic scientists, whose scepticism and cynicism about spirituality would survive such an experience.

The form of spirituality I am referring to is fully compatible with any level of intelligence, education, and specific knowledge of the information amassed by such disciplines as physics, biology, medicine, and psychology. None of the sophisticated subjects I have worked with found any conflicts between their spiritual experiences and the information they had about the physical world. However, they often had to give up certain undefendable generalizations and unfounded metaphysical assumptions that had been part of their academic education. There exists these days extensive literature suggesting that many revolutionary advances in modern science point to a radically new worldview. Although we are still far from a comprehensive synthesis, significant elements of this emerging paradigm show far-reaching convergence with the worldview of the great mystical traditions (Grof 1984).

However, it is important to emphasize that this does not necessarily mean convergence of science and religion. The spirituality that emerges spontaneously at a certain stage of experiential self-exploration should not be confused with the mainstream religions and their beliefs, doctrines, dogmas, and rituals. Many of them lost entirely the connection with their original source, which is a direct visionary experience of transpersonal realities. They are mainly concerned with such issues as power, money, hierarchies, and ethical, political, and social control. It is possible to have a religion with very little spirituality, complete absence thereof, or even one that interferes with genuine spiritual quest.

A good friend of mine, Walter Houston Clark, a retired professor of religion and author of a well-known text on the psychology of religion had profound mystical experiences after many years of teaching religion in a university setting. As a result of these experiences, he came to understand the relationship between true spirituality and religion. I have heard him talk about it using an interesting image. He said that much of mainstream religion reminded him of vaccination. One goes to church and gets "a little something that then protects him or her against the real thing." Thus many people believe that regular attendance of church on Sundays and holidays, saying the prayers, and listening to the sermons is sufficient for being truly religious. This false sense of having already arrived then prevents them from starting on a journey of spiritual discovery. Carl Gustav Jung expressed a similar opinion (Jung 1958); according to him, the main function of formalized religion is to protect people against the direct experience of God.

Spiritual experiences that become available in deep self-exploration typically do not bring the subject closer to the established church and do not inspire more frequent attendance of formalized divine service, whether the religion involved is Christianity, Judaism, or Islam. More frequently, it brings to a clear relief the problems and limitations of established churches and mediates understanding as to where and why religions went astray and lost contact with true spirituality. However, direct spiritual experiences are perfectly compatible with the mystical branches of the great religions of the world, such as the different varieties of Christian mysticism, Sufism, and Kabbalah or the Hassidic movement. The really important division in the world of spirituality is not the line that separates the individual mainstream religions from each other, but the one that separates all of them from their mystical branches.

Mainstream religions typically advocate concepts of God where the divinity is a force that is outside of human beings and has to be contacted through the mediation of the church and the priesthood. A preferable place for this interaction then is the temple. In contrast, the spirituality revealed in the process of focused self-exploration sees God as the Divine Within. Here the individual uses various techniques that mediate direct experiential access to transpersonal realities and discovers his or her own divinity. For spiritual practice of this kind, it is the body and nature that play the function of the temple.

The temples can play an important role in facilitating true spirituality, only if their architecture and interior decoration are of such exquisite beauty and perfection that they bring visitors closer to the transcendental realm, or if elements of divine service that they offer, such as organ music, choir chanting, and the luster of liturgical objects, mediate direct transpersonal experience. The great Gothic cathedrals of Europe can be mentioned here as salient examples.

The most important aspects of the above discussion of the relationship between religion and spiritual experience can be illustrated by the following account from a session of a writer who took the amphetamine-related empathogens MDMA and 2CB in a group setting (Adamson 1986). Another part of his experience is described on p. 67.

> It was as though I were hovering, several layers of obfuscating reality above a great howling source of light. As levels of misconception, misrepresentation, illusion, consensuality diffused and dissipated like a clearing fog, the sound grew louder and louder. It was the sizzling of an arc-light of billions of volts, it was a roaring of a thousand suns, it was the sound of the universe ablaze. As it became more apparent, it was a huge, round ball that I was now orbiting. To call it white light would be to pale and daub this light monochromatic. It blazed with a radiance that was primordial, with an intensity that was absolute.
>
> I came to know — not through language but through innate cognition — that this roaring explosion was life itself. It shrieked and

pulsed through everything living, it was the source of the crystalline movement of life. It was the precursor to the original ball of starseed that exploded and created everything that exists in our big-banging or, depending on your cosmology, pulsating universe. And it flowed through me. I was connected with it as if by an immense shuddering optical fiber of not only light, but energy.

This was a pre-religious experience. Religion now seemed superfluous next to being in the presence of this source of life. Spirituality had become a limp representation of the fury and power of life. It was not awesome, it was awe itself. It was not godly, but godding. It was not goodly, but was the way it was; it was the pure absolute that was not right, or loving, or benign, but was just the way it was — life alive.

Of course one loves all other living creatures. Of course one feels that everything is all right with creation. Of course we are all united. We are simply all part of the fire of life. If this source of energy that flows through us did not exist, neither would we. Love, spirituality, and peace follow from this experience as surely as one breath leads to another. No big deal. It is merely our nature.

There exists ample evidence that the transcendental impulse is the most vital and powerful force in human beings. Systematic denial and repression of spirituality that is so characteristic for modern Western societies can be a critical factor contributing to the alienation, existential anxiety, individual and social psychopathology, criminality, violence, and self-destructive tendencies of contemporary humanity. For this reason, the recent increase of interest in various forms of self-exploration, which can mediate direct spiritual experiences, is a very encouraging trend and a development of great potential significance.

The importance of the spiritual quest can be explained in terms of the model discussed earlier in this book (p. 238). I have suggested that to describe human beings in a way that conforms with the observations from modern consciousness research, one has to use a paradoxical complementary model that bears a certain resemblance to the wave-particle paradox of subatomic physics. The two modes of consciousness corresponding to these two complementary aspects of human nature are the hylotropic, or matter-oriented mode, and the holotropic mode, aiming for totality and wholeness.

To live fully up to one's potential, it is essential to acknowledge both aspects of one's being, cultivate them, and become familiar and comfortable with both of them. In practice, this means to be in touch with one's inner life and to complement the daily activities by focused self-exploration of one's unconscious and superconscious. This can be achieved through meditation, techniques of humanistic and transpersonal psychotherapy, participation in shamanic rituals and trance events, a stay in a sensory isolation tank, supervised psychedelic work, or some other means.

In this way, one's life becomes an active dialogue between the hylotropic and the holotropic mode. This is really just a reformulation of Carl Gustav Jung's idea that the most vital human need is to discover one's own inner reality through the cultivation of symbolic life and to live in active, dynamic contact with the collective unconscious and the Self. This makes it possible to draw on the enormous resources and wisdom of ages that lie in the collective psyche.

A person whose entire existence is limited to the hylotropic mode, even if free from manifest clinical symptoms and thus mentally healthy from the point of view of traditional psychiatry, is cut off from these inner resources and incapable of drawing on them. This leads to chronic frustration of higher transcendental needs and a sense of lack of fulfillment. Holotropic experiences encountered in the process of in-depth self-exploration have intrinsic healing potential. Those that are difficult and painful in nature — if completed and well-integrated — seem to eliminate sources of disturbing emotions and tensions that would otherwise interfere with everyday life. Ecstatic and unitive holotropic experiences then remove the sense of alienation, create feelings of belonging, infuse the individual with strength, zest, and optimism, and enhance self-esteem. They cleanse the senses and open them for the perception of the extraordinary richness, beauty, and mystery of existence. The experience of fundamental oneness with the rest of creation increases the tolerance and patience toward others, lowers the level of aggression, and improves the capacity for synergy and cooperation.

The discovery of the hidden aspects of reality and of the challenges associated with them adds fascinating new dimensions to existence. It makes one's life much richer and more interesting and frees some of the energies that have been previously tied up in various quixotic ambitious endeavors and directs them to the adventure of self-discovery. Repeated experiences of the transpersonal domain can have a profound impact on the individual involved. They tend to dissolve the narrow and limited perspective characterizing the average Westerner and make one see the problems of everyday life from a cosmic perspective.

Some of the experiences encountered during the inner quest have such an extreme intensity that they change the individual's baseline for the experience of life and the concept of what one can endure, cope with, and integrate. In addition to actual healing that occurs in the process, this drastic change of perspective, context, and baseline for evaluation of one's life experience can represent an important asset in life and transform the quality of everyday existence.

In view of these facts, the increase of interest in spirituality and in inner quest is certainly one of the few hopeful developments in our troubled world. If this trend continues, inner transformation of humanity could become a major force in averting the present suicidal trend and the global catastrophe toward which the world seems to be moving at a frightening pace. The rapidly processing convergence between the new science and the mystical traditions of perennial philosophy offers an exciting perspective of a future comprehensive worldview that will heal the gap between scientific research and spiritual quest. Such an encompassing new paradigm could become an important catalyst in the evolution of consciousness that seems to be a critical condition for the survival of life on this planet.

Appendix A

PSYCHEDELICS IN PSYCHOTHERAPY AND SELF-EXPLORATION

THE USE of psychedelic substances for healing, divination, and communication with both the supernal and chthonic realms can be traced back to the dawn of human history. From time immemorial, plants and, in rare instances, animal materials containing powerful mind-altering alkaloids have been administered for ritual and magical purposes both in aboriginal and high cultures in various parts of the world.

Psychedelic Plants and Substances

IN the history of Chinese medicine, reports about psychedelic substances can be traced back at least 3,500 years. Of special historical interest is the legendary divine plant and potion called *haoma* in the ancient Persian Zend Avesta and *soma* in the old Indian literature. Introduced to India by the nomadic Aryan invaders, it had a profound influence on the development of the Hindu religion and philosophical thought. One hundred and twenty verses of the *Rig Veda* are dedicated to soma and praise the extraordinary effects that this divine potion had on worshippers. Those who drank it were overcome by ecstatic rapture, where "half of them was on earth, the other half in the heavens." Their bodies were strengthened, their hearts were filled with courage, joy and enthusiasm, their minds were enlightened, and they received assurance of their immortality.

Another common and widespread plant with psychedelic properties that has been used for sacred and recreational purposes is *hemp*. Leaves, blossoms, and resin from its varieties, such as *Cannabis sativa* and *Cannabis indica*, have been smoked and ingested under various names — *hashish, kif, charas, bhang, ganja, marijuana* — in the Middle East, Africa, India, China, Tibet, North and South America, and in the Caribbean for pleasure, healing, and for ritual purposes. Hemp has served as an important sacrament for such diverse groups as the African aboriginal tribes, Indian Brahmins, Tibetan Tantric Buddhists, some orders of the Sufis, ancient Scythians, and the Jamaican Rastafarians.

The psychedelic pharmacopeia has been particularly rich in Central America, where various Pre-Columbian cultures (Aztecs, Toltecs, Mayans) and contemporary Indian groups (Huichols, Yaquis, Mazatecs) have used at least sixteen different plants with distinctly mind-altering properties. The most famous of these plants are the peyote cactus (*Lophophora williamsii*), the sacred mushrooms *teonanacatl* or "flesh of the gods" (*Psilocybe mexicana* and *cubensis*), and *ololiuqui*, which is the native name of the morning glory seeds (*Turbina corymbosa*).

The ceremonial use of peyote continues today particularly among the Huichol, Yaqui, Cora, and Tarahumara Indians of Mexico. After the Civil War in the United States, the peyote religion passed north from the Rio Grande area into the United States and became assimilated by more than fifty Native American tribes. According to some estimates, more than a half of American Indians (250,000) belong at present to the Native American Church, a syncretistic religion that combines the peyote cult with Christian elements. Ceremonial use of Psilocybe mushrooms among the Mexican Mazatec Indians was publicized world-wide after the famous *curandera* Maria Sabina revealed their secret to the American banker and mycologist Gordon Wasson and his wife.

The most famous South American psychedelic is *ayahuasca* or *yage*, prepared from the bark of the jungle *liana Banisteriopsis caapi* and known in Brazil, Peru, Ecuador, and Columbia under many native names, such as Vine of Death, Vine of the Soul, and Vine-Rope of Death (*soga de muerte*). It is administered in dramatic puberty rituals that involve intense flagellation and is also renowned for its powerful purgative, healing, visionary, and telepathic effects. The most popular among the South American psychedelic snuffs are *cohoba*, made from the sap of *Virola theiodora* or *Virola cuspidata*, and *epená* from *Virola calophylla* and *Virola theiodora*. The Virola snuffs are used among many Indian groups in the Amazonian regions of Venezuela, Columbia, and Brazil for communication with the spirit world, diagnosis and treatment of diseases, prophecy, divination, and other magico-religious purposes. The San Pedro cactus (*Trichocerus pachanoi*) is similar in its effects to peyote with which it shares the active alkaloid mescaline. It has been used by shamans of the Andean Ecuador for more than three millenia for divination and healing.

Equatorial Africa contributes to the world of psychedelic plants the shrub *eboga* (*Tabernanthe iboga*). Its roots are sought after by wild boars, gorillas, and porcupines whose behavior it dramatically alters. Shavings of the bark from the roots are used by the natives under the name *eboga* or *iboga*. In small quantities, it is an aphrodisiac and psychostimulant; warriors on military path and lion hunters take it to keep themselves awake during night watches. The iboga cults consisting of male (Bwiti) and female (Mbiri) participants employ large doses in all-night ceremonies that involve dancing and drumming for religious purposes to mediate communication with ancestral spirits.

The last major psychedelic plant I would like to mention is the fly-agaric (*Amanita muscaria*), the red, white-speckled mushroom which appears in Lewis Carroll's *Alice in Wonderland* and many other Western fairy-tales. It has been widely used by Siberian shamans of the Koryak, Samoyed, Ostyak, and Chukchee tribes, North American Indian groups around the Great Lakes, particularly the Ojibway, and certain Scandinavian peoples. Some researchers have tried to link the old Viking reports about the so-called *Berserksgang*, military frenzy of a group of bearskin-clad warriors described in the Nordic sagas, to the ingestion of fly-agaric mushrooms (Fabing 1956). Gordon Wasson (1967) has collected evidence from various disciplines suggesting that *Amanita muscaria* was the legendary plant and potion soma of the Vedic period. Some unclarity and controversy about the psychedelic effects of fly-agaric has arisen, and Wasson's theory, although very interesting and popular, has not reached general acceptance.

I would like to close the discussion of the most famous psychedelic materials by a brief reference to mind-altering substances of animal origin. The "dream fish" (*Kyphosus fuscus*) found off Norfolk Island in the South Pacific has a reputation among the natives for causing powerful nightmarish visions. Joe Roberts, a photographer for the *National Geographic Magazine*, broiled and ate some in 1960 and confirmed these claims. He experienced a powerful hallucinatory state with many elements of science fiction. (Roberts 1960). The psychoactive properties of toad skin and its secretions explain its popularity in medieval witches' brews and ointments used in the context of the Witches' Sabbath or Walpurgis' Night. The mind-altering effects of these animal products can be explained by high contents of psychedelic tryptamine derivatives such as dimethyl-tryptamine (DMT), 5-methoxy-DMT, and bufotenin (dimethyl-serotonin). Among the main ingredients of the Sabbath preparations were the plants from the nightshade family: the deadly nightshade (*Atropa belladonna*), thornapple (*Datura stramonium*), mandrake (*Mandragora officinarum*) and henbane (*Hyoscyamus niger*).

The long history of ritual use of psychedelic substances contrasts sharply with a relatively short period of scientific interest in these materials and their systematic laboratory and clinical investigation. Louis Lewin, often referred to as the father of modern psychopharmacology, collected specimens of peyote, brought them to Germany and isolated several of its alkaloids. In 1897, his colleague and rival, Arthur Heffter, succeeded in chemical identification of the psychoactive principle of peyote and called it *mezcaline* (mescaline). The early pioneering experiments with peyote were conducted by Weir Mitchell, Havelock Ellis, and Heinrich Kluever. This research culminated in 1927 in the publication of the book *Der Meskalinrausch (The Mescaline Intoxication)* by Kurt Beringer (Beringer 1927).

In the following years, very little psychedelic research was done until the early 1940s. The golden era in the history of psychedelics began in April 1942, when the Swiss chemist Albert Hofmann made the serendipitous discovery of the extraordinary psychoactive properties of miniscule dosages of the diethylamid of lysergic acid (LSD-25). This new semisynthetic ergot derivative, active in incredibly minute quantities of millionths of a gram (micrograms or gammas), became overnight a scientific sensation. The research inspired by Hofmann's discovery did not remain limited to LSD; it led to a renaissance of interest in the previously known psychedelic plants and substances and an avalanche of new knowledge about them.

One after another, the secrets and mysteries of the psychedelic world were yielding to systematic team efforts of modern scientific inquiry. The active principles from the most famous psychedelic plants were chemically identified and prepared in the laboratory in pure form. Albert Hofmann himself developed deep interest in the chemistry of psychedelic plants after his initial accidental intoxication by LSD-25 and the subsequent planned self-experiment with this substance. He succeeded in solving the mystery of the Mexican sacred mushrooms by isolating their active alkaloids, psilocybine and psilocin. Before his scientific work in this area was terminated by the unfortunate political and administrative measures caused by the existence of the psychedelic black market and unsupervised mass self-experimentation of the young generation, he was also able to trace the activity of the morning glory seeds to their content of d-lysergic acid amid and related ergot derivatives.

The main active principle from *ayahuasca* or *yage'* is the alkaloid harmaline, also called banisterine, yageine, or telepathine. Although its chemical structure has been known since 1919, modern chemical and pharmacological research disclosed some important new data. Of particular interest is the fact that harmaline bears close resemblance to substances that can be obtained from the pineal gland, such as 10-methoxy-harmaline. This provided the basis for some fascinating speculations, since the mystical traditions attribute great significance to the pineal gland in relation to the "opening of the third eye," visionary states, and psychic abilities. Harmala alkaloids have also been found in cohoba and epena snuffs and in the Syrian rue (Peganum harmala).

Ibogaine, the most important psychoactive alkaloid of the African eboga plant (Tabernanthe iboga), was isolated in 1901, but the understanding of its chemical structure was not completed until the late 1960s. After many difficulties, modern chemists also deciphered the chemical secrets of hashish and marijuana by tracing their typical effects to a group of tetrahydrocannabinols (THC).

A theoretically important contribution to the understanding of various psychedelic materials of plant and animal origin was the research of psychoactive tryptamine derivatives, initiated in Budapest, Hungary, by Böszörmönyi and Szara. Dimethyltryptamine (DMT), diethyltryptamine (DET), dipropyltryptamine (DPT), and other related compounds are among the simplest molecules with psychedelic effects. They are responsible for the mind-altering properties of the South American snuffs *cohoba, epená*, and *paricá* and contribute to the efficacy of *ayahuasca* mixtures. In the animal kingdom, as I have already mentioned earlier, they are the active principles in the toad skin and its secretions and in the meat of the Pacific "dream fish" (*Kyphosus fuscus*).

The theoretical interest of tryptamine derivatives lies in the fact that they occur naturally in the human organism, are derivatives of the important aminoacid tryptophane, and are chemically related to neurotransmitters. For these reasons, they are logical candidates for endogenous psychotomimetic substances that might be produced by the metabolic processes in the body and have often been discussed in the context of biochemical theories of psychoses. Among the naturally occurring tryptamine derivatives are also the active alkaloids from the Mexican sacred mushrooms, psilocybine and psilocin, mentioned above.

Modern chemical research has thus solved the problems of most psychedelic substances that have played important roles in the history of humanity. Only the Vedic *soma* has remained a mystery, both botanically and chemically. Beside Wasson's theory that links it to *Amanita muscaria*, there are others implying the Syrian rue (*Peganum harmala*), the Chinese pine (*Ephedra sinica*), and other plants. It is regrettable that the enthusiastic efforts of anthropologists, botanists, pharmacologists, chemists, psychiatrists, and psychologists that characterized the psychedelic research of the 1950s and 1960s were so drastically stymied before some of the remaining secrets of the psychedelic world could yield to scientific curiosity.

The recent widely publicized controversy concerning methylene-dioxy-methamphetamine (MDMA), popularly known as XTC, Ecstasy, or Adam, attracted attention of mental health professionals, as well as lay audiences, to a large group of psychoactive substances that have a molecular structure resembling mescaline, dopamine, and amphetamine. Most of these substances that are of interest for psychiatry are semisynthetic. They do not occur in nature as such, but their chemical precursors are volatile oils found in nutmeg, saffron, sassafras, and other plants and botanical products. The best known of these amphetamine related psychedelics or "empathogens" are MDA (3,4-methylene-dioxy-amphetamine), MMDA (3-methoxy-4,5-methylene-dioxy-amphetamine), MDMA (3,4-methylene-dioxy-methamphetamine), DOM or STP (2,5-dimethoxy-4-methyl-amphetamine), TMA (3,4,5-trimethoxy-methyl-amphetamine), and 2-CB (4-bromo-2,5-dimethoxy-phenethylamine).

Ketamine hydrochlorid (Ketalar, Ketanest, Ketajet), is a fully synthetic compound that is chemically related to the infamous phencyclidine (PCP or "Angel Dust"), an anesthetic used in veterinary medicine and known as a dangerous drug of street abuse. In spite of its chemical similarity to phencyclidine, ketamine differs from it considerably in its psychological effects. It is produced and distributed by Parke-Davis as a dissociative anesthetic and is generally considered to be one of the safest substances used in surgical practice to produce general anesthesia. In the early years of its existence, it was administered to hundreds of thousands of patients with uncertain medical history requiring immediate emergency surgery. In spite of its biological safety, it fell gradually in disfavor of the surgical community, because it often produced the so-called "emergence syndrome," basically very unusual and powerful perceptual and emotional changes experienced by patients during their return to normal consciousness. Psychiatrists investigating this phenomenon discovered that Ketamine is a very powerful psychedelic substance that in quantities much smaller than those used by surgeons (about one-tenth to one-sixth of the anesthetic dose) can be used for extraordinary psychiatric explorations, training of professionals, and for therapeutic purposes.

Ritual and Therapeutic Use of Psychedelics

ANTHROPOLOGISTS who have studied ritual use of psychedelics in various aboriginal cultures have described a broad spectrum of extraordinary claims associated with these substances.

Among these have been diagnosing of diseases and emotional or psychosomatic healing; communication with the world of spirits, ancestors, deities, and demons; black magic and hexing; return to one's origins; opening of extrasensory channels of perception (telepathy, clairvoyance, psychometry, astral projection); transcendence of death with subsequent loss of fear of dying; profound personal transformation and rejuvenation; communion with natural forces, animals and plant life; enhancement of social cohesion in the community, and others.

In view of the enormous variety and scope of these phenomena, most of which lie far beyond the conceptual framework of traditional psychology and the philosophy of Western science, it is not surprising that Western scientists and educated laypersons alike tend to take these claims with a grain of salt. However, laboratory and clinical research of psychedelics during its golden era in the 1950s and 1960s brought unexpected confirmation of the beliefs concerning the effects of psychedelics held by ancient and aboriginal cultures, while simultaneously undermining many fundamental assumptions and preconceptions of Newtonian-Cartesian science.

The first step in this direction was the recognition that the major psychedelics do not produce specific pharmacological states (toxic psychosis), but are *unspecific amplifiers of mental processes*. Exploration of the human psyche with these powerful catalyzing agents has shown beyond any doubt that the biographical model developed by Freud's "depth" psychology barely scratches the surface of mental dynamics. To account for all the extraordinary experiences and observations in psychedelic states, it was necessary to develop a vastly expanded cartography of the human mind. This cartography, described in the first part of this book and illustrated by many clinical examples, can be used as a unifying conceptual framework that introduces new light into the rich world of psychedelic observations and brings them to a common denominator.

The new model is so encompassing that it includes all or most of the phenomena described in various historical periods and various countries of the world in situations involving psychedelics. However, different cultural and historical frameworks emphasize and cultivate certain specific experiential domains and their combinations. Thus, for example, the *ancient mysteries of death and rebirth*, such as the Eleusinian mysteries, that were conducted for almost two millenia in Greece, seemed to focus on the profound transformation associated with perinatal dynamics: confrontation with death, transcendence, and the resulting changes in one's experience of life, hierarchy of values, and relationship to the cosmos. These changes were deeply connected with the loss of fear of death. Wasson, Hofmann, and Ruck collected in their book *Road to Eleusis* impressive evidence suggesting that the sacred potion *kykeon* used in Eleusis contained ergot derivatives chemically close to LSD. (Wasson, Hofmann, and Ruck 1978).

The so-called rites of passage, powerful ritual events, enacted by various aboriginal cultures at the time of important biological and social transitions, revolve around the triad of birth, sex, and death, and involve experiences characteristic for the third perinatal matrix (BPM III). In this context, the initiates undergo powerful experiences of psychological death and rebirth that are then typically interpreted as dying to the old biological or social role and being born into the new one. Thus, for example, in puberty rites boys and girls are seen as dying to the role of children and being born as adults. In addition, different cultures might emphasize various transpersonal realms of experience as parts of the symbolic context of these rites, for example, cosmological mythological themes, reclaiming the ancestral heritage, connection with the totem animal, participation of specific deities or demons in the rituals, and others.

During the "shamanic illness" that begins the career of many shamans, powerful perinatal elements usually dominate the experiences. The death-rebirth process takes the form of the descent into the underworld, torture, dismemberment and annihilation by demons, and subsequent ascent to the upper world. The associated transpersonal experiences typically focus on elements of nature — deep connection with cosmic forces, animals and animal spirits, plant life, and even inanimate objects. Development of ESP, creative inspiration, and the ability to diagnose and heal diseases are additional typical transpersonal concomitants of profound and well-integrated shamanic experiences.

Some other ritual frameworks highlight other types of transpersonal experiences, such as communication with or even possession by deities or demons and other archetypal beings, healing mediated by spirit guides or animal helpers, various forms of parapsychological phenomena, and racial or collective experiences. Here the cultural and social context and the techniques used seem to provide selective channels to various levels and domains of the cartography described earlier. Experiences of deep empathy or meaningful connection with others and a sense of group belonging can often be observed after powerful perinatal experiences, as well as in connection with various types of transpersonal phenomena.

It is important to emphasize that the above experiences characteristic of death-rebirth mysteries, rites of passage, shamanic "illness," and other ritual situations occur in frameworks using psychedelic materials, as well as in those that involve powerful nonpharmacological means. This supports the main thesis of this book that there is no basic difference between psychedelic experiences and nonordinary states of consciousness induced by other techniques, such as respiratory maneuvers, chanting and drumming, trance-dancing, meditative practice, and others.

I have already mentioned above that psychedelic research has in general confirmed the claims concerning psychedelic states made by various non-Western cultures. Modern psychologists, psychiatrists, and anthropologists are now facing the challenge of reinterpreting these observations so that they are consonant with modern Western psychology and philosophy of science. In view of the main thrust of this book it is of special interest to explore how the claims about the healing potential of psychedelic drugs withstood the test of modern research.

The often dramatic and profound effects of psychedelics on experimental subjects in laboratory and clinical settings suggest naturally the possibility that they might be useful as therapeutic agents. For some reason, this avenue was not pursued during the first wave of interest in psychedelics in the first decades of this century, when research focused primarily on mescaline. The general understanding of the effects of this drug at that time was that it induced a toxic psychosis, a state that was of no therapeutic interest.

The possibility of therapeutic use of LSD was first suggested by Condrau in 1949, only two years after Stoll had published in Switzerland the first scientific study of LSD (Condrau 1949). In the early 1950s, several researchers independently recommended LSD as an adjunct to psychotherapy that can deepen and intensify the therapeutic process. The pioneers of this approach were Busch and Johnson (1950) and Abramson (1955) in the United States, Sandison, Spencer, and Whitelaw (1954) in England, and Frederking (1953) in West Germany.

The early reports of these researchers attracted considerable attention and stimulated psychiatrists and psychologists in various countries of the world to conduct their own therapeutic experimentation with LSD and other psychedelics. Many of the reports published over a period of about twenty years confirmed the initial claims that psychedelics could expedite the psychotherapeutic process and shorten the time necessary for the treatment of various emotional and psychosomatic disorders.

In addition, there appeared numerous studies indicating that LSD-assisted psychotherapy could reach certain categories of psychiatric patients usually considered poor candidates for psychoanalysis and other types of psychotherapy. Many individual researchers and therapeutic teams reported various degrees of success with chronic alcoholics, narcotic drug addicts, sociopaths, criminal psychopaths, sexual deviants, and subjects suffering from serious character disorders.

In the early 1960s, a new and exciting area was discovered for psychedelic psychotherapy: the care of patients with terminal cancer and some other incurable diseases. Studies of dying individuals indicated that this approach was able to bring not only alleviation of the emotional suffering and relief from severe physical pain associated with cancer, but also dramatically transform the concept of death and change the attitude toward dying (Grof and Halifax 1977).

The efforts to use LSD and other psychedelics in the treatment of emotional disorders now span a period of more than three decades. Since the appearance of the early clinical reports, much time and energy has been invested in research of their therapeutic potential and many hundreds of professional papers have been published on the subject. As has to be expected in any new area of such enormous complexity and revolutionary significance, the history of psychedelic therapy has its share of trials and errors.

Many different techniques of therapeutic use of LSD and other psychedelics have been proposed and tested during the past thirty years. Some of these approaches did not withstand the test of time and were abandoned; others were refined, modified, and assimilated by other therapists into more sophisticated treatment procedures. It would be beyond the scope of this presentation to try to follow this complicated process through its different stages. The interested reader can find a more comprehensive discussion of this subject in my book *LSD Psychotherapy* (Grof 1980). In this context, I will try only a brief critical review of the clinical use of psychedelics, following the most important streams and focusing on those treatment modalities that deserve attention from the point of view of our current knowledge.

Among the approaches that were abandoned, because they proved to be too simplistic and did not do justice to the complexity of the effects of psychedelics are those that saw these substances just as another group of chemical agents and wanted to exploit their pharmacological properties. Here belong attempts to use LSD as an antidepressant, shock-inducing compound, abreactive agent, or a drug that can activate chronic and stationary clinical conditions and make them more responsive to traditional psychiatric treatment.

The researchers who maintained their trust in psychedelic therapy through the various conflicting reports of the initial era all came to the conclusion that psychedelic substances are more or less unspecific amplifiers and that the therapeutic success depends critically on a variety of factors of nonpharmacological nature (extrapharmacological variables). The most important among these are the personality structure of the subject, the personality of the guide or sitter, the therapeutic relationship, the nature and degree of specific psychotherapeutic help, and the physical and interpersonal context of the session.

All that psychedelic drugs can do in and of themselves is to activate the psyche and mediate emergence of the unconscious and superconscious contents into consciousness. Whether this process will be therapeutic or destructive and disorganizing is then determined by an entire spectrum of other influences that have nothing to do with the pharmacological effects of these compounds. Since the factors of the set and setting are of such paramount importance, no magic results should be expected from a simple administration of psychedelics; they should always be used in the framework of a complex psychotherapeutic program.

Even if we narrow the therapeutic use of psychedelics to the use of these substances in the context of psychotherapy, the two elements can be combined in many different ways, some of them more effective than others. Among the less interesting possibilities is the use of small dosages to facilitate psychotherapeutic process, occasional psychedelic sessions in the course of drug-free psychotherapy to overcome defenses and resistances, use of small dosages in group psychotherapy, and a combination of hypnosis and psychedelics, or *hypnodelic therapy* (Levine and Ludwig 1967). The two techniques of drug-assisted psychotherapy that have received most attention and are most interesting, are the psycholytic and the psychedelic treatment.

Psycholytic Therapy. The term psycholytic was coined by the British researcher and pioneer in LSD therapy, Ronald A. Sandison. Its root, *lytic* (from the Greek *lysis* = dissolution) suggests a process of releasing tensions, or resolving conflicts in the psyche. This treatment method represents in theory, as well as in practice, a modification and extension of Freudian analysis. It involves administration of an entire series (15–100) of medium dosages of psychedelics in one- to two-week intervals.

Psycholytic therapy represents a gradual exploration of increasingly deep levels of the unconscious. The therapist is usually present for several hours during the culmination period of the sessions, giving support and specific interpretations when necessary. All the phenomena that occur during the drug sessions or in the free intervals between them are approached with the use of basic Freudian therapeutic principles.

Psychedelic Therapy. The term psychedelic was first suggested by the psychiatrist and *LSD* researcher Humphrey Osmond and was inspired by his correspondence with Aldous Huxley. It means literally mind-manifesting (derived from the Greek *psyche* and *delein* = to make manifest). Psychedelic therapy differs in several important aspects from the psycholytic approach. Its main objective is to create optimal conditions for the subject to have a profound transformative experience of a transcendental nature. For most subjects, this takes the form of the experience of ego death and rebirth with subsequent feelings of cosmic unity and other types of transpersonal phenomena.

Among the factors that facilitate such an experience are special preparation, use of higher dosages of psychedelics, internalization of the process by the use of eyeshades, high fidelity stereophonic music played throughout the session, and emphasis on spirituality, art, and natural beauty in the set and setting. Verbal exchange is limited to periods before the drug sessions and following them; during the actual psychedelic experiences, talking is discouraged, since it interferes with the depth of emotional and psychosomatic self-exploration. Psychedelic therapists do not believe in brilliant and properly timed verbal interpretations or other interventions reflecting the belief system of a particular school. They encourage the client to let go of the usual defenses and to surrender to the spontaneous healing potential of the deeper dynamics of the psyche.

Most of the psychiatrists and psychologists who conducted clinical research with psychedelics have clearly precipitated either toward the psycholytic or psychedelic treatment modality. In my opinion, both of these approaches practiced in a pure form have their distinct disadvantages. In psycholytic therapy, it is the theoretical limitation to the biographical conceptual framework of Freudian psychoanalysis, lack of recognition of the perinatal and transpersonal dimensions of the psyche, and externalization of the process with excessive use of verbal ploys.

In contrast, in psychedelic therapy not enough attention is paid to the biographical material when it emerges in the sessions and too much is expected from a single transformative experience. While the use of the "single overwhelming dose" characterizing psychedelic therapy is generally very effective with alcoholics, narcotic drug addicts, depressed persons, and individuals dying of cancer, major therapeutic changes in patients suffering from various psychoneuroses, psychosomatic diseases, and character disorders require typically systematic working through in an entire series of psychedelic sessions.

In the following section, I will describe the form of drug-assisted psychotherapy, which I found most effective in my own clinical work. This approach combines the advantages of psycholytic and psychedelic therapy and avoids their disadvantages. Its basic principles are very similar to those of holotropic therapy which was described in detail in an earlier chapter. This should not be surprising, since holotropic breathing is conceptually and philosophically a direct derivative of the clinical work with psychedelics.

Principles of LSD Psychotherapy

THE psychedelic treatment procedure consists of three separate, but interrelated phases. The first of these is the preparation period; it involves a series of drug-free interviews during which the subject is prepared for the psychedelic experience. The amount of time that is necessary to achieve this goal depends on the nature of the problems involved, on the personality of the subject, on the drug used, and on some other circumstances. The purpose of this phase is to obtain sufficient information about the nature of the emotional difficulties and the personal history of the subject. An even more critical task is to develop a relationship of trust between the therapist and the client, which is the single most important factor determining the course and the outcome of the session.

When these objectives have been met, a special meeting should be scheduled to discuss various specific issues related to the drug session. These involve detailed information about the effects of the drug that will be administered, its potential benefits and risks, and the types of experiences that it might induce. At this time, the therapist should explain to the client the philosophy of the treatment, its general strategy, and the rules for conducting psychedelic sessions. At the end of this meeting, the client should sign an informed consent.

The second phase is the psychedelic session itself. It should take place in a protected environment, where the client is not disturbed by external influences and, in turn, has unlimited freedom of full expression, if necessary. The treatment facility should be homelike, comfortably furnished, and tastefully decorated. If possible, it should be located in a beautiful natural setting, since return to nature is an important aspect of the psychedelic experience. The bathroom facilities should be easily available. As music is an important part of psychedelic therapy, a good music system and an extensive collection of tapes or records belong to standard and absolutely indispensable items in any psychedelic treatment suite.

Before a psychedelic session, the client should fast or have only a very light meal. Fasting facilitates unusual states of consciousness and reduces the incidence of gastrointestinal problems. Quiet, relaxed, and meditative time immediately preceding the session is preferable to stressful and chaotic activities. After the administration of the psychedelic substance, the client should remain in a reclining position with eyeshades and headphones for most of the duration of the pharmacological action. As long as the dosages are low, it is possible to have rewarding externalized sessions, during which the subject keeps his or her eyes open. This is particularly the case with the amphetamine psychedelics such as MDA or MDMA. They can enhance the sensory perception of the environment, deepen interpersonal relations, and result in spiritualization of everyday life. However, when higher dosages are used, internalized sessions are generally much more profound and less confusing; they are conducive to a better integration of the experience. The basic safety rule for psychedelic sessions is that all the material which has been released from the unconscious has to be faced, fully experienced, and integrated. This condition is not met in externalized sessions, where various sensory distractions interfere with the awareness of the inner process.

During the time of intense psychedelic experiences, verbal exchange is kept at a minimum. The client keeps the eyes closed for most of the session, with the exception of bathroom breaks. Ideally, a male-female team pays undivided attention to the client through the entire session. At least one of the sitters should always be present to change music, attend to the subject's needs, offer support if necessary, and cover all aspects of external reality.

Constant presence of the sitters is an essential prerequisite for a good and safe psychedelic experience, even if an uncomplicated session requires from them only minimum action. They choose appropriate pieces of music according to the nature of the client's experience, check in briefly about every half-an-hour, bring water, Kleenex, or a plastic bag if necessary, and help the subject to the bathroom if assistance is needed.

During the peak hours specific interventions are required only if the subject is resisting the experience, refuses to stay in the eyeshades and headphones, and shows a tendency to project and act out. The description of these situations and discussion of the appropriate interventions can be found in my book *LSD Psychotherapy* (Grof 1980).

At the time when the pharmacological effects of the psychedelic substance are wearing off, the guides should check in with the client and get a sense of the nature of his or her experience. In most instances, the session reaches a spontaneous closure with a good resolution of all the issues brought up that particular day. An extensive talk about the experience in the late hours of the session or on the following day can help to facilitate the integration. Also writing a report, drawing and painting, or meditation can be very useful in this regard.

If there is a lack of resolution at the time when the pharmacological effects are subsiding, active intervention might be necessary. Here the sitters can use the techniques of holotropic therapy described earlier. A shorter period of faster breathing combined with focused body work on places where there is energy blockage usually leads to a rapid resolution of any residual emotional or psychosomatic issues. If necessary, uncovering work can be continued on the following day until good integration is attained.

The third phase, the post-session work, consists typically of several nondrug interviews in which the client discusses the experience with the guide(s) and explores how it could best be integrated into everyday life. Group interaction or various artistic expressions of the psychedelic experience are additional options. The occasional need for nondrug experiential sessions or body work was already mentioned earlier. In extreme cases, it might be indicated to schedule another psychedelic session within a week or so to complete the unfinished gestalt. Ideally, the course of psychedelic therapy should involve an open-ended situation where the number of sessions is not *a priori* limited by the research design or some other factors. The therapist and the client should be able to use their judgment and plan an additional session if and when necessary. In general, uncovering work is always preferable to tranquilizing medication that under these circumstances tends to freeze the process in its difficult stages and prevent resolution.

Psychedelic substances are extremely powerful tools for opening the depths of the unconscious and the heights of the superconscious. They have great positive potential and can also present grave dangers, depending on circumstances. The work with them should be approached with great seriousness and respect. As the history of the psychedelic movement shows, research in this field can present dangerous pitfalls not only for experimental subjects, but also for experienced researchers. If psychedelics are ever again used in clinical practice, their use should occur in the context of team work with peer control and mutual supervision.

Holotropic therapy, although generally not as profound as high dose psychedelic sessions with LSD or psilocybine, provides access to similar experiential territories and to remarkable healing mechanisms. The fact that the experiences develop gradually and are generated by sustained effort of the subject, makes the approach much safer and easily applicable on a large scale. If in the future psychedelic work becomes again possible, holotropic therapy could be a very useful preparation for both psychedelic therapists and clients. Being accustomed to and feeling comfortable with various powerful emotional and psychosomatic manifestations, they would find the introduction of a psychedelic catalyst into the treatment situation a logical and useful step.

This situation would differ from that of the 1950s, when the advent of LSD found most professionals entirely unprepared. Used to the tame atmosphere of Freudian free associations, face-to-face interviews, or behaviorist deconditioning and caught in the strait-jacket of the Newtonian-Cartesian paradigm, they were unable to assimilate the alien world of LSD phenomena into their theory and practice. Whatever happens in the future with psychedelic therapy *per se*, it is difficult to ignore the fact that similar challenging observations do not require strange and exotic drugs, but can be triggered by such simple means as breathing and sound. It should be only a matter of time until this fact is acknowledged, and the consequences will revolutionize psychiatry, psychology, and psychotherapy.

The above discussion focused on some very general principles of therapeutic work with psychedelics. Although these substances activate in a relatively nonspecific way the biographical, perinatal, and transpersonal experiential realms in the human psyche, they differ in certain aspects of their pharmacological action and in selective emphasis on certain parameters of the psychedelic experience. In the following text, I would like to add a few specific notes about the most important substances that have been explored in psychotherapeutic work.

LSD-25 (diethylamid of lysergic acid) remains after several decades of clinical research the most remarkable and interesting of all psychedelics. Its incredible efficacy and biological safety is unparalleled by any other psychoactive substance. A dose as small as 25 micrograms (gammas or millionths of a gram) can induce noticeable psychological changes lasting 6–8 hours. The optimal dosage for the therapeutic procedure described above is between 250 and 500 mcg. The major disadvantage of LSD is that it can, in higher dosages, lead occasionally to profoundly disorganizing experiences that under the wrong circumstances and without expert handling can lead to dangerous acting out.

Psilocybine, the pure alkaloid from the Mexican sacred mushrooms, is in its effects very similar to LSD. Both researchers conducting double-blind studies and experienced subjects have found it difficult to distinguish these two substances from each other, except by the shorter time of action for psilocybine. The dosage that seems optimal for therapeutic purposes ranges between 25 and 35 mg. In spite of the fact that the Mazatec *curandera* Maria Sabina endorsed a laboratory sample of psilocybine as being a valid surrogate for sacred mushrooms, many experienced subjects prefer the natural product. Fresh or dried Psilocybe mushrooms have in the psychedelic circles the reputation of the gentlest and smoothest mind-altering substance available. They have often been recommended as an ideal means of introducing neophytes into the world of psychedelic experiences.

Mescaline sulphate, the pure principle responsible for the psychedelic effects of peyote, resembles in its action the two previously mentioned substances. The most important difference seems to be the unusual richness of colors in mescaline visions and high incidence of gastrointestinal difficulties, particularly nausea and vomiting. Mescaline has never reached popularity as a therapeutic agent. One of its great disadvantages, beside the gastrointestinal side effects, is its toxicity and narrow safety range. Even administration of dosages commonly used in clinical work (150–500 mg) has an influence on the liver and causes distinct changes in laboratory tests. The toxicity of mescaline reaches dangerous levels when the dose approaches 1000 mg. In contrast, natural peyote has a great reputation among the Indians as a medicinal agent. It has so many medical uses that it almost approaches a panacea. Its remarkable healing potential is acknowledged even by those Indians who are opposed to its use in religious rites. The bitter taste of peyote and its nauseating effects serve as a self-limiting factor controlling the quantity of ingested material.

Among the short-acting tryptamine derivatives two deserve special attention. *Dipropyltryptamine (DPT)* has been systematically researched as an adjunct to psychotherapy in alcoholics and cancer patients and found to be comparable to LSD (Grof et al. 1973, Richards et al. 1979). Like all tryptamine derivatives, it has to be administered by injection; the alternative route by inhalation is not considered sufficiently predictable to be used in scientific experiments. The optimal therapeutic dosages are 75 mg–125 mg and the effects end abruptly in four hours. *5-methoxy-DMT* is a therapeutically interesting substance, since it makes it possible to have a powerful and compelling experience in the course of one single hour. Depending on dosage, it can be used for biographical work, perinatal and transpersonal exploration, or for a profound transforming experience of an entirely abstract, contentless, yet all-containing nature that subjects often compare to the Primary Clear Light described in the *Tibetan Book of the Dead*.

Among the ayahuasqueros in northwestern South America, yage is known as the "great medicine," believed to be curative whether it is swallowed by the patient or the healer. However, there have been only very limited efforts to test these claims in a Western clinical context. The most important study of therapeutic effects of *yage'* and the harmala alkaloids comes from Claudio Naranjo (Naranjo 1973). He described dramatic therapeutic changes in ten of his thirty subjects who took harmaline. A fascinating aspect of the harmala alkaloids is unusually high incidence of certain specific images from the collective unconscious, particularly large cats, snakes, and naked black women. These occur together with other more usual experiences, such as passage through the uterus, death, visions of sexual organs, cosmic vistas, and others. The effective dose of harmaline, according to Shulgin lies between 300 and 400 mg orally.

The therapeutic experiences with ibogaine are equally limited as those with the harmala group. The main source of data is again the report by Claudio Naranjo based on forty sessions with thirty patients using either ibogaine or total iboga extract (Naranjo 1973). According to him, ibogain tends to bring out the instinctual side of the psyche, as indicated by predominance of aggressive and sexual themes and images of animals or primitives. The optimal dosage for ibogain seems to be between 3 and 5 mg per kilogram.

In contrast with LSD, which is biologically very safe but can have a deeply shattering psychological impact, the psychedelic amphetamines (with the exception of DOM or STP) are psychologically very benign, while their physiological properties can present problems. They have a narrow safety range and their sympathomimetic effects make them potentially dangerous for people with cardiovascular disorders, particularly heart disease or hypertension. Most psychedelic amphetamines (empathogens) cause only minimum changes in sensory perception, while strongly enhancing emotional responses, stimulating philosophical thought, and inducing profound spiritual feelings. They open channels of empathy and increase the sense of connection with other people and with the natural environment. They can be used with advantage in groups in an entirely or partially externalized way.

During the recent wave of professional and public interest in MDMA (Adam, Ecstasy), this substance achieved a high acclaim as a love drug, opening the heart chakra. Before its widespread use alarmed the legislators who put it on emergency schedule I, it was used by many professionals with great success in marital counseling and family therapy, as well as a means of restoring faith in human relations (e.g., in victims of physical abuse or rape). Therapeutic work with empathogens requires a different choice of music than psychotherapy with LSD or psilocybine. Sweet, gentle, and flowing music seems to best correspond to the mode of action of these substances. Two of the empathogens deserve special notice: *DOM or STP* for the power and excessive duration of its action (up to several days) and *2-CB* because it combines the general empathogenic effects with rich changes in visual perception, which places it somewhere between MDMA and LSD.

Ketamine hydrochlorid, a substance combining anesthetic and psychedelic properties, is extremely interesting from the heuristic point of view. It opens access to most extraordinary realms of experiences, offers remarkable philosophical and spiritual revelations, and mediates fascinating insights into the cosmic processes by which reality itself is created. Its disadvantage is that the subject feels strongly drugged, has poor coordination, and his or her capacity for verbal communication, as well as subsequent recall, are distinctly impaired. Ketamine also seems to be the least interesting psychedelic substance from the therapeutic point of view, since the experience results in very little lasting emotional and psychosomatic transformation. Its greatest value is in a profound and lasting change of one's worldview and a radically new understanding of the process of death. The optimal dosage is about one-tenth to one-sixth of the anesthetic dose; it ranges between 100 and 150 milligrams intramuscularly. The music used for ketamine sessions should be slow, expansive, and "cosmic" in nature to reflect the quality of the experience.

Some of the disadvantages of ketamine could be possibly overcome by separating its two optically-active components. Ketamine is a racemic preparation, that is, a mixture of the dextro- and levorotatory fraction. Preliminary clinical research suggests that the anesthetic and psychedelic properties are selectively associated with the propensity of the two components to rotate polarized light to the right and to the left. Since these two can be separated, the psychedelic effects of ketamine can be studied in isolation from the anesthetic ones.

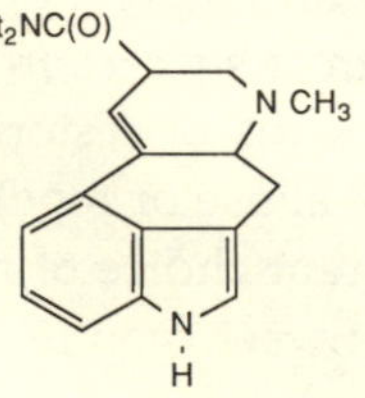

LSD-25

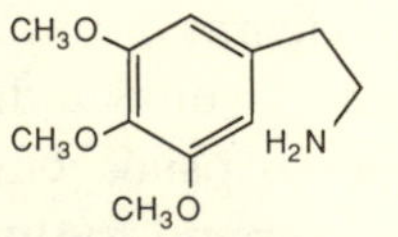

MESCALINE

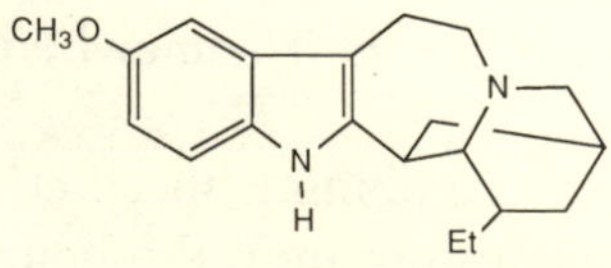

IBOGAINE

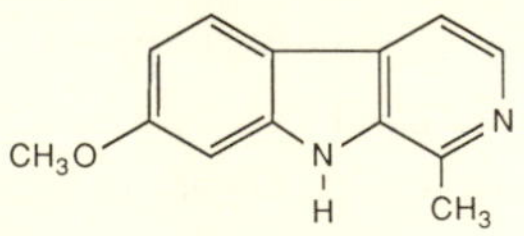

HARMINE

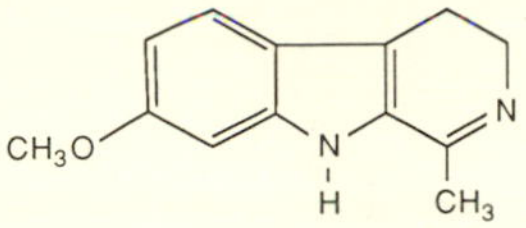

HARMALINE

TRYPTAMINES:

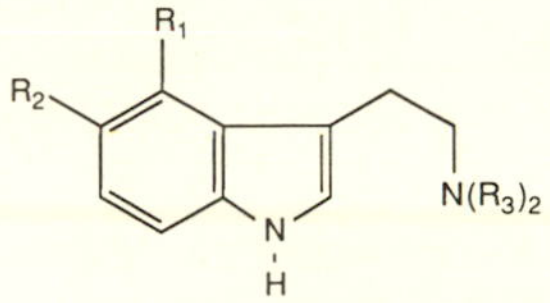

Dimethyltryptamine (DMT)	$R_1 = H$, $R_2 = H$, $R_3 = CH_3$
Diethyltryptamine (DET)	$R_1 = H$, $R_2 = H$, $R_3 = CH_2CH_3$
Dipropyltryptamine (DPT)	$R_1 = H$, $R_2 = H$, $R_3 = CH_2CH_2CH_3$
Bufotenine	$R_1 = H$, $R_2 = OH$, $R_3 = CH_3$
5-Methoxy-DMT	$R_1 = H$, $R_2 = OCH_3$, $R_3 = CH_3$
Psilocybin	$R_1 = OP(O)(OH)_2$, $R_2 = H$, $R_3 = CH_3$
Psilocin	$R_1 = OH$, $R_2 = H$, $R_3 = CH_3$

AMPHETAMINE EMPATHOGENS

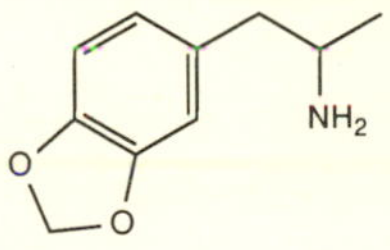

MDA

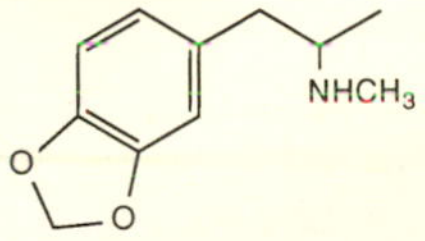

MDMA (ADAM, ECSTASY)

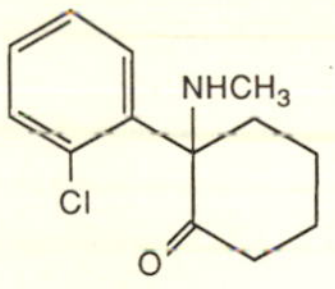

KETAMINE

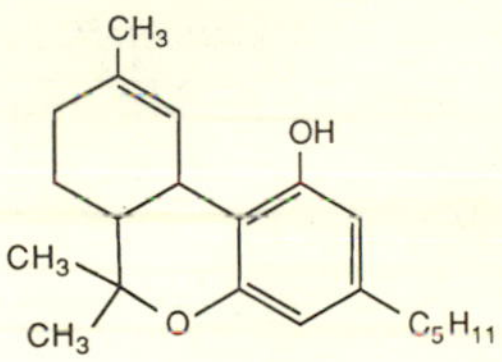

Δ^9-TETRAHYDROCANNABINOL (THC)

References

Abramson, H. A.: LSD-25 As An Adjunct to Psychotherapy with Elimination of Fear of Homosexuality. *J. Psychol.* 39:127, 1955.

Beringer, K.: *Der Meskalinrausch. Seine Geschichte und Erscheinungsweise.* Berlin, Springer, 1927.

Busch, A. K. and Johnson, W. C.: LSD As An Aid in Psychotherapy. *Dis. nerv. Syst.* 11:241, 1950.

Condrau, G.: Klinische Erfahrungen an Geisteskranken mit LSD-25. *Acta psychiat. neurol. Scand.* 24:9, 1949.

Fabing, H. D.: On Going Berserk: A Neurochemical Inquiry. *Amer. J. Psychiat.* 113:409, 1954.

Frederking, W.: Intoxicant Drugs (Mescaline and LSD-25) in Psychotherapy. *J. nerv. ment. Dis.* 121:262, 1953.

Grof, S. et al.: DPT As An Adjunct in Psychotherapy of Alcoholics. *International Pharmacopsychiatry*, 8:104, 1973.

Grof, S.: *LSD Psychotherapy.* Pomona, CA: Hunter House, 1980.

Grof, S. and Halifax, Jr.: *The Human Encounter with Death.* New York: E. P. Dutton, 1977.

Hofmann, A., Ruck, C., and Wasson, R. G.: *The Road to Eleusis.* New York: Harvest Books, 1978.

Levine, J. and Ludwig, A. M.: The Hypnodelic Treatment Technique. In: *The Use of LSD in Psychotherapy and Alcoholism*, (edited by H. A. Abramson), New York: Bobbs-Merrill, 1967.

Naranjo, C.: *The Healing Journey.* New York: Pantheon Books, 1973.

Richards, W. et al.: Psychedelic Drug (DPT) As An Adjunct in Brief Psychotherapy with Cancer Patients. *Omega*, 2:9, 1979.

Sandison, R. A.; Spencer, A. M.; and Whitelaw, J. D. A.: Further Studies in the Therapeutic Value of LSD-25 in Mental Illness. *J. ment. Sci.* 103:332, 1957.

Wasson, R. G.: *Soma: Divine Mushroom of Immortality.* New York: Harcourt & Brace, 1968.

APPENDIX B

TABLE OF BASIC PERINATAL MATRICES

BPM I	BPM II	BPM III	BPM IV
RELATED PSYCHOPATHOLOGICAL SYNDROMES			
Schizophrenic psychoses (paranoid symptomatology, feelings of mystical union, encounter with metaphysical evil forces); hypochondriasis (based on strange and bizarre physical sensations); hysterical hallucinosis and confusing daydreams with reality	Schizophrenic psychoses (elements of hellish tortures, experience of meaningless "cardboard" world); severe inhibited "endogenous" depressions; irrational inferiority and guilt feelings; hypochondriasis (based on painful physical sensations); alcoholism and drug addiction, psoriasis; peptic ulcer	Schizophrenic psychoses (sadomasochistic and scatological elements, automutilation, abnormal sexual behavior); agitated depression, sexual deviations (sadomasochism, male homosexuality, drinking of urine and eating of feces); obsessive-compulsive neurosis; psychogenic asthma, tics, and stammering; conversion and anxiety hysteria; frigidity and impotence; neurasthenia; traumatic neuroses; organ neuroses; migraine headache; enuresis and encopressis	Schizophrenic psychoses (death-rebirth experiences, messianic delusions, elements of destruction and recreation of the world, salvation and redemption, identification with Christ); manic symptomatology; female homosexuality; exhibitionism
CORRESPONDING ACTIVITIES IN FREUDIAN EROGENOUS ZONES			
Libidinal satisfaction in all erogenous zones; libidinal feelings during rocking and bathing; partial approximation to this condition after oral, anal, urethral, or genital satisfaction and after delivery of a child	Oral frustration (thirst, hunger, painful stimuli); retention of feces and/or urine; sexual frustration; experiences of cold, pain and other unpleasant sensations	Chewing and swallowing of food; oral aggression and destruction of an object; process of defecation and urination; anal and urethral aggression; sexual orgasm; phallic aggression; delivering of a child, statoacoustic eroticism (jolting, gymnastics, fancy diving, parachuting)	Satiation of thirst and hunger; pleasure of sucking; libidinal feelings after defecation, urination, sexual orgasm, or delivery of a child

ASSOCIATED MEMORIES FROM POSTNATAL LIFE

Situations from later life in which important needs are satisfied, such as happy moments from infancy and childhood (good mothering, play with peers, harmonious periods in the family, etc.), fulfilling love, romances; trips or vacations in beautiful natural settings; exposure to artistic creations of high aesthetic value; swimming in the ocean and clear lakes, etc.	Struggles, fights, and adventurous activities (active attacks in battles and revolutions, experiences in military service, rough airplane flights, cruises on stormy ocean, hazardous car driving, boxing); highly sensual memories (carnivals, amusement parks and nightclubs, wild parties, sexual orgies, etc.); childhood observations of adult sexual activities; experiences of seduction and rape; in females, delivering of their own children	Fortuitous escape from dangerous situations (end of war or revolution, survival of an accident or operation); overcoming of severe obstacles by active effort; episodes of strain and hard struggle resulting in a marked success; natural scenes (beginning of spring, end of an ocean storm, sunrise, etc.)

PHENOMENOLOGY IN LSD SESSIONS

Undisturbed intrauterine life: realistic recollections of "good womb" experiences; "oceanic" type of ecstasy, nature at its best ("Mother Nature"); experiences of cosmic unity; visions of Heaven and Paradise; *disturbances of intrauterine life:* realistic recollections of "bad womb" experiences (fetal crises, diseases, and emotional upheavals of the mother, twin situation, attempted abortions), universal threat; paranoid ideation; unpleasant physical sensations	Cosmic engulfment; immense physical and psychological suffering; unbearable and inescapable situation that will never end; various images of hell; feelings of entrapment and encagement (no exit); agonizing guilt and inferiority feelings; apocalyptic view of the world (horrors of wars and concentration camps, terror of the Inquisition; dangerous epidemics; diseases; decrepitude and death, etc.); meaninglessness and absurdity of human existence	Intensification of suffering to cosmic dimensions; borderline between pain and pleasure; "volcanic" type of ecstasy; brilliant colors; explosions and fireworks; sadomasochistic orgies; murders and bloody sacrifice, active engagement in fierce battles; atmosphere of wild adventure and dangerous explorations; intense sexual orgiastic feelings and scenes of harems and carnivals; experiences of dying and being reborn; religions involving bloody sacrifice
		Enormous decompression; expansion of space; "illuminative" type of ecstasy; visions of gigantic halls; radiant light and beautiful colors (heavenly blue, golden, rainbow, peacock feathers); feelings of rebirth and redemption; appreciation of simple way of life; sensory enhancement; brotherly feelings; humanitarian and charitable tendencies; occasionally manic activity and grandiose feelings, transition to elements of BPM I); pleasant feelings

("hangover," chills and fine spasms, unpleasant tastes, disgust, feelings of being poisoned); encounter with demonic entities and other metaphysical evil forces

tence; "cardboard world" or the atmosphere of artificiality and gadgets; ominous dark colors and unpleasant physical symptoms (feelings of oppression and compression, cardiac distress, hot flashes and chills, sweating, difficult breathing)

(Aztecs, Christ's suffering and death on the cross, Dionysus, etc.); intense physical manifestations (pressures and pains, suffocation, muscular tension and discharge in tremors and twitches, nausea and vomiting, hot flashes and chills, sweating, cardiac distress, problems of sphincter control, ringing in the ears)

can be interrupted by *umbilical crisis*: sharp pain in the navel, loss of breath, fear of death and castration, shifts in the body, but no external pressures

STAGES OF DELIVERY

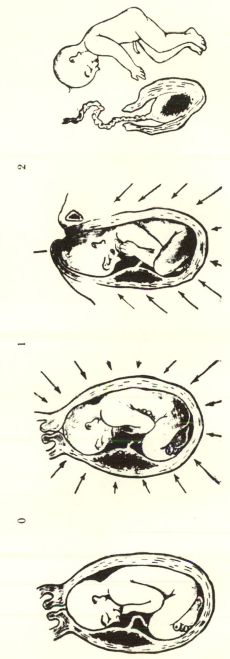

0   1   2   3

Bibliography

Aaronson, B. and Osmond, H.: *Psychedelics: The Uses and Implications of Hallucinogenic Drugs.* Anchor Books, Doubleday and Co., New York, 1970.

Adamson, S.: *Through the Gateway of the Heart.* Four Trees, San Francisco, CA, 1986.

Alexander, F.: Buddhist Training as Artificial Catatonia. *Psychanalyt Review.* 18:129, 1931.

Asimov, I.: *Fantastic Voyage — The Novel.* Houghton Mifflin, Boston, 1966.

Bacon, F.: *De Dignitate* and *The Great Restauration,* Vol. 4., *The Collected Works of Francis Bacon,* eds. J. Spedding, L. Ellis, and D. D. Heath, Longmans Green, 1870.

Bastians, A.: *Der Mann im Konzentrationslager und der Konzentrationslager im Mann.* Mimeographed manuscript, not dated.

Bateson, G.: *Steps to An Ecology of Mind.* Ballantine Books, New York, 1972.

_____. *Mind and Nature.* E. P. Dutton, New York, 1979.

Bell, J.: On the Problem of Hidden Variables in Quantum Physics. *Review of Modern Physics* 38:447, 1966.

Bender, H.: *Umgang mit dem Okkulten.* Aurum Verlag, Freiburg im Breisgau, 1984a.

_____. *Telepathie, Hellsehen, und Psychokinese.* R. Piper and Co., Munich and Zurich, 1984b.

_____. *Verborgene Wirklichkeit.* R. Piper and Co., Munich and Zurich, 1985.

Benson, H. *et al.*: "Body Temperature Changes During the Practice of g Tummo Toga," *Nature* 295:232, 1982.

Berendt, J. E.: *Das dritte Ohr: vom Hören der Welt.* Rowohlt Verlag, Reinbek bei Hamburg, 1958.

Bohm, D.: *Wholeness and the Implicate Order.* Routledge & Kegan Paul, London, 1980.

Bonny, H. and Savary, L. M.: *Music and Your Mind*. Harper and Row, New York, 1973.

Bleuler, E.: *Die Psychoide als Prinzip der organischen Entwicklung* . Springer Verlag, Berlin, 1925.

Campbell, J.: *Hero with A Thousand Faces*. World Publishing Co., Cleveland, OH, 1970.

_____. *The Way of the Animal Powers*. Harper and Row, New York, 1984.

Capra, F.: *The Tao of Physics*. Shambhala Publications, Berkeley, CA, 1975.

_____. *The Turning Point*. Simon & Schuster, New York, 1982.

Croissant, J.: *Aristôte et les mystères*. Faculte de Philosophie et Lettres, Liège, 1932.

Davies, P.P.: *God and the New Physics*. Simon and Schuster, New York, 1983.

Driesch, H.: *The Science and Philosophy of the Organism*. A.C. Black, London 1929. London, 1929.

Eisenbud, J.: *The World of Ted Serios*. William Morrow & Co., New York, 1967.

Elgin, D.: *Voluntary Simplicity*. William Morrow & Co., New York, 1981.

Eliade, M.: *Shamanism: The Archaic Techniques of Ecstasy*. Pantheon, New York, 1964.

Eysenck, H. J. and Rachman, S.: *The Causes and Cures of Neurosis*. R. R. Knapp, San Diego, CA, 1965.

Ferenczi, S.: "Thalassa," *Psychoanalytic Quarterly*, New York, 1938.

Ferguson, M.: "Music Medicine," A special double issue of the *Brain/Mind Bulletin*, Vol. 10., January 21 and February 11, 1985.

Fodor, N.: *Search for the Beloved: A Clinical Investigation of the Trauma of Birth and Prenatal Condition*. University Books, New Hyde Park, NY, 1949.

Frankl, V.: *Theorie und Therapie der Neurosen: Einfuehrung in die Logotherapie und Existenzanalyse*. Urban & Schwarzenberg, Vienna, 1956.

Freud, S. and Breuer, J.: *Studies on Hysteria*. Nervous and Mental Diseases Publishing Co., New York, 1936.

Greyson, B. and Flynn, C. P.: *The Near-Death Experience*. Charles C. Thomas, Chicago, IL, 1984.

Grof, C. and Grof, S.: Spiritual Emergency: Understanding and Treatment of Transpersonal Crises. *Re-Vision Journal* 8:7, 1986.

Grof, S.: *Realms of the Human Unconscious: Observations from LSD Research*. Viking Press, New York, 1975.

_____. *LSD Psychotherapy*. Hunter House, Pomona, CA, 1980.

_____. (ed.) *Ancient Wisdom and Modern Science*. State University of New York Press, Albany, NY, 1984.

_____. *Beyond the Brain: Birth, Death, and Transcendence in Psychotherapy*. State University of New York Press, Albany, NY, 1985.

_____. and Grof, C.: *Beyond Death: The Gates of Consciousness*. Thames & Hudson, London, 1980.

_____. and Halifax, J.: *The Human Encounter with Death*. E. P. Dutton, New York, 1977.

Guillamont, A. *et al.*: *The Gospel According to Thomas* (translation of an original Coptic text). Harper, New York, 1959.

Hamel, P. M.: *Through Music to the Self*. Element Books, Dorset, 1978.

Hanzliček, L.: *Biologické terapie psychóz*. (*Biological Therapies of Psychoses*) Čsl. zdravotnické nakladatelství, Prague, 1961.

Harner, M.: *The Way of the Shaman*. Harper & Row, New York, 1980.

_____. The Sound of Rushing Water. In: *Hallucinogens and Shamanism* (M. Harner, ed.). Oxford University Press, New York, 1973.

Hastings, A.: The Oakland Poltergeist. *Journal of the American Society for Psychic Research* 72:233, 1978.

_____. A Counseling Approach to Parapsychological Experience. *Journal of Transpersonal Psychology* 15:143, 1983.

Huxley, A.: *The Doors of Perception and Heaven and Hell*. Penguin Books, 1971.

_____. Visionaere Erfahrung. In: *Moksha: Auf der Suche nach der Wunderdroge*. R. Piper and Co. Verlag, Munich and Zurich, 1983.

_____. *The Perennial Philosophy*. Harper & Row, New York, 1945.

James, W.: *Varieties of Religious Experience*. Collier, New York, 1961.

Jantsch, E.: *The Self-Organizing Universe*. Pergamon Press, New York, 1980.

Jung, C. G.: *Psychology and Religion: East and West*. In: *Collected Works*, Vol. 11., Bollingen Series XX., Princeton University Press, Princeton, NJ, 1959.

_____. *The Archetypes and the Collective Unconscious*. In: *Collected Works*, Vol. 9.1., Bollingen Series XX., Princeton University Press, Princeton, NJ, 1959.

_____. *Synchronicity: An Acausal Connecting Principle*. In: *Collected Works*, Vol. 8., Bollingen Series XX., Princeton University Press, Princeton, NJ, 1960.

_____. *Memories, Dreams, Reflections*. Pantheon Books, New York, 1961.

_____. Letter to Bill W.: The Bill W.–Carl Jung Letters. *Grapevine*, January 1963.

_____. *Flying Saucers: A Modern Myth of Things Seen in the Skies*. In: *Collected Works*, Vol. 10., Bollingen Series XX., Princeton University Press, Princeton, NJ, 1964.

_____. *Psychological Types*. In: *Collected Works*, Vol. 6., Bollingen Series XX., Princeton University Press, Princeton, NJ, 1971.

_____. Letter to Carl Selig, February 25, 1953. *C. G. Jung's Letters*, Vol. 2., Bollingen Series XCV., Princeton University Press, Princeton, NJ, 1973.

_____. *Psychological Commentary on Kundalini Yoga*. Spring Publications, New York, 1975.

_____. "Septem Sermones Ad Mortuos." In: Holler, S.: *The Gnostic Jung and the Seven Sermons to the Dead*. Quest Book. The Theosophical Publication House, Wheaton, IL, 1982.

Kalff, D.: Sandplay: *Mirror of A Child's Psyche*. Hendra and Howard, San Francisco, CA, 1971.

Kardec, A.: *The Mediums' Book*. Livraria Allan Kardec Editora Ltda. (LAKE), Sao Paulo 1975a.

_____. *The Spirits' Book*. Livraria Allan Kardec Editora Ltda. (LAKE), Sao Paulo, 1975b.

Katz, R.: The Painful Ecstasy of Healing. *Psychology Today*, December 1976.

Kellogg, J.: The Use of Mandala in Psychological Evaluation and Treatment. *American Journal of Art Therapy* 16:123, 1977.

Kelsey, D. and Grant, J.: *Many Lifetimes*. Doubleday Publishing Co., Garden City, NY, 1967.

Korzybski, A.: *Science and Sanity: An Introduction to Non-Aristotelian Systems and General Semantics*. The International Non-Aristotelian Library Publishing Co., Lakeville, CT 1933.

Krippner, S.: *The Song of the Siren: A Parapsychological Oddyssey*. Harper & Row, New York, 1977.

_____. *Human Possibilities*. Anchor Books, Doubleday and Co., Garden City, NY, 1980.

Krishna, G.: *Kundalini: The Evolutionary Energy in Man*. Shambhala Publications, Berkeley, CA, 1970.

Kübler-Ross, E.: Death: The Final Stage of Growth. A presentation at the Ninth Annual Conference of the International Transpersonal Association (ITA), Kyoto, Japan, April 1985.

Lamb, F. B.: *The Wizard of the Upper Amazon: The Story of Manuel Córdova-Rios*, Houghton-Mifflin Co., Boston, 1971.

Lawson, A.: Perinatal Imagery in UFO Abduction Reports. *Journal of Psychohistory* 12:211, 1984.

Leboyer, F.: *Birth Without Violence*. A. A. Knopf, New York, 1975.

Lee, R. B. and DeVore, I. (eds.): *Kalahari Hunter-Gatherers: Studies of the !Kung San and Their Neighbors*. Harvard University Press, Cambridge, MA, 1976.

Lilly, J.: *The Center of the Cyclone*. Julian Press, New York, 1972.
_____. *The Scientist: A Novel Autobiography*. J. B. Lippincott Co., Philadelphia and New York, 1978.

Lovelock, J.: Gaia: *A New Look at Life on Earth*. Oxford University Press, New York, 1979.

Marçalo Gaetani, V. R.: *Gasparetto: Nem santo, nem genio, medium*. Grafica Editora Aquarela, S. A., São Paulo, S.P., Brazil, 1986.

Maslow, A.: *Toward A Psychology of Being*. Van Nostrand, Princeton, NJ, 1962.

_____. *Religions, Values, and Peak-Experiences*. State Univeristy of Ohio, Cleveland, 1964.

Masters, R. E. L.: and Houston, J.: *Varieties of Psychedelic Experience*. A Delta Book. Dell Publishing Co., New York, 1966.

Maturana, H. R. and Varela, F. J.: *Autopoiesis and Cognition*. D. Reidel Publishing Co., Dordrecht, Boston, London, 1980.

Matus, Thomas: *Yoga and the Jesus Prayer: An Experiment in Faith*. Paulist Press, Ramsey, NJ, 1984.

McCririck, P.: *The Importance of Fusion in Therapy and Maturation*. Unpublished mimeographed manuscript, not dated.

McGee, D. *et al.*: "Unexperienced Experience: A Critical Reappraisal of the Theory of Repression and Traumatic Neurosis," *Irish Journal of Psychotherapy* 3:7, 1984.

Metzner, R.: *The Ecstatic Adventure*. The Macmillan Co., New York, 1968.

Miller, A.: *For Your Own Good: The Hidden Cruelty in Child-Rearing and the Roots of Violence*. Farrar, Strauss, and Giroux, New York, 1983.

Monroe, R.: *Journeys Out of the Body*. Doubleday and Co., New York, 1971.

Moody, R.: *Life After Life*. Mockingbird Books, Atlanta, GA, 1975.

_____. *Reflections on Life After Life*. Mockingbird Books, Atlanta, GA, 1977.

Mookerjee, A.: *Kundalini: Arousal of Inner Energy*. Thames & Hudson, London, 1982.

Muktananda, Swami: *Play of Consciousness*. SYDA Foundation, South Fallsburg, NY, 1974.

_____. *Kundalini: The Secret of Life*. SYDA Foundation, South Fallsburg, NY, 1979.

Murphy, M. and White, R.: *The Psychic Side of Sports*. Addison-Wesley, Menlo Park, CA, 1978.

Muses, C.: *Destiny and Control in Human Systems: Studies in the Interactive Connectedness of Time (Chronotopology)*. Kluwer-Nijhoff, Boston, Dordrecht, Lancaster, 1985.

Nalimov, V. V.: *Realms of the Unconscious: The Enchanted Frontier*. ISI Press, Philadelphia, PA, 1982.

Neher, A.: "Auditory Driving Observed with Scalp Electrodes in Normal Subjects." *Electroencephalotography and Clinical Neurophysiology* 13:449, 1961.

_____. "A Physiological Explanation of Unusual Behavior Involving Drums," *Human Biology* 34:151, 1962.

Origenes Adamantius (Father Origen): *De Principiis (On First Principles)*. G. W. Butterworth (trans.), Peter Smith, Gloucester, MA, 1973.

Orr, L. and Ray, S.: *Rebirthing in the New Age*. Celestial Arts, Millbrae, CA, 1977.

Pauli, W.: "The Influence of Archetypal Ideas on the Scientific Theories of Kepler," *The Interpretation of Nature and the Psyche*. Bollingen Series LI. Panthon, New York, 1955.

Peerbolte, L.: "Prenatal Dynamics," *Psychic Energy*. Servire Publ., Amsterdam, Holland, 1975.

Pietsch, H.: *Shufflebrain*. Houghton Mifflin Co., Boston, MA, 1981.

Plato: "Phaedrus," In: *Collected Dialogues of Plato*. Bollingen Series LXXI. Princeton University Press, Princeton, NJ, 1961.

Pribram, K.: *Languages of the Brain*. Prentice-Hall, Englewood Cliffs, NJ, 1971.

_____. "Holonomy and Structure in the Organization of Perception," *Images, Perception, and Knowledge* (J. M. Nicholas, ed.). Reidel Publishing Co., Dordrecht, 1977.

Prigogine, I. and Stengers, I.: *Order Out of Chaos: Man's Dialogue with Nature*. Bantam Books, New York, 1984.

Radin, P.: *The Autobiography of A Winnebago Indian*. Dover Publications, New York, 1920.

Rank, O.: *The Trauma of Birth*. Harcourt Brace, New York, 1929.

Reich, W.: *Character Analysis*. Noonday Press, New York, 1949.

_____. *The Function of the Orgasm: Sex-Economic Problems of Biological Energy*. Farrar, Strauss, and Giroux, New York, 1961.

Ring, K.: *Life at Death*. Coward, McCann & Geoghegan, New York, 1980.

_____. *Heading Toward Omega*. William Morrow & Co., New York, 1984.

Rosen, D.: "Suicide Survivors: A Follow-Up Study of Persons Who Survived Jumping from the Golden Gate and San Francisco-Oakland Bay Bridges," *Western Journal of Medicine* 122:289, 1973.

Roszak, T.: *Person/Planet*. Doubleday Anchor Books, New York, 1978.

Russell, P.: *The Global Brain: Speculations on the Evolutionary Leap to Planetary Consciousness*. J. P. Tarcher, Los Angeles, CA, 1983.

Sabom, M.: *Recollections of Death*. Simon and Schuster, New York, 1982.

Sannella, L.: *Kundalini: Psychosis or Transcendence*. H. R. Dakin, San Francisco, CA, 1976.

Schweickart, R.: Space-Age and Planetary Awareness: A Personal Experience. *Re-Vision Journal* 8:69, 1985.

Sheldrake, R.: *A New Science of Life*. J. P. Tarcher, Los Angeles, CA, 1981.

Sidenbladh, E.: *Water Babies: The Igor Tjarkovsky Method for Delivering in Water* (W. Croton, trans.), St. Martin, New York, 1983.

Silverman, J.: "Shamans and Acute Schizophrenia," *American Anthropologist* 69:21, 1967.

Simonton, C., Matthews-Simonton, S. and Creighton, J.: *Getting Well Again*. J. P. Tarcher, Los Angeles, CA, 1978.

Stafford, P.: *Psychedelics Encyclopedia*. J. P. Tarcher, Los Angeles, CA, 1983.

Stevenson, I.: *Twenty Cases Suggestive of Reincarnation*. University of Virginia Press, Charlottesville, VA, 1966.

_____. *Unlearned Language*. University of Virginia Press, Charlottesville, VA, 1984.

Targ, R. and Puthoff, H.: *Mind Reach: Scientists Look At Psychic Ability*. Delta Books, New York, 1978.

_____. and Harary, K.: *The Mind Race*. Villard Books, New York, 1984.

Tart, C.: "Out-of-the-Body Experiences," *Psychic Explorations* (E. Mitchell and J. White, eds.), Putnam, New York, 1974.

_____. *Learning to Use Extrasensory Perception*. The University of Chicago Press, Chicago, 1975a.

_____. *States of Consciousness*. E. P. Dutton, New York, 1975b.

_____. *PSI: Scientific Studies of the Psychic Realm*. E. P. Dutton, New York, 1977.

Vallée, J.: *UFOs in Space: Anatomy of a Phenomenon*. Ballantine Books, New York, 1965.

Varela, F. J.: *Principles of Biological Autonomy*. Elsevier Publishing Company, New York, 1979.

Vaughan, F.: "Transpersonal Psychotherapy: Context, Content, and Process," *Beyond Ego* (R. N. Walsh and F. Vaughan, eds.) J. P. Tarcher, Los Angeles, CA, 1980.

Vonnegut, K.: *Slaughterhouse Five*. Dell Publishing Co., New York, 1974..

Watts, A.: *The Joyous Cosmology: Adventures in the Chemistry of Consciousness.* Pantheon, New York, 1962.

White, J. (ed.): *Kundalini: Evolution and Enlightenment.* Anchor Books, Garden City, NY, 1979.

Wilber, K.: *The Spectrum of Consciousness.* The Theosophical Publication House, Wheaton, IL, 1977.

_____. *The Atman Project: A Transpersonal View of Human Development.* The Theosophical Publication House, Wheaton, IL, 1980.

Young, A.: *The Reflexive Universe: Evolution of Consciousness.* Delacorte Press, New York, 1976.

Index